Advance praise for

The Dharma Bum's Guide to Western Literature

"What a wise and wonderful book, an exploration of some of our greatest writers through the seemingly simplest and most noble questions: Who am I? What am I doing here? What is the nature of consciousness? What energies and forces supersede my transient ones? Bravo!"

— **Ken Burns**, filmmaker

"*The Dharma Bum's Guide to Western Literature* beautifully demonstrates how inspiration and spiritual insight can be found anywhere, at any time, in any situation. Dean Sluyter's unveiling of the sacred within the secular is wonderful to experience, a satisfying feast for the mind and soul. Savor it."

— **Michael Bernard Beckwith**, founder and spiritual director, Agape International Spiritual Center

"This book is both wise and funny, inspired and inspiring, delightful and light filled. It opens up whole new ways of seeing."

— **Connie Zweig, PhD**, author of *The Inner Work of Age*

"With sensitivity, humor, and clarity, Dean Sluyter draws out the inner meaning of familiar literature, revealing at its heart the nondual understanding that underlies the world's great wisdom traditions. He shows us a pathway through the literary past to the recognition of our own essential nature."

— **Rupert Spira**, author of *Being Aware of Being Aware*

"This book holds the magic to convert literary junkies into mystic warriors and the power to turn spiritual seekers into lovers of letters. A must for bookworms and psychonauts, devotees as well as neophytes."

— **Michael Imperioli**, actor-writer-filmmaker

"Enlightening! A brilliant and beautifully written tour of the spiritual wisdom in great literature, and an insightful and inspiring guide to bringing this wisdom into one's own life. A delight to read, and witty too."

— **Peter Russell**, author of *Letting Go of Nothing* and *From Science to God*

"Funny, wry, curious, and wise, *The Dharma Bum's Guide to Western Literature* winds like a lyrical highway through the twists and turns of the life of the spirit. It doesn't just tell us but *shows* us that reading can be a radical, liberative act — that books can wake us up and leave us changed forever."

— **Willa Blythe Baker, PhD**, founding teacher, Natural Dharma Fellowship

"Lighthearted ... original ... pleasantly breezy. Those with an appreciation of literature and spirituality will appreciate Sluyter's fresh takes."

— *Publishers Weekly*

"I loved this insightful, compelling, thoroughly original book. Putting aside the bland conventions of mainstream guides, it reveals the perennial wisdom found in all great literature, Western and Eastern. No matter how often you've read these books, Dean Sluyter introduces you to them anew."

— **Rabbi Rami Shapiro**, author of
Perennial Wisdom for the Spiritually Independent

"This is not your ordinary Dharma book or lit book either. It's a brilliant, insightful, playful, sometimes irreverent journey for discovering Dharmic pathways in Western literature. Dean Sluyter is the lit professor you wish you'd had, and this is a trip worth taking. The guide is compelling, the company stellar, the view cosmic, and what we take back home is radical hope."

— **Yogacharya Ellen Grace O'Brian**, spiritual director of the Center for Spiritual Enlightenment and author of *The Jewel of Abundance*

"This is *Dead Poets Society* meets the Buddha. Dean Sluyter has a miner's gift for extracting nuggets of wisdom that no one else sees. I have no doubt that Blake, Salinger, Dickinson, and the rest of Sluyter's all-star authors would be delighted to have their work appreciated from this deep level of enlightened insight — and joy."

— **Philip Goldberg**, author of *American Veda*

"This amazing book does it all, providing the back story, the front story, and the over story for more than two dozen masterpieces of English and American literature. Dean Sluyter brings the big picture into focus by juxtaposing the work of perennial favorites from John Donne to Toni Morrison and celebrating the joy and wisdom we receive through fiction and poetry. It will inspire educators and students alike to keep reading, keep reflecting, and keep faith in humankind."

— **Christopher Key Chapple**, Doshi Professor of Indic and Comparative Theology at Loyola Marymount University and author of *Living Landscapes*

"Dean Sluyter is a powerful and revelatory writer. In his latest work, he shines his light, his wisdom, and his exuberant wit on the great literary classics of the West. With an ultrawide lens ranging from Shakespeare to Dr. Seuss, he shows us that we don't need to travel far to find the sacred teachings and ancient truths."

— **Jai Uttal**, sacred music composer-vocalist-instrumentalist

THE
DHARMA BUM'S
Guide to
Western Literature

THE
DHARMA BUM'S
Guide to
Western Literature

FINDING NIRVANA IN THE CLASSICS

DEAN SLUYTER

New World Library
Novato, California

New World Library
14 Pamaron Way
Novato, California 94949

Text design by Tona Pearce Myers

The illustration credits on page 279 are an extension of the copyright page.

Library of Congress Cataloging-in-Publication data is available.

First printing, March 2022
ISBN 978-1-60868-769-5
Ebook ISBN 978-1-60868-770-1
Printed in Canada on 100% postconsumer-waste recycled paper

New World Library is proud to be a Gold Certified Environmentally Responsible Publisher. Publisher certification awarded by Green Press Initiative.

10   9   8   7   6   5   4   3   2   1

For Charles Genoud

*Thank you to Jack Kerouac,
from whom I borrowed the first three words
of my title, and to Gary Snyder for lending them to Jack.*

CONTENTS

"There's lotsa keys, but only one door."

— JACK KEROUAC, *The Dharma Bums*

INTRODUCTION

Let's Take Our Shoes Off

I found my first guru on the cover of *Mad* magazine.

I was twelve years old. We were going to see a drive-in movie that night, and my mom had sent me to the garage to clear out the back seat of our Nash Rambler station wagon. Picking through the mess of toys and comic books that my brothers and I had left there, I was in my usual state of vague agitation, a nonspecific *Uh-oh, something's wrong* feeling, like the rumble of a garbage truck that's been idling on your block for so long you forget what's making the pit of your stomach churn like that.

Among the comic books was a copy of *Mad*, the wacky satire magazine. On the cover was their cheerful, dim-witted mascot, Alfred E. Neuman, with his gap-toothed grin and his motto: "What — Me Worry?"

Oh.

My mind stopped. Time stopped. Everything went deeply, deliciously silent. In the silence I saw that my churning anxiety — my worry — had not been

1

happening *to* me. I'd been doing it, habitually revving that garbage truck engine myself, but now I'd taken my foot off the pedal. The word *bliss* may sound woo-woo (this whole story may sound woo-woo), but bliss is what it was, as if the top of my cranium had opened and my brain had merged with the sky. All afternoon and all evening I floated in sky-merged, shimmering bliss. By morning the vision had faded, but some echo remained, some sense that liberation was possible: from agitated Me-Worry into wide-open luminosity.

So yeah, that was my first clear foretaste of *nirvana*, enlightenment. Maybe that inclined me toward finding it in unexpected places — and inoculated me against getting too solemn about it, or thinking it could be out of anyone's reach, or that any one sage or savior could have a monopoly on it.

•

I found my second guru in a Southern California classroom. I had been getting happily lost in books since my Winnie-the-Pooh days, and had loved puns and rhymes and tongue twisters practically since I could speak, but John Frisius (*FREE-zee-us*), my English teacher at Van Nuys High School, showed me that words could open into fathomless depths. He was a genuine wild man, with a big gut, a prematurely gray crew cut, and a serious drinker's flushed complexion. He wore cheap white dress shirts with two breast pockets and a pack of Tareytons in each, always. He was copious in his profanity and ferocious in his skewering of hypocrites. Local ministers had pressured the school board more than once to fire him, but having gone straight from high school into combat in World War II, he was not easily intimidated.

He had a trove of bad jokes and outdated slang that he repeated ritualistically. He called himself Uncle John, alluded often to his crush on the screen goddess Hedy Lamarr (here he gave a wolf whistle), and responded to any goopy sentimentality with "I almost tossed my cookies." When you gave a good answer, he shouted, "Ex-*ac*-a-tick-a-lee!" When you gave a bad answer, he shook his big head till his jowls flapped.

Mr. Frisius was driven to convey the astonishing power of words to express the joys and sorrows of human life. He was in his full glory when reading poetry aloud, his soaring Laurence Olivier elocution punctuated by Groucho Marx asides. When reading, say, a grim sonnet by Keats — dying at twenty-five, burning with hopeless love and lust — he would look up with wide-eyed anguish that sharpened a moment later into a glare, a silent accusation that we'd insufficiently appreciated the doomed poet's tragedy. Then he'd growl, "That's rougher than a damned cob." When he reached the end of a poem he would say, "OK, let's take our shoes off and run through it," then go back to the beginning and unpack it phrase by phrase, revealing all the subtle gears and levers of poetic technique, occasionally pausing to mutter, "God *damn*, that's good!"

He was skeptical of all over-the-counter spirituality, but once he told us about the time he drowned and, before being resuscitated, had an experience of ecstatic, limitless ease. And once in a dream he met God — not the vindictive Sunday school bully that he mocked and defied, but an invisible God that was rolling peals of infinite laughter.

At some point I knew I wanted to be Uncle John, or at least have his job. I eventually settled in New Jersey, where I taught English at a top-drawer prep school. I called myself Uncle Dean and couldn't explicate a poem without first saying, "OK, let's take our shoes off and run through it." Everyone knew my classroom: it was the one with a circle of comfy couches instead of rows of desk chairs. For thirty-three years I got paid to sit around reading books and talking about them with smart young people. (And oh yeah, marking papers. That part sucked.)

By then I'd found other gurus, actual awakened sages, from the East and the West, sometimes spending months with them in deep retreat, sometimes in ashrams where the first thing you do is take your shoes off. (Hmmm.) I had also read texts like the Upanishads and the Gospels, the dialogues of Plato and the sutras of the Buddha. I learned that spontaneous openings like my *Mad* episode are not just odd neurological blips. They've been recognized through the ages as glimpses of the beingness that is the essence of all beings, just as colorless light is the essence of all colors. And I learned that there are methods, "skillful means," for going beyond teasing glimpses. The simplest method is meditation, which turns out to be surprisingly easy if you take it easy, letting it pull you rather than pushing. Fifteen-year-olds can do it, as I found out by slipping it into the curriculum.

The sages taught, and I've gradually confirmed, what happens if we keep opening to the light of being, washing our lives in it day by day. We can deal gracefully with all life's noise and busy-ness on the outside, while on the inside we're as silent and crystal clear as an empty mirror. I had, in short, stumbled onto the Dharma, the path of awakening, and then just stayed on the path. It never occurred to me to do otherwise.

•

In time I began to see the connection between this awakening and the books and poems I loved, between the silence and the words. One exciting discovery was Emily Dickinson's testimony:

If I feel physically as if the top of my head were taken off, I know that
is poetry.

There it was, the open-cranium *samadhi* I had tasted at age twelve. The stuff,
the juice, the light that makes literature (or soccer or architecture or anything)
sublime turns out to be the same clear light of enlightenment. And that light
illuminates all the big questions — birth and death, hope and despair, love
and fear — that literature explores.

Some writers, like Dickinson or Salinger or Blake, are explicit about it.
Their writing, like their lives, is consumed by the joy of diving into the light
and the anguish of being cast again into darkness. With others, like Mark
Twain or Toni Morrison, the light breaks in only occasionally, unbidden,
through a side door. But they're astute observers, and even when they observe
the pain of its absence, that pain implies the presence that should be. When
Gatsby pines for Daisy, and Ahab for the White Whale, and Vladimir and
Estragon for Godot, they're all pining for the same light. So are their creators,
and so are their readers.

As it turns out, this light is never actually absent, only somehow overlooked. If the infinite is infinite, there can't be anywhere it isn't. That's recognized in the spiritual traditions of the West as well as the East:

Where can I go from your Spirit?
    Where can I flee from your presence?
If I go up to the heavens, you are there;
    if I make my bed in the depths, you are there....
Even the darkness will not be dark to you;
    the night will shine like the day,
    for darkness is as light to you.
        — Psalm 139

•

My aim in this book, then, is to lead a guided tour of literature as a path
of awakening to the light. There are, of course, many powerfully awakening
books from the East. I'm skipping them all. They pretty much speak for themselves, and several have found their place in our culture: these days, Rumi is
one of America's bestselling poets, and CEOs keep manuals of Taoist wisdom
on their desks. Instead, I want to look through the Dharma eye and find the
one light in the most familiar Western literature — the books that we read,
or were supposed to read, in high school or college. (So yes, most of our texts

will be by white male authors, and a few may be considered controversial. I leave those debates to the many more highly qualified commentators while I quietly tend the neglected garden of Dharma lit.)

I won't assume you have an advanced background in either literature or Dharma, but if you do, I believe you'll find some fresh ways of seeing what you already knew, or thought you knew. I'll also follow Elmore Leonard's advice and try to leave out the part that readers tend to skip. This won't be rigorous scholarship. Our tour won't be tidy or comprehensive or even chronological. We'll just play with the light-filled books I can't wait to play with.

We'll stick to works written in English because it's the only language I can competently read. And we'll digress. Like Holden Caulfield,

> I *like* it when somebody digresses. It's more *int*eresting and all.... I like it when somebody gets excited about something.

So we'll let excitement be our guide. Like ski bums following the snow, or surf bums following the waves, we'll be Dharma bums following the light wherever it leads us, wherever we find the juiciest action, the most fun. If it's not fun, what's the point?

·

The remarkable thing about my *Mad* experience is that it was provoked by simply reading words, three of them: "What — Me Worry?" I had done no yoga or meditation, sung no mantras. But I had encountered a cockamamie, purebred Western version of what Indian philosophy calls *mahavakya*, "great utterance," a statement of such incandescent truth that, for the right unsuspecting person at the right unpredictable moment, it sparks genuine awakening. When mere words become the catalyst for our release into the spacious dimension beyond words, beyond everything, it's a sort of miracle. With luck, perhaps the words of Keats or Shakespeare, Virginia Woolf or Walt Whitman, will work some such miracle for you.

1. Eternity's Sunrise

WILLIAM BLAKE

I've experienced sand blowing in my eyes, and it hurt. For William Blake, it's an ecstatic revelation.

> You throw the sand against the wind,
> And the wind blows it back again.
>
> And every sand becomes a Gem
> Reflected in the beams divine

To a natural-born visionary like Blake, the divine is revealed by — the divine *is* — every ordinary object. We can try to reject it, but it's always up in our face, like blowing sand. As he famously put it:

If the doors of perception were cleansed every thing would appear to
man as it is, Infinite.

Blake's own doors of perception were cleansed early — blown wide open,
really. He grew up in the Soho section of London in the mid-eighteenth century. When he was four years old, he saw God leaning his forehead against the
window, and it left him screaming. By age eight he'd grown more at home with
his expanded perception and could enjoy the sight of a tree filled with shining
angels. Later, as he watched his brother Robert die, he saw Robert's soul rise
joyfully through the roof and into the heavens. No big surprise, then, that his
contemporaries dismissed him as a lunatic; it took more than a century till he
became a beacon to Dharma bums everywhere.

There's a theory that Blake suffered from ergotoxicosis, a condition that
gives rise to hallucinations — or spiritual visions, depending on your point
of view. Known among peasants since the Middle Ages as Saint Anthony's
fire, it's caused by eating rye bread infested by purple ergot fungus, which, in
the twentieth century, was refined into LSD. (The Doors got their name from
the Blake passage above, as did Aldous Huxley's pioneering account of his
mescaline trips, *The Doors of Perception*.) But Blake's highest epiphanies were
also the purest, with no psychedelic special effects required. Once again, it's
as plain as sand.

To see a World in a Grain of Sand
And a Heaven in a Wild Flower
Hold Infinity in the palm of your hand
And Eternity in an hour

That's steep but simple. Just as ocean is present in every wave, the infinity of existence is present in every object that exists, and eternity in every
moment of time. This is not some hippie spiritual fantasy but a confirmable
hypothesis, and Blake has assigned us the lab work to confirm it. You have
to *look*. Put a grain of sand, or a wildflower, or a crumpled gum wrapper, or
anything else in the palm of your hand. Or just look at your hand. (Blake had
at least one actual student in these matters, his wife Catherine, who learned
to see as he did.)

Look and keep looking for an hour, or eternity, whichever comes first.
Eternity comes not at the end of a zillion zillion years. It comes — or, rather,
comes to be noticed — in a moment, any moment when time melts away.
That's happened to you before, whenever you got so lost in dancing with your
headphones on, or pulling the weeds, or practicing your jump shot, or gazing

at a star, that time evaporated. It happens whenever you get so lost in *en-joying* that you're *in joy* and out of time, when you're so present that past and future are delightfully absent, off on a well-earned vacation.

Anything we experience in this eternity discloses infinity. The timeless, weightless *whooooooshhh* that you and your lover (or you and your cat) feel when you relax and melt into each other's eyes, when the edges between "I" and "you" go blurry, is a glimpse of release from the matrix of time and space.

That limitlessness is what we all seek, consciously or not. Failing to find it, we usually settle for a consolation prize, some worthy achievement or tasty snack, something. Still, though, a vague dissatisfaction persists, and sometimes it reveals itself as the deepest of longings.

> Ah Sun-flower! weary of time,
> Who countest the steps of the Sun:
> Seeking after that sweet golden clime,*
> Where the travellers journey is done.

> Where the Youth pined away with desire
> And the pale Virgin shrouded in snow
> Arise from their graves and aspire
> Where my Sun-flower wishes to go.

Helianthus annuus, the common sunflower, is so named for two reasons. It looks like the sun, and it's heliotropic: it follows the sun as it moves across the sky. It "countest the steps of the Sun," plugging along like a hardworking clock, marking the hours and days till it's "weary of time." And don't we all grow weary of time? Don't we quietly dream of a "sweet golden clime / Where the travellers journey is done" — where we're done slogging through the routine, the responsibilities, the hopes and fears? Until we learn to be timeless, we're all doing time.

For some people, represented here by Blake's Youth and pale Virgin, the pining may never give way to fulfillment in this world. Right now, numberless beautiful souls weep alone in their rooms, convinced that their body shape or personality quirks disqualify them from being loved. Numberless gentle souls languish in prison, knowing that the violent confusion that landed them there has long since passed. But for all souls, the deepest yearning can still be fulfilled. That sweet golden clime is always available.

Where? In the palm of your hand. Even closer than that. The clue is in

---

*   Clime: climate, region.

the name. "Sunflower" contains "sun." We infinity-seekers contain — in our essence we *are* — infinity. As we awaken to what we are, we arise from our graves of dejection and "aspire / Where my Sun-flower wishes to go." Right here.

•

Infinity is sometimes called God. And people who see God everywhere know it can't be confined within anyone's temple or book. The proprietors of the temples and books often fear (correctly) that visionaries like Blake threaten their monopoly: the freelancers are poaching on their turf. In ages past, the solution was to punish them as heretics — or declare them saints, an equally effective way to push their experience out of the reach of ordinary consumers. Since Blake's time, the Age of Reason, the easiest method has been to pathologize the visions. *Oh, Blake? That guy's crazy.* Problem solved.

Fine. Blake had as little use for the church as it had for him. In his view, its ministers knew the infinite only as a stale rumor. Too blind or repressed to savor life's delights, they vented their frustration by attacking the delights of others.

> As the catterpillar chooses the fairest leaves to lay her eggs on, so the priest lays his curse on the fairest joys.

ALBION ROSE

These fairest joys are both spiritual and physical, which are inseparable. The body is the expression of divine energy, as in Blake's engraving *Albion Rose*. Albion is a cosmic Original Man, reveling in the glory of physical and spiritual nakedness — unlike Adam, who covers his shame with fig leaves. Light shines not only from Albion's head, like the halos of chaste Christian saints, but from his whole body. He's unbridled 360-degree joy, beyond fear and shame.

That's the ideal that Blake aspired to in his own life. He was probably his own model for Albion. (Compare his self-portrait at the head of this chapter — and while you're there, look deep into those deep eyes.) Once a neighbor, a government clerk named Thomas Butts, came calling and stumbled across Blake and his wife, luxuriating unclothed in their unpruned, Eden-wild garden, reading *Paradise Lost*. Impressed by the way the poet lived his poetry, Butts became one of his few patrons.

•

Blake's 1789 book *Songs of Innocence* ushers us into that Eden, a place where body and spirit, humans and nature, and pictures and words flow together as one organic whole. It's presented as the spontaneous, unselfconscious song of an innocent child. But producing the book — handmade from start to finish — required painstaking craft, using a new method, "Illuminated Printing," revealed in visions, said Blake, by his deceased brother.

Each page was conceived as an integrated design of images and calligraphy, which Blake composed — backward! — on copper plates, with brushes and quill pens dipped in varnish. He etched the plates with nitric acid to recess the unvarnished parts, and then, with his wife's help, printed pages from the plates and hand-painted each copy with watercolors. (Few spiritual misfits or outsider artists are lucky enough to have a patient, supportive spouse like Catherine Blake.) The books were tiny, about three by four-and-a-half inches, and Blake sold them one by one. I've seen a few of the surviving copies; they're like little jewels from another planet.*

---

*   You can see hi-res scans, with their one-of-a-kind paint jobs, at blakearchive.org.

The essence of *Songs of Innocence* is conveyed in "The Lamb." The text is framed by two saplings, joined at the top in a tangled embrace, and appears almost to grow out of their spiraling tendrils. Beneath the text, before a hillock and a rustic cottage, a child stands with a flock of grazing sheep, addressing a lamb that listens with sweet, upraised face. The child is as innocently naked as Albion or the sheep themselves.

> Little Lamb who made thee
>   Dost thou know who made thee
> Gave thee life & bid thee feed.
> By the stream & o'er the mead;
> Gave thee clothing of delight,
> Softest clothing wooly bright;
> Gave thee such a tender voice,
> Making all the vales rejoice;
>   Little Lamb who made thee
>   Dost thou know who made thee

Yes, this sounds syrupy. Blake is deliberately imitating the saccharine style of eighteenth-century children's verse, but with a deep purpose: to extrapolate from the Lamb to God. Since the Lamb, as one finite thing in the universe, one wave on the ocean of existence, has certain qualities — "tender," "bright," "delight" — then the God who made the Lamb, the ocean that gave rise to the wave, must be infinite tenderness, infinite brightness, infinite delight.

The second half of the poem, by answering the question posed in the first half, makes the point explicit.

> Little Lamb I'll tell thee,
>   Little Lamb I'll tell thee;
> He is called by thy name,
> For he calls himself a Lamb;
> He is meek & he is mild,
> He became a little child:
> I a child & thou a lamb.
> We are called by his name.
>   Little Lamb God bless thee.
>   Little Lamb God bless thee.

In the Christian tradition, Christ is, of course, the Lamb of God — God manifest as a man, the infinite as finite. He's also the loving Good Shepherd, tending us, the sheep. (Other traditions have equivalents, such as Govinda, "protector of the cows," Krishna's name as a young cowherd boy.) And Christ also "became a little child," which identifies him with "I," the speaker of the poem. Abracadabra — in a few simple lines, Blake merges "he" (Christ), "I" (the speaker and the reader), and "thou" (the Lamb). Divinity, humanity, and nature are now one big, happy jumble.

This is communion in the most wide-open sense: not just taking the wine and wafer to *become* one with the divine, but discovering that we innately *are* one with the divine, and with the natural world that is its manifestation. No priest required. Our seeming alienation was just some temporary confusion, and now we've cleared it up through the profound magic of being "meek" and "mild" — innocent, uncontrived, simple enough to just be.

This agendaless *just being* is sometimes called *meditation*, a word that, like *God*, may bring up a tangle of associations. Please just set those aside. Meditation, like God, is simple beyond all simplicity. Both are just being. Trying is counterproductive. To commune with the lambs, be meek and mild…lamblike.

•

But if simply communing with the lambs seems too easy, too naïve in its neglect of the shadow side of existence, Blake agrees. Five years after *Songs of Innocence*, he produced an expanded edition, called *Songs of Innocence and of Experience*. To demonstrate that the infinite is truly all-embracing, he had to go beyond childhood, outside the gates of Eden. He had to confront hard cases. Many of his songs of experience answer back to specific songs of innocence. Answering "The Lamb" is "The Tyger," pictured beneath a barren tree trunk, the stanzas of the poem separated by dead, leafless branches.

> Tyger Tyger, burning bright,
> In the forests of the night;
> What immortal hand or eye,
> Could frame thy fearful symmetry?*

The challenge is clear from the outset: to extrapolate to God, this time not from the gentle Lamb but from the devourer of lambs. What divine hand

---

* Why does Blake spell *Tyger* with a *y*? By his time that spelling was passé, but it does make the tiger more mysterious, more mythic. Also, since for Blake words and pictures are inseparable, he probably liked the *y* because it has a tail. And now, if you're like me, the *i* spelling will look deficient to you for the rest of your life.

could "frame" the Tyger, as a human builder frames out a house? What divine eye could have a big enough frame of reference to see the Tyger's ferocity as part of a universal harmony, a grand symmetry?

The Tyger is "burning bright" with its own fiery light. Logically, that makes no sense; psychologically, it makes perfect sense. "The forests of the night" are not just some dark jungle but life's — and our own — heart of darkness. There the Tyger lurks, burning with pure animal hunger, driven to kill and eat the weaker beings in its path, slaking its bloodlust with perfect disregard for their lives or their screaming deaths. Maybe you've heard, in the middle of the night, the screams of a rabbit or cat being eaten by a fox or coyote. Predators are wired to be perfectly fine with that. A lot of violence in our world is just business as usual. Sometimes we're the coyote and sometimes we're the rabbit.

Like the throbbing here-comes-the-shark theme in *Jaws* (ba-*dum*...ba-*dum*), the glow of the burning Tyger epitomizes all the scary things that are coming, sooner or later, for our blood. But it also epitomizes our own burning bloodlust, and for that matter all our lusts, with their capacity for selfish gratification. Many people will grab that last piece of cake before anyone else gets a chance. A few people will murder their spouses to cash in the insurance and run off with a younger, sexier partner. There's your forest of the night.

By the same logic as in "The Lamb," the Tyger's "fearful symmetry" — the jaws and claws, the springing power of the legs, all the sleek efficiency of this ferocious killing machine — must proceed from a source that is infinite ferocity. That would be a source so incomprehensible we hardly know where to look for it.

> In what distant deeps or skies.
> Burnt the fire of thine eyes?
> On what wings dare he aspire?
> What the hand, dare seize the fire?

In an effort to conceive of this inconceivable power, the next two stanzas picture it as a mighty blacksmith God, forging the Tyger in his blast furnace and hammering out its form on the anvil of creation.

> And what shoulder, & what art,
> Could twist the sinews of thy heart?
> And when thy heart began to beat,
> What dread hand? & what dread feet?

> What the hammer? what the chain,
> In what furnace was thy brain?
> What the anvil? what dread grasp,
> Dare its deadly terrors clasp!

The forests of the night were already a stark contrast to the sunny pastures of the Lamb. But in the next stanza, as the poem's emotion intensifies, they become a world of storm, in which the lightning and rain are the spears and tears of the stars. It's as if the realization that our world must have Tygers as well as Lambs has set the entire cosmos to warring and grieving. And into those stormy skies the poet hurls the poem's big question.

> When the stars threw down their spears
> And water'd heaven with their tears
> Did he smile his work to see?
> Did he who made the Lamb make thee?

There it is: the unanswerable challenge to the hallelujah God of sweetness and light, the dreadful question that I still hear in the voice of my English teacher John Frisius, who had waded through the blood of war at age nineteen. His face contorted with disgust, he clutched his book, staring past the roomful of startled tenth-graders at some unspeakable horror, and stretched out the verb like the filthiest of obscenities. "Did he *smile* his work to see?"

Whew. Nowhere to go from there. Except back to the beginning. The last stanza is almost identical to the first. Only a single, crucial word is different.

> Tyger Tyger burning bright,
> In the forests of the night:
> What immortal hand or eye,
> Dare frame thy fearful symmetry?

"Dare." There's so much packed into that word: *How dare you, God? Out of all possible universes, you create one in which beings are condemned to inflict and endure hideous agonies — and then you expect them to fall on their knees and praise you? Where do you get the nerve? Damn you, God.*

Or is that too easy, too obvious a response? As the poem concentrates its energy into that final, devastating "dare," is it in fact, as Mr. Frisius presumed, slamming up against a creator who has cruelly betrayed his creatures? Or is it slamming up against the limits of our own dualistic concepts of good and bad, black and white, and for that matter, creator and creature? Could Blake be marveling at the high daring of an infinite so vast that it encompasses infinite contradiction? After all, he never disavowed his songs of innocence, never declared that his songs of experience superseded them. He later wrote a book titled *The Marriage of Heaven and Hell*. God's reality must include and transcend all contradictory human realities. Infinity, having no frame, has room for all finite frames of reference to coexist.

Then the question "Did he who made the Lamb make thee?" is elevated from a disillusioned Christian's complaint to a koan, a mind-busting paradox like "What was your face before your parents were born?" But it's less abstract than the koans of Zen, more passionately *felt*. Why did God make our lovely green world and then insist that it include cancer? Why does nature give us rainbows and dolphins and then throw in monsters like the Lamb-devouring Tyger?

Part of the answer is that it's all relative. To the many species that are color-blind, a rainbow is nothing special. To a fish, a dolphin is a fish-devouring monster. To a nursing tiger cub, the Tyger is Mom. If we're having trouble wrapping our mind around the Lamb/Tyger paradox, that's an invitation to expand our mind, to widen our perspective toward the big-picture God's-eye view that dares to see all of life and death as a fearful but grand symmetry.

Once my wife came home to find that a crow had just eaten the nestful of newly hatched baby doves outside the kitchen window and was now terror-izing the bereft parents, cawing loudly and chasing them off a nearby branch. For weeks afterward, she wanted to kill every crow she saw — until, on a back road one evening, she came across a crow with a broken wing, horribly mangled, desperately flailing as it tried to fly away. She could only stand by and witness its agony. "But I got it," she says. "Crows and everything else. And everyone else. All just trying to get by and not be the next one to suffer."

•

Blake was a troublemaker. Politically woke as well as spiritually awake, he denounced war, slavery, and gender inequality way before it was cool. He was friends with dangerous radicals like Thomas Paine and flaunted his support of the French Revolution by wearing a liberty cap through the streets of London when that was asking for a fight. Once he did get into a fight with a British soldier and wound up in court, accused of sedition. Another time he joined a mob of protesters that stormed Newgate Prison, set it afire, and freed the prisoners. This is the man who wrote, "The road of excess leads to the palace of wisdom."

By most measures, he was a failure. He sold only a few dozen copies of *Songs of Innocence and of Experience* in his lifetime. His later books, with their elaborate, bewildering mythological systems, are still rarely read. (But they were avidly enjoyed, he said, by the angels that inspired them.) In business, he was repeatedly let down or cheated. Much of his work was destroyed, burned after his death by a zealous Christian. An artist first and only incidentally a poet, he could work for months preparing an exhibit and not sell a single painting.

He eked out a living by illustrating other people's books: on the day he died, he was still working away, trying to complete a set of watercolors for Dante's *Divine Comedy*. Being married to him must have been as exasperating as it was inspiring. But Catherine remained devoted, in spite of poverty, ridicule, and having, as she once said, "very little of Mr. Blake's company. He is always in Paradise." On his deathbed, he finally put aside the Dante work and made his last drawing — of Catherine. "You have ever been an angel to me," he said.

Blake never knew that someday a handful of his poems and aphorisms would motivate the spiritual lives of seekers all over the world. Nowadays you can find them online, quoted and misquoted on T-shirts and coffee mugs. He certainly never dreamed (unless he did) that one of his poems, "Jerusalem," would become a Church of England hymn and England's unofficial national anthem, more popular than "God Save the Queen." It's sung at royal weddings and in stadiums full of flag-waving, beer-sloshing, face-painted soccer fans — presumably unaware that they're repeating the words of a misfit radical nudist, a church-hating blasphemer, an eccentric (and possibly ergot-tripping) visionary artist. To make things even stranger, the poem is based on an oddball legend that the boy Jesus visited England during his "lost years" to plant the seeds of heaven on earth.

> And did those feet in ancient time,
> Walk upon Englands mountains green:
> And was the holy Lamb of God,
> On Englands pleasant pastures seen!

But the poem becomes universal — and irresistible — in the third stanza, which aches with the sum of all human yearning and thunders with the determination to fulfill it.

> Bring me my Bow of burning gold:
> Bring me my Arrows of desire:
> Bring me my Spear: O clouds unfold!
> Bring me my Chariot of fire!

The final stanza ends with a vow not to rest "Till we have built Jerusalem, / In Englands green & pleasant Land." The real Jerusalem — or Mecca or Lhasa or Varanasi — the real holy land is something we must build ourselves, here in our own "green & pleasant Land," our own backyard. We think the Ultimate Something for which we yearn is remote, in some faraway guru's ashram, or some solemn robe-and-sandals past, or some utopian future after the Rapture or the Aquarian Age kicks in. That gets us off the hook.

It's up to us to find the kingdom of heaven inside, then build it out with the bricks of daily living — to find the sacred and then integrate it into the (so-called) mundane. That takes some warrior spirit. Before you command the clouds of ignorance and suffering to unfold, you need to call for your bow and arrows, your spear and chariot. *But I'm so busy.* Really? Shush, please, and sit. Perhaps our grandparents bled on the beaches to defeat fascism or were beaten in the streets fighting racism. You're being called to put down your phone for twenty minutes, sit on a cushion or chair, and be.

•

After Blake's death, a little unpublished poem titled "Eternity" — scrawled in pencil, with cross-outs and revisions — was retrieved from his notebook.

Its four lines neatly summarize the entire Dharma teachings of the Buddha, which were unknown in Blake's England. He had to find them through his own clear seeing.

The starting point is the acknowledgment that human life is pervaded by unhappiness. This is what the Buddha called the First Noble Truth, the truth of suffering: all those weary sunflowers. The next step is to investigate the source of that unhappiness.

>He who binds to himself a joy
>Does the winged life destroy

The objects of our happiness, the joys that come into our life, are like delicate winged things — fluttering butterflies perhaps, or shimmering angels. Naturally, our impulse is to try to grasp and hold them forever, to bind them to ourselves. But in the very act of grasping, the child crushes the butterfly, the eager lover suffocates the angel. This is the Second Noble Truth, that the origin of suffering is grasping. The Buddha called it *tanha*, literally "thirst." (It's often translated as "desire," but "hankering" or "craving" gives a better sense of it.) Even today we call needy, grasping people "thirsty," and we understand that there's something clueless and self-defeating about that.

Then what to do? Renounce our human joys? Repress our desires? Become a monk? Even the Buddha, though a monk himself, didn't advocate that for everyone. His Third Noble Truth, the truth of the cessation of suffering, points to a subtler, more skillful solution. Don't push away the joys. In fact, love them — but stop grasping at them. Blake imparts that same wisdom in the second half of the poem and, as usual, makes it simple, elegant, luminous.

>But he who kisses the joy as it flies
>Lives in eternity's sunrise.

Love it all, even as you accept that it will all go away, that it *is* going away in every moment. As you read this, your favorite shirt is turning into a dust rag. The hot guys or girls you lusted after in high school are putting on weight. Your adorable kittens are becoming…cats. Oh, and everyone you know is dying. But once we recover from our initial shock, from the shattering of the dream of permanence, we start awakening to a liberation undreamt of.

To awaken fully takes some practice. That's the Fourth Noble Truth, the truth of the path, but it doesn't mean we postpone joy till enlightenment dawns in some hypothetical future, some remote Jerusalem. Even as you walk the path, kiss the joy in whatever form it assumes, right now, in this moment, the only moment, the pulsing eternity of now. Relax your grip on the hopes and fears of the vanished past and the imagined future. That's how we shed what is stifling and stale, and come to live in the fresh breeze and the cool, perpetual glow of the real: eternity's sunrise.

2. Unutterable Visions

F. SCOTT FITZGERALD • THE GREAT GATSBY

There appears to be a law requiring that all discussions of *The Great Gatsby* mention three words, so let's take care of that right off: Great American Novel. If by that we mean a big story that captures, in some fresh and compelling way, the genius and the madness of the American psyche and how they play out in American lives, then yes to *Gatsby*, and yes to the other two perennial nominees, *Huckleberry Finn* and *Moby-Dick*.

F. Scott Fitzgerald — that is, Francis Scott Key Fitzgerald — would certainly seem to have the right DNA for the job: his great-great-uncle wrote "The Star-Spangled Banner." He practically applied for the job when he settled on his final title for this book, *Under the Red, White, and Blue* (too late, fortunately, for the publisher to make the change). And his Roaring Twenties opus is certainly dazzling in its depiction of our I-did-it-my-way dreams and our anvil-falling-on-your-head rude awakenings. But it also taps into something beyond nationality, where Americans are like everyone else — just more so, as if we were issued the standard human script but sprinkled with an extra fistful of exclamation marks. We do whatever humans do, only louder.

Humans yearn. Gatsby's greatness is in his great yearning. We see it in his very first appearance, through the eyes of the narrator, Nick Carraway:

> The silhouette of a moving cat wavered across the moonlight, and, turning my head to watch it, I saw that I was not alone — fifty feet away a figure had emerged from the shadow of my neighbour's mansion and was standing with his hands in his pockets regarding the silver pepper of the stars.... It was Mr. Gatsby himself, come out to determine what share was his of our local heavens.
>
> ...But I didn't call to him for he gave a sudden intimation that he was content to be alone — he stretched out his arms toward the dark water in a curious way, and as far as I was from him I could have sworn he was trembling. Involuntarily I glanced seaward — and distinguished nothing except a single green light, minute and far away, that might have been the end of a dock. When I looked once more for Gatsby he had vanished, and I was alone again in the unquiet darkness.

End of chapter 1. You can't beat that for a dramatic entrance and magical exit, or for an indelible image of yearning. The object of Gatsby's yearning is at first a mystery, as are most things about him. He lives like a poor man's idea of a rich man, on Long Island's moneyed North Shore, in a colossal imitation French castle "with a tower on one side... and a marble swimming pool and more than forty acres of lawn and garden." He owns a hydroplane and a car that's "swollen... monstrous... with a labyrinth of windshields that mirrored a dozen suns." He speaks of his (alleged) days at Oxford and calls people "old sport"; his "elaborate formality of speech just missed being absurd." He hosts extravagant parties at which he's barely seen but to which all of high and low society throng, to drink too much bootleg liquor, dance to the wild new jazz music, and trade rumors about Gatsby.

Eventually, we discover that he's a gangster, involved in rum-running, shady stock deals, and more. This becomes clear when Nick meets Gatsby's mentor, Meyer Wolfsheim, "the man who fixed the World's Series back in 1919." (He's modeled after Arnold Rothstein, reputed mastermind of the Black Sox scandal.) Wolfsheim wears cuff links made from a pair of human molars; we don't want to think about who was relieved of them, or how. "Gat," of course, is slang for "gun," making "Gatsby" a sly mash-up of gangster violence and Oxford pretension. Yet, for all this, there's something in Gatsby — a sincerity, a naïve purity — that prevents us, and Nick, from closing our hearts to him.

What Gatsby yearns for is a lost love: Nick's cousin Daisy. Nick has recently moved from his native Midwest to "learn the bond business," and he has rented a modest bungalow next door to Gatsby's pleasure palace, in the new-money enclave of West Egg (Fitzgerald's fictional name for Great Neck). Daisy lives across Long Island Sound in old-money East Egg (Manhasset Neck). She's lovely and shallow. She dresses elegantly, makes bantering small talk, gushes over people indiscriminately, and calls for another round of drinks. As usual with romantic obsessions, the allure is in the eye of the obsessed.

Daisy's husband Tom Buchanan is — how to put this delicately? — an asshole. To be precise, he's a big, hulking, rich, arrogant, hypocritical, racist, unbearably stupid asshole, who spends his life playing polo, cheating on Daisy, and looking down at people who weren't clever enough to be born rich like him. Even Daisy calls him "a brute of a man." When we first meet him, he welcomes Nick to his mansion by saying, "I've got a nice place here." The high point of his life was playing football at Yale, a sport that allowed him to hurt people. The one time his mistress gives him sass, he breaks her nose.

We eventually learn that five years earlier, when Gatsby was stationed at an army base in Louisville, he and Daisy had a brief involvement. She broke it off because he didn't have money, and after some serious crying and drinking, she married Tom. Gatsby — actually Jimmy Gatz, a poor boy from nowhere South Dakota — went off to the Great War and came home determined to find a shortcut to riches and to win back Daisy, like a knight rescuing a princess from a dragon. The house in West Egg and the lavish parties are all part of the plan. Meanwhile, he yearns for her across the dark water, stretching out his arms toward the green light at the end of her dock.

•

Red means stop. That's blood, danger, as our cave-dwelling ancestors well knew. Yellow is fire. Maybe it's the warming cook fire at the mouth of the cave, maybe it's a forest fire — proceed with caution. But go toward the green. Green is the grove, the orchard, the oasis with its shade and fresh water. It's safety and abundance, the lush flourishing of life. The green light at the end of Daisy's dock evokes all that, and for Gatsby, Daisy embodies all that. She's the go-for-it of his life. She's the oasis, the flowering garden, the reclaimed Eden.

She's also cash, what capitalists raise instead of lettuce. "Her voice is full of money," Gatsby tells Nick.

Daisy is Gatsby's missing piece, the object of his obsession, and we've celebrated romantic obsession for so many centuries that it's almost mandatory. If we haven't pined night and day for some unattainable lover — if we haven't felt sure that without them we'll die of misery, that out of eight billion they're *the one*, with the unique essence that will heal our pain and make our life magical — then there must be something wrong with us.

An impulse that's so pervasive and compelling yet makes so little sense logically may make sense biologically, may offer some survival advantage for the species. We're most often seized by this kind of emotional tunnel vision in our teens and twenties, when hormones are raging, perhaps so we'll focus long enough on a single mate to beget and raise the next generation. By middle age, when reproduction is a fading issue (and when our cave ancestors, having fulfilled their reproductive destiny, were usually dead), we may find ourselves wondering what all the fuss was about.

But even then we may project similar fantasies onto our favorite rock stars or movie stars, artists or authors, gurus or (God help us) politicians. We believe that they're magical beings, and we crave transfusions of their magic. I once found myself in a car with a quite renowned guru, who was driving to the retreat center where I and several hundred other students would spend a week receiving his teachings. He paused at a stop sign and then started to nose into the intersection, when suddenly a car he hadn't noticed honked. It was coming through on the cross street, and the driver was quite correctly asserting his right of way. As the guru hit the brakes, he grumbled a rueful "Yeah, yeah" — just like a regular human. That was the best teaching I got all week. (A close second: on the way, he insisted that we stop at a little market that sold excellent ham sandwiches and coffee.)

The belief that someone else has a special essence that we lack perpetuates our sense of incompleteness. It keeps us, like Gatsby, stretching out our arms toward the dark water of separation and the green light of the dream lover, or feeding off the secondhand radiance of our favorite superstar. We yearn for the light as Blake's sunflower yearns for the sun. But just as the word *sunflower* contains *sun*, we contain the light for which we yearn. Jesus said, "You are the light of the world." The Buddha, in his very last words, said, "Be your own light."

That's not just a nice sentiment. It's an exhortation to practice — to look deeper, beneath our doing and thinking and feeling, to being, which is perfect, empty, self-sufficient, luminous, free. Identifying the light with any external thing is dangerous, not only because we might not get the thing but because we might. Then we'll find out that having can't match the grandness of our yearning. We first see this when, with Nick's help, Gatsby manages to arrange a romantic reunion with Daisy at his mansion. It's been raining, and they gaze out at the water:

> "If it wasn't for the mist we could see your home across the bay," said Gatsby. "You always have a green light that burns all night at the end of your dock."
>
> Daisy put her arm through his abruptly but he seemed absorbed in what he had just said. Possibly it had occurred to him that the colossal significance of that light had now vanished forever. Compared to the great distance that had separated him from Daisy it had seemed very near to her, almost touching her. It had seemed as close as a star to the moon. Now it was again a green light on a dock. His count of enchanted objects had diminished by one.

Fitzgerald himself was, famously, a case study in the hazards of getting what you want. Like Gatsby, he was an empty-handed boy from the Midwest who achieved spectacular early success in the East, in his case as the chronicler of the booming, partying Jazz Age (a term he coined) — followed by a rapid fall when first *The Great Gatsby* tanked and then the Depression put his twenties brand out of style. Also like Gatsby, he specialized in romantic yearning. He once said of his service during the war, "I didn't go overseas — my army experience consisted mostly of falling in love with a girl in each city I happened to be in."

ZELDA SAYRE FITZGERALD

In one of those cities, he managed to win his yearned-for golden girl: Zelda Sayre, the belle of Montgomery, Alabama, wild child of a state supreme court judge. After a few years as the It Couple of New York and the Riviera, they spiraled into a hell of alcoholism, debt, and dueling adulteries, as Zelda's wildness went from alluring to unhinged. Scott died, broken, at age forty-four, and Zelda lived out her few remaining years in a mental institution.

·

When we find ourselves yearning for a heaven, or at least to get out of hell, we often clutch at an idealized past. Demagogues exploit that impulse, promising to restore the glory of Rome or to make America great again. Of course it never works, for nations or for individuals. At one point, after yet another big party, Gatsby realizes — briefly — that his cherished image of yesteryear's Daisy is colliding with present reality.

> "And she doesn't understand," he said despairingly. "She used to be able to understand. We'd sit for hours —"
> He broke off and began to walk up and down a desolate path of fruit rinds and discarded favors and crushed flowers.
> "I wouldn't ask too much of her," I ventured. "You can't repeat the past."
> "Can't repeat the past?" he cried incredulously. "Why of course you can!"
> He looked around him wildly, as if the past were lurking here in the shadow of his house, just out of reach of his hand.
> "I'm going to fix everything just the way it was before," he said, nodding determinedly. "She'll see."

The psychological accuracy here is dead-on. The veil of self-deception starts to lift, we're alarmed by what it reveals, and then we quickly pull it down again. That scaredy-cat reaction, by the way, meshes nicely with Gatsby's peculiar little-boy innocence, seen here in the way he nods his head and insists, "She'll see." It's why neither we nor Nick can fully condemn him, despite his crimes. He's like a seven-year-old playing at being a gangster, as my father and his little buddies on the streets of Brooklyn played at being Al Capone and Lucky Luciano.

The past to which Gatsby wants to rewind — and the book's juiciest passage from a Dharma perspective — is his first kiss with Daisy, in their Louisville days. We hear the story in Nick's paraphrase, allowing Fitzgerald to relate it in the high lyrical style it requires, expressing what Gatsby feels but could never articulate.

One autumn night, five years before, they had been walking down the street when the leaves were falling, and they came to a place where there were no trees and the sidewalk was white with moonlight. They stopped here and turned toward each other. Now it was a cool night with that mysterious excitement in it which comes at the two changes of the year. The quiet lights in the houses were humming out into the darkness and there was a stir and bustle among the stars. Out of the corner of his eye Gatsby saw that the blocks of the sidewalk really formed a ladder and mounted to a secret place above the trees — he could climb to it, if he climbed alone, and once there he could suck on the pap of life, gulp down the incomparable milk of wonder.

All this florid language may sound over the top, but not for those who've *been* to the transcendental secret place and gulped the milk of wonder. (The Indian poet-sage Kabir sang, "Kabir saw that for fifteen seconds, and it made him a servant for life.") It is sometimes glimpsed at peak moments of romantic excitement — here facilitated by the magical atmosphere of white moonlight, the "stir and bustle among the stars," and a vision that's a wild visual pun, the sidewalk rising ninety degrees to become a ladder to the sky. But there's a catch: "he could climb to it, if he climbed alone." Peak moments are fragile highs, which can quickly evaporate if we try to share them. ("Two's a crowd," as the Stones put it in "Get Off of My Cloud.")

His heart beat faster and faster as Daisy's white face came up to his own. He knew that when he kissed this girl, and forever wed his unutterable visions to her perishable breath, his mind would never romp again like the mind of God. So he waited, listening for a moment longer to the tuning fork that had been struck upon a star. Then he kissed her. At his lips' touch she blossomed for him like a flower and the incarnation was complete.

Man, that's good — and bold. Fitzgerald has taken it upon himself to utter the vision that is unutterable. Almost at the same moment that his best frenemy Hemingway is eulogizing men getting their balls blown off in the Spanish Civil War and Sinclair Lewis is satirizing the entire American middle class, Fitzgerald writes about romping like the mind of God. That's an unapologetic declaration of spiritual ecstasy — from *ek-stasis*, "outside of place," no longer constrained within the shell of the body, romping free.

Because this freedom — this samadhi — is supremely democratic, it can happen to anyone, including a social-climbing, romantically obsessed gangster, or a social-climbing, romantically obsessed novelist. (Only someone who has tasted this ecstasy could write about it with such clarity and conviction.) We can't earn this amazing grace. But we can be open to it. The childlike purity that makes Gatsby so receptive to the vision is what redeems and blesses him, so that "Gatsby turned out all right at the end," says Nick, despite whatever "foul dust floated in the wake of his dreams."

For Gatsby, though, the vision is lost in the instant of its revelation. This is not just a matter of a goddess-worshipping bachelor trading in his fantasy for the morning-breath disillusionments of domesticity. At the moment of the kiss, Gatsby's formless, sky-wide samadhi narrows and descends to take the form of Daisy. "At his lips' touch she blossomed for him like a flower and the incarnation was complete." The word "incarnation" here is profound — from *in-carnis*, in meat, enfleshed. The imperishable, boundless spirit, the light, incarnates as an imperfect, impermanent, perishable human girl.

There's also the hint of another visual pun: as she grounds the light, its wavelength is stepped down from daisy yellow (caution) to carnation red (stop, no more romping). And, particularly for Fitzgerald, who was raised Catholic, there's a sardonic echo of the doctrine of the Incarnation, the belief that in Jesus the divine spirit takes human, physical form. "And the Word was made flesh." That's fine if your savior leads you from the physical realm, the meat world, back to his spirit kingdom of heaven. Gatsby's perishable savior has nowhere to lead him but to drinks on the veranda.

Nick wraps up Gatsby's vignette on a note of embarrassment, apologizing for its gushing tone. But he can't deny that it rings a distant bell.

> Through all he said, even through his appalling sentimentality, I was reminded of something — an elusive rhythm, a fragment of lost words, that I had heard somewhere a long time ago. For a moment a phrase tried to take shape in my mouth and my lips parted like a dumb man's, as though there was more struggling upon them than a wisp of startled air. But they made no sound and what I had almost remembered was uncommunicable forever.

Nick is essentially us, the uninvolved witness to the book's events. But here he can't remain uninvolved. Gatsby's story resonates for him and for us as some elusive, undefinable something because sky-romping ecstasy is our essential nature. The fall from that grace is our primal trauma. The sense of loss of something we can't name is universal: that bell tolls for thee.

This samadhi experience appears to require heightened, florid language, and to be unshareably fragile, only when it's unfamiliar. For practicing Dharma bums who sit down regularly to cultivate samadhi rather than just stumble into it now and then, the revelation loses its artificial specialness and fragility. To romp like the mind of God is simply to lose the illusion that you're an isolated little wave, to notice that there's no boundary between wave and ocean. That turns out to be the most natural thing in the world. And it doesn't have to be sacrificed to connect with others; it's the discovery of our deepest, most authentic connection. There's only one ocean, and when I and you are both nonseparate from it, we no longer feel compelled to bridge the nonexistent gap between us with romantic myths or concocted performances.

The epigraph to *The Great Gatsby* is all about performance.

> Then wear the gold hat, if that will move her;
>   If you can bounce high, bounce for her too,
> Till she cry "Lover, gold-hatted, high-bouncing lover,
>   I must have you!"

All that bouncing and posing in hats feels mandatory for children like Gatsby. But it has nothing to do with love, and in time it becomes exhausting. Either you grow out of it (through Dharma practice and/or the commonsense wisdom of maturity) or, one way or another, you crash out of it.

"Love is patient, love is kind," writes Saint Paul. "It is not jealous, it does not parade itself, it is not puffed up." The bouncing and gold-hatting are all parade, all puffery. Saint Paul's exclusion of jealousy from his definition of love would have been useful news for Gatsby, who demands that Daisy pledge not only that she loves him but that she never loved Tom. This disastrous insistence, like most romantic disasters, is premised on the notion of love as a single, narrow, intense stream, like a fire hose, which when it turns toward one person must turn away from all others. But (to riff on Saint Paul) love is relaxing. Love is not intense. It's not like a fire hose but a warm bath, with room for more friends than you can count — innumerable sentient beings, as the Buddhist texts call them. Hence the term "*in* love": we're soaking *in* that big, yummy, warm tub, our imagined boundaries softening up as we all relax together.

Certainly some friends will sit closer to us in the tub than others. That's just human. Certainly we may have a special friend who sits closest, a partner, with whom life on earth is way more fun. As our delight in just being deepens, love becomes uncomplicated. It's just being… together. Being is the real magic, and magic shared is magic squared. Still, the love-friend is not the solution to our problem, which is the human problem: consciously or not, we crave the infinite. *That's* what our yearning, Gatsby's yearning, is for, and so long as we keep trying to fill that infinite space with finite things, we keep finding all the ways that that doesn't work.

·

The great discovery is that anyone can relax into this bathtub of beingness at any time. Just sit down for a little while and relax your grip on any thought or feeling or sensation you find yourself gripping. Don't try to get rid of it, which is a backhanded way of continuing to engage with it. Just relax your grip and relax back into yourself, into spacious beingness.

Sooner or later you'll notice that it's not even a matter of "doing" it. Beingness is naturally right here all the time, available to be enjoyed, in the background of all your encounters in the world, and it takes the grind and the sting out of them, leaving delicious open space in their place. This, for lack of a better word, is called enlightenment.

·

The Great Gatsby is a tragedy, the fall of a great man — one who is larger than life, greatly yearning, greatly aspiring. It was written smack in the middle of the twenties, as the stock market soared, bob-haired flappers danced and romanced with their beaus, and Prohibition succeeded in prohibiting nothing. Like all terrific parties, it seemed like it would never end.

But as Fitzgerald's characters drive their shining cars from Long Island carousings to Manhattan carousings and back again, he makes them drive beside "a certain desolate area of land." Based on the Corona dumps, in Flushing, Queens, this is where garbage from all over the city was deposited, along with the ashes of the coal-fired furnaces then in use.

> This is a valley of ashes — a fantastic farm where ashes grow like wheat into ridges and hills and grotesque gardens, where ashes take the forms of houses and chimneys and rising smoke and finally, with a transcendent effort, of men who move dimly and already crumbling through the powdery air.

With perhaps an echo of the ruins of Pompeii — the figures of the doomed, buried in crumbling volcanic ash — this valley is a prophecy, foreshadowing the crash of the twenties bash, and of Gatsby, and of Fitzgerald himself. It's the ashes-to-ashes destiny of all human achievement. In the Buddha's *second*-to-last utterance, he said, "All composite things fall apart."

Please take a moment to contemplate what in your life is composite.

Yep, everything but the beingness. I'm afraid it's simple physics, cosmic truth, as attested by the "blue and gigantic" eyes of Dr. T. J. Eckleburg, the faded ruin of a huge optometrist's sign that peers out over the valley of ashes, a pair of disembodied, bespectacled eyes, like the eyes of God bearing silent witness to the way of all flesh.

For the sake of those who've never read it, we won't go into the details of how Gatsby's tragedy unfolds. But we must consider Nick's final thought, which ends the book.

> Gatsby believed in the green light, the orgastic future that year by year recedes before us. It eluded us then, but that's no matter — tomorrow we will run faster, stretch out our arms farther.... And one fine morning —
> So we beat on, boats against the current, borne back ceaselessly into the past.

That's Gatsby, that's America, that's humanity except for a few sages, ever pursuing some imagined future happiness, some ultimate Christmas-morning euphoria so rapturously orgastic that we'll be rendered postcoitally incapable of ever desiring anything else again. But like the carrot dangling before the donkey, that future recedes before us at every step. And like the donkey following the carrot, we persevere. It's what we know how to do.

Fitzgerald, of course, says it more beautifully. This is magnificent, heartbreaking prose. The last sentence, with its "boats against the current," is inscribed on the slab over the grave that Scott and Zelda share in a Rockville, Maryland, cemetery, and it's the most quoted line of this much-quoted book.

But it's wrong.

We can't be borne back into the past, any more than we can deliberately repeat the past, any more than we can run fast enough to catch the future. Even after all of his hero's (and his own) suffering, Fitzgerald didn't get it. We can, of course, never be anywhere but the present. When we try to grasp the mirage of the future and fail, we fall back into the present, and it *feels* like we're being borne back into the past. But that's also a mirage. As they say on those maps, "You are here." When we let ourselves fully, ungraspingly *be* here, fully present in the present, we discover that it's all incomparable milk of wonder.

3. Tribulation

FREDERICK DOUGLASS · THE SLAVE NARRATIVE

One afternoon in 1990, for a writing project about teachers and mentors, I interviewed Amiri Baraka: poet, playwright, and a leading figure of Black cultural nationalism. He had risen to fame for his role in the 1967 Newark rebellion, as some people called it (or race riot, as others called it), when the cops beat him nearly to death. I grew up as a white kid in the very white Los Angeles suburbs, but with parents who hosted Friends of the Black Panthers meetings in their living room, so I felt at home.

Baraka and I sat together in his basement, which doubled as a theater and arts space for the Newark community, and chatted for an hour or two about the teachers who had been key to his development. At one point I mentioned that I taught American literature at a mostly white prep school, and that all the writers in the syllabus I'd inherited were white. Who was the first Black writer I should add? He answered without hesitation: "Fred Douglass."

My colleagues and I put Douglass's slave narrative on our reading list and used it to help give our students an intimate view of the bondage and liberation of the enslaved and of the historical roots of the struggles of Black Americans. The central themes of Dharma, of course, are also bondage and liberation — *inner* bondage and liberation, but with some close parallels to the outer kind. Douglass's story made America look at some deep, searing truths. And if the principles of Dharma are really the basic facts of life they claim to be, we should be able to find them at the core of any true human story.

•

Slave narratives — first-person accounts of slavery — were an established literary genre in England and the United States as early as the 1770s. But when Douglass's appeared in 1845, with the title *Narrative of the Life of Frederick Douglass, an American Slave, Written by Himself*, it caused a sensation. His sober, detailed documentation of the physical and psychological horrors of slavery, and of his grim determination to escape, made the book one of America's first great bestsellers. It also provoked controversy. Before the Civil War, actual conditions in the South were still widely disputed by denialists and apologists. Many readers took Douglass's eloquence as proof that the book must be a forgery, fake news concocted by radical white abolitionists. Obviously, no Black man could be so intelligent and articulate.

Before Douglass wrote his story he told it, at abolitionist meetings throughout the North (putting himself in danger of being recaptured), and his speech was as powerful as his writing. One witness attested:

> His voice is full and rich, and his enunciation remarkably distinct and musical. He speaks in a low conversational tone most of the time, but occasionally his tones roll out full and deep as those of an organ. The effect is electrical.

The meetings were open to the public, and brawls were common, the Black Lives Matter vs. Proud Boys clashes of their time.

It's not surprising that Douglass's story stirred people up. He begins his book by describing his childhood on a Maryland plantation, where, by local custom, he was separated from his mother at an early age, meeting her only a few times before she died. She had to walk twelve miles to visit him and twelve miles back, always under cover of night. He knew that his father was white and was probably his master. (Please take a moment and try to imagine the hideous emotional confusion of growing up with that knowledge.) Young

Freddy and the other slave* children were given no pants or shoes, only "two coarse linen shirts per year." They slept on the damp floor and subsisted on cornmeal mush, which they ate without spoons from a wooden trough set on the ground, "like so many pigs....He that ate fastest got most."

When still a young child, he witnessed the first of many acts of horrific violence. His master, Captain Anthony, caught young Freddy's beautiful Aunt Hester in the company of a male slave whom he had forbidden her to see. Anthony, it is implied, considered her his exclusive sexual property. Douglass calls the scene of her punishment, with its sick fusion of lust and rage, "the blood-stained gate, the entrance to the hell of slavery, through which I was about to pass."

> He took her into the kitchen, and stripped her from neck to waist, leaving her neck, shoulders, and back, entirely naked....He made her get upon the stool, and tied her hands to the hook....Her arms were stretched up at their full length, so that she stood upon the ends of her toes. He then said to her, "Now, you d----d b---h, I'll learn you how to disobey my orders!"...No words, no tears, no prayers, from his gory victim, seemed to move his iron heart from its bloody purpose. The louder she screamed, the harder he whipped; and where the blood ran fastest, there he whipped longest.

Douglass ends the episode with one more note:

> I was so terrified and horror-stricken at the sight, that I hid myself in a closet....I expected it would be my turn next.

Witnessing domestic violence typically infects children with this kind of fear. According to the clinical literature, it commonly results in anxiety or depression, fighting, bullying, lying, cheating, learning problems, and unstable relationships. In this case, the trauma was visited on an entire population for some ten generations, with a potential for psychological damage that's incalculable. Such a legacy doesn't vanish magically or quickly.

---

*   Today, *slave* has become a freighted term, often replaced by *enslaved person* to acknowledge that slavery is a superimposed condition, that no one is legitimately or intrinsically a slave — eventually a crucial insight for Douglass. For now, I'm using *slave*, *master*, and so on, consistent with his understanding and his terminology at this point in the narrative.

One of the most chilling parts of the book is the story of the slave Demby. Baraka told me that it was still, a century and a half later, the key to understanding the outlook of Black Americans — the psychology of desperation, of nothing left to lose. The episode is instigated by a harsh overseer appropriately named Gore.

> Mr. Gore once undertook to whip one of Colonel Lloyd's slaves, by the name of Demby. He had given Demby but few stripes, when, to get rid of the scourging, he ran and plunged himself into a creek, and stood there at the depth of his shoulders, refusing to come out. Mr. Gore told him that he would give him three calls, and that, if he did not come out at the third call, he would shoot him. The first call was given. Demby made no response, but stood his ground. The second and third calls were given with the same result. Mr. Gore then, without consultation or deliberation with any one, not even giving Demby an additional call, raised his musket to his face, taking deadly aim at his standing victim, and in an instant poor Demby was no more. His mangled body sank out of sight, and blood and brains marked the water where he had stood.

Gore suffers no consequences for this murder, asserting that Demby had become "unmanageable" and "was setting a dangerous example to the other slaves."

He argued that if one slave refused to be corrected, and escaped with his life, the other slaves would soon copy the example; the result of which would be, the freedom of the slaves, and the enslavement of the whites.

This kind of warped rationale, where oppressors justify their oppression in the name of self-defense, is still a favorite of racists today.

THE SHOOTING OF DEMBY,
FROM *LIFE AND TIMES OF*
FREDERICK DOUGLASS,
1892 EDITION

Eventually, Captain Anthony died and Douglass became the property of a Thomas Auld. By the time Douglass was about sixteen, Auld found him difficult to "manage" and rented him for a year to Edward Covey, a poor local farmer with a reputation as a great "breaker" of slaves. One day, after six months of savage treatment, Covey worked Douglass till he passed out from exhaustion, then proceeded to kick him and beat him with a heavy stick, demanding yet more work. Finally, Douglass managed to flee, bleeding badly.

> I walked through the woods…through bogs and briers, barefooted and bareheaded, tearing my feet sometimes at nearly every step; and after a journey of about seven miles, occupying some five hours to perform it, I arrived at master's store. He asked me what I wanted. I told him, to let me get a new home;…that Covey would surely kill me; he was in a fair way for it. Master Thomas ridiculed the idea that there was any danger of Mr. Covey's killing me, and said that he knew Mr. Covey; that he was a good man, and that he could not think of taking me from him; that, should he do so, he would lose the whole year's wages.

We see here, as we do through most of the book, not only the intensity of the slave's suffering, but its hopelessness, its apparent inescapability. Several times young Douglass contemplates the phrase "a slave for life." Its note of heavy, inexorable doom helps us understand why Demby might have chosen his way out.

●

The word for suffering that's used in Buddhist and some Hindu texts is *dukkha*. Dukkha as a stubborn, universal reality is, in particular, the point of departure for the teachings of the Buddha — the First Noble Truth, as we've seen. He goes to great lengths to expound its pervasiveness throughout human experience.

> Birth is dukkha, aging is dukkha, death is dukkha; sorrow, lamentation, pain, grief, and despair are dukkha; association with the unbeloved is dukkha; separation from the loved is dukkha; not getting what is wanted is dukkha.

This may sound perversely gloomy, especially if we're lucky enough to live comfortable lives in prosperous countries. Then birth seems like an excellent deal. (Would the Buddha have changed his tune if he'd had antibiotics, modern dentistry, and indoor plumbing?) But the reality of dukkha cuts deeper than that. When we say that something's a pain in the neck, or that something makes us sick, or that someone broke our heart, or that we're aching for this or hurting from that, we're not talking about physical injury or pain, but it's suffering nonetheless.

The word *dukkha*, oddly, is derived from roots that mean "axle hole." In the ancient Indo-European cultures, where people traveled in horse- or ox-drawn carts, if a hole was too big for its axle you got uncomfortably bumped with every turn of the wheel. In our own little jaunt through life, we may pass through the loveliest of scenery in the most deluxe of vehicles (nice homes, schools, careers, premium entertainment channels), but if one wheel keeps bumping we'll have a rough ride. So while dukkha does include the kind of obvious physical suffering that Douglass endured (what the Buddha called *dukkha-dukkha*), a better translation might be "discomfort," "unsatisfactoriness," "distress," "grief," "sorrow," "disappointment," or "anguish." It's really too big a reality to stuff into any one definition.

That's also true of enlightenment, for which my favorite (though still inadequate) definition is "boundless OK-ness." Boundless OK-ness doesn't mean everything goes our way. We can still stub our toe or lose our job or be crucified, and those nails still hurt. But at the same time, there's a simple, deep, completely inexplicable OK-ness that makes even the heaviest of fates somehow weightless.

In the world ye shall have tribulation, but be of good cheer: I have overcome the world.
— John 16:33

For the enlightened, crucifixion and resurrection are coextensive — that's the real miracle. After the great twentieth-century Indian sage Sri Nisargadatta Maharaj was diagnosed with terminal throat cancer, he just went on teaching and didn't bother getting treated. His body was in tribulation but he had overcome the world, of which the body is a part.

This is not a mere belief or attitude, but a fundamentally different mode of experiencing whatever comes along. It's as uncontrived and neurologically real as our cheerful clarity after a great night's sleep. But until this boundless OK-ness dawns for us, some bumping of the wheel always remains. It's the free-floating dissatisfaction that humans are cursed with till they awaken and blessed with because it *motivates* them to awaken.

The Buddha counted dukkha as one of the Three Marks of Existence, the basic facts of life, all of which we see in Douglass's story. Another of the Three Marks is *anitya*: impermanence. Everything is constantly changing and passing away, melting and transforming. The throngs of people you see on the streets of the city will be gone in a hundred years, replaced by a fresh shift that won't know or care you were ever here. You'll be older when you get to the end of this sentence than you were at the beginning. We know all this in a general, abstract way, yet we keep feeling ambushed by the specifics. Just when I make peace with the fact that my hair is thinning in the back, it starts thinning in front.

Anitya means, then, that we ultimately can't rely on anything. And just as with dukkha, we can see anitya more clearly in the extreme forms it took in Douglass's life of slavery. He couldn't rely on having a warm place to sleep, decent meals, medical care — things that most of us take for granted (until we can't). He couldn't rely on anyone: not his mother, whom he barely knew, certainly not his father, and cruelly, not even his fellow sufferers, as the master would plant spies among them to casually ask how they were being treated. Giving a truthful answer was always a mistake:

> The poor man was then informed by his overseer that, for having found fault with his master, he was now to be sold to a Georgia trader. He was immediately chained and handcuffed; and thus, without a moment's warning, he was snatched away, and forever sundered, from his family and friends, by a hand more unrelenting than death.

But anitya is double-edged. If all things must pass, that includes all oppressive things. Then the sentence of "a slave for life" is also not an absolute, forever truth. This insight was key to Douglass's liberation.

There's one more insight that was probably the most important of all for Douglass, and certainly is for us. As Sri Nisargadatta put it:

> All that a guru can tell you is: My dear Sir, you are quite mistaken about yourself. You are not the person you take yourself to be.

Although bondage on the physical level is externally imposed, on a deeper level it's a function of faulty self-definition, a case of mistaken identity. Everyone, friend or foe, Black or white, told Douglass that he was a slave, that a slave was what he *was*, as water is water and fire is fire. That was all he knew.

But when he was some seven or eight years old, that wall of ignorance began to crack. He was sent to serve the Hugh Auld family, his master's relatives in Baltimore — a city, something he had never seen before. Far from the isolation of backward plantation life, this was a wider reality. He was decently clothed and fed, and treated with relative kindness by the lady of the house, who taught him his ABCs and the rudiments of reading. But that didn't last.

> Just at this point of my progress, Mr. Auld found out what was going on, and at once forbade Mrs. Auld to instruct me further, telling her, among other things, that it was unlawful, as well as unsafe, to teach a slave to read.... "It would forever unfit him to be a slave...." These words sank deep into my heart....I now understood what had been to me a most perplexing difficulty — to wit, the white man's power to enslave the black man. It was a grand achievement, and I prized it highly.

Understanding that literacy was the key to his freedom, he secretly continued learning to read and write, bribing and conning lessons out of the white boys in the neighborhood, copying pages out of the Aulds' young son's lesson book, and eventually obtaining an anthology of speeches, *The Columbian Orator*, that opened whole worlds to him — and foreshadowed his career as a thundering orator for the abolitionist cause.

The ultimate lesson of Douglass's reading was that he was not a slave. He was a person who had been enslaved. He was not a farming implement or a beast of burden, but *somebody*. He reports in the book that he didn't know his exact age or his birthday. That information was intentionally withheld:

> I do not remember to have ever met a slave who could tell of his birthday. They seldom come nearer to it than planting-time, harvest-time, cherry-time, spring-time, or fall-time.

Beasts and farm tools don't have birthdays; only people do. In fact, in later life Douglass tried, earnestly but unsuccessfully, to learn his date of birth.

Yet he became the most prominent and respected Black American of his time: the crusading editor of several abolitionist newspapers, a famous speaker on both sides of the Atlantic, the author of three autobiographies, and an advisor and gadfly to President Lincoln. When the Civil War broke out, he recruited Black soldiers to fight in the Union army, including two of his own sons. After the war, he held a number of posts in the federal government, including an ambassadorship to Haiti — all unprecedented for an African American — and was the first Black nominee for vice president.

A tireless crusader for both freedmen's and women's rights, Douglass was the only Black attendee at the first Women's Rights Convention in Seneca Falls, where he helped convince reluctant women to demand the vote. He was the most photographed American of the nineteenth century, and in every shot he strikes the pose: dignified, immaculately dressed, life-or-death serious, and ferociously determined, modeling the kind of formidable, force-to-be-reckoned-with somebody a Black person could be.

Today, there are schools and institutions named for Douglass throughout the country; there's a statue of him in the US Capitol with the words "If there is no struggle there is no progress" inscribed on the base; and if one version of the DC statehood campaign succeeds, the District of Columbia will become Douglass Commonwealth. (His fame did bring its own problems, including a steady stream of former slaves who assumed he was fabulously wealthy and morally obligated to lend them money or buy them a house.)

But what does the news that "You are not the person you take yourself to be" mean for *us*? Certainly, like young Douglass, we may have accepted limiting self-definitions that keep us from being bigger, better somebodies, and seeing through those limitations can be life-changing. But the Dharma teaching here, the third Mark of Existence, is more profound than that. The Buddha called it not bigger self or better self, but *no* self, no solid, separate person: *anatta*.

Now, it doesn't take a buddha to grasp the reality of dukkha and anitya — every reasonably clear-eyed adult knows that shit happens but doesn't last forever — but anatta is less obvious. It may sound frightening at first, but in fact it's the best of all possible news. It means there's no one for the shit to happen to. Douglass's great liberation came from realizing that he was not chattel, not a slave, but a person who had been enslaved. In this deeper liberation, we realize that we're not a person but luminous, aware, open space that has been enpersoned.

You've experienced this, in those moments of eternity when you become so absorbed in dancing or gardening or anything else that time melts away. When that happens, the self — the sense of a separate identity, an ego zipped into a bag of skin — melts along with it. If I were to ask you just then about things that usually seem deeply baked into your identity — your past, your future, your beliefs, your fears — you might just give me an indulgent little smile and a shrug. If you glimpsed your body in a mirror, you might even smile again and think, "Oh, *that* thing! Is that still hanging around here?"

Along with time and self, the sense of dukkha also melts. This is the root of the "second wind" that athletes know so well, where pain and fatigue don't so much go away as suddenly cease to matter. If in that moment we could interrogate them about other forms of dukkha in their lives, the things they discuss with their therapists, we would probably find that they also had eased. Time, pain, self: it all becomes weightless, insubstantial. We still function — we can still talk and drive and do math, we still respond to our name — but our sense of self and of everything else is less oppressively solid, less like stuff and more like a play of light.

•

As important as books were in sparking Douglass's liberation, and as important as Dharma books may be in sparking ours, reading alone rarely brings about full combustion. At some point we must *choose* liberation and then pursue it with stubborn persistence. To discourage this kind of commitment, the slavers engaged in what may be the worst of their many sins: to deliberately poison the minds of their slaves against freedom. They gave them a holiday between Christmas and New Year's Day, where they egged them on with whiskey-drinking contests and wrestling matches, all designed to end in a vomitous melee.

> Their object seems to be, to disgust their slaves with freedom, by plunging them into the lowest depths of dissipation…, artfully labelled with the name of liberty.… So, when the holidays ended, we staggered up from the filth of our wallowing, took a long breath, and marched to the field — feeling, upon the whole, rather glad to go, from what our master had deceived us into a belief was freedom, back to the arms of slavery.

For Douglass, the crisis came at the age of sixteen, just after the incident where he walked seven miles, bleeding and barefoot, to complain to his master about his brutal treatment at the hands of Mr. Covey. When his plea fell on deaf ears, he had to walk back to Covey's farm. A day later he was in the stable tending the horses when suddenly Covey appeared with a long rope, caught hold of his legs, and tried to tie him up to be beaten. Like Demby, Douglass had now been pushed to his limit. But he responded not with resignation but with resolution, and put up a fight that turned into a grueling two-hour battle. Finally, Covey gave up.

> I felt as I never felt before. It was a glorious resurrection, from the tomb of slavery, to the heaven of freedom. My long-crushed spirit

rose, cowardice departed, bold defiance took its place; and I now resolved that, however long I might remain a slave in form, the day had
passed forever when I could be a slave in fact.

The heroes of spiritual liberation display a similar determination, whether
it's Jesus spending forty days and nights in the desert or the Buddha's seven
weeks of meditation under the fig tree. As the Buddha took his seat he vowed:

Though my skin, my nerves, and my bones shall waste away and my
life blood go dry, I will not leave this seat until I have attained the
highest wisdom, called supreme enlightenment, that leads to ever-
lasting happiness.

Nowadays meditation retreats offer considerably more comfort, but it still
takes some perseverance to keep sitting for several hours a day. Years ago, on
a retreat in Mallorca that lasted five months, my pals and I adopted an unofficial slogan: "No Refunds."

But even if your Dharma practice consists of fifteen minutes of meditation a day in your easy chair, you can apply the Buddha's spirit of determination. The Dalai Lama has said that once we've decided absolutely to
practice till enlightenment, the outcome is assured: it's just a matter of how
long it will take. And, he added, if meanwhile we're growing in awareness and
the love and compassion that are its expression, it doesn't matter if it takes
ten thousand lifetimes. Otherwise, we're just fooling around, and even one
lifetime is too many.

•

As America belatedly comes to learn that Black lives matter, it becomes even
clearer what a pioneer and prophet Frederick Douglass was, and what an ex-
emplary model of the lifelong agitator and activist. I've been around passionate political activists for much of my life. Some of them remain engaged and
effective for decades, some burn out, and some are consumed by their own
anger or despair.

Activists are often suspicious of spirituality. They may condemn religion
as the opium of the people (as my parents did), and indeed, Douglass saved
his sharpest indignation for the religious hypocrites who selectively quoted
and twisted the Bible to rationalize slavery. But sincere immersion in the
spirit was indispensable to him. In later life he became a licensed lay preacher
in the AME Zion Church and a deep student of world religions.

Today's activists often shun anything spiritual or meditative, fearing it will drain the rage they think is essential to their activism. But the greatest activists have all been anchored in inner silence, not rage: Gandhi, obviously, but also Dr. King, Rosa Parks, Nelson Mandela, Vaclav Havel, Malala Yousafzai. You can feel it — there's something at their core that's profoundly settled, and it makes them strong, not weak. Even the creators of the silliest action films make their top ninjas and secret agents unflappably steady, unshaken no matter how much they're stirred. When revolutionaries without inner silence succeed in their revolutions, they usually become monsters.

The canonical version of this teaching is found in the Bhagavad Gita, ancient India's user's manual for a life of enlightened action. The teacher is Lord Krishna, an embodiment of the infinite whose name happens to mean "black one" or "dark one." He imparts life's essential wisdom to his worthy student — not a monk in a cave but a warrior, the mighty Arjuna, on a battlefield just before the fighting starts. Krishna, who (luckily) has been serving as Arjuna's charioteer, gives him eighteen chapters' worth of detailed advice, but at one point he sums it up in a single sentence: *Yogastah kuru karmani.* Established in beingness, do what you have to do.

Take care of business, kick butts as necessary, engage in righteous conflict on the battlefield of life. But first center yourself in the silence that is beyond conflict, beyond suffering, and beyond a self that can suffer. Then you'll keep

your cool in the heat of battle, see with clarity through the fog of war, fight as the moment requires, and know when to stop. You won't get carried away, and it won't be personal.

In this regard, a few people are naturals. The rest of us have to practice.

KRISHNA AND ARJUNA

4. Future Buddhas of America

THOREAU, EMERSON & FRIENDS

In June of 1967, I dropped out — out of college but also out of plans, out of society, out of any activity that wasn't directly aimed at sustaining the Beatific Vision. I became a kind of do-it-yourself *sadhu*, a wandering holy man. Crisscrossing the country, I hitchhiked, hopped freight trains, hung out in communes and crash pads, slept on floors and under bushes. When people asked where I was from, I said, "I'm from nowhere — now here."

Some of my now-here's were in jail cells; turns out the cops had limited sympathy for long-haired visionaries invading their towns. (The nicest jail was the federal lockup in Grand Canyon National Park, a sweet little cabin with bars on the windows.) Once, after several days alone in the woods, I walked into the local general store to buy a few groceries with a traveler's check. When I went to sign it, it took me a moment to remember my name. *Excellent*, I thought. *I'm breaking free of the self to abide in nameless selflessness.*

The little canvas bag slung over my shoulder contained a rolled-up army poncho, a toothbrush, a bottle of Dr. Bronner's liquid soap (with the inscrutable small print on the label), carrots, peanut butter, and two paperback books: the Tao Te Ching and Henry David Thoreau's *Walden.* The Tao Te Ching, in its pared-down language, urged me to pare down my life. "The way to do is to be." Good — sign me up. Thoreau,* in his account of his dropped-out existence in a shack beside Walden Pond, offered the same wisdom elaborated into a narrative. It was all-American proof that it could really be done: a life of simplicity and solitude, devoted to penetrating to the essence of life itself. As I thumbed rides, I thumbed through the pages:

My greatest skill has been to want but little.

I would rather sit on a pumpkin and have it all to myself, than be crowded on a velvet cushion.

I went to the woods because I wished to live deliberately, to front only the essential facts of life, and see if I could not learn what it had to teach, and not, when I came to die, discover that I had not lived. . . . I wanted to live deep and suck out all the marrow of life, . . . to drive life into a corner, and reduce it to its lowest terms.

Our life is frittered away by detail. Simplify, simplify, simplify!

Thoreau's advice to simplify became the cue to minimize my material life, till only the spiritual remained.

Anyway, that was the theory.

•

Living through the ferment of the sixties, we had a strong sense of what George Carlin called *vújà de*: "the strange feeling that somehow none of this has ever happened before." But it pretty much had, in the time of Thoreau's young adulthood, roughly the late 1830s through the mid-1850s.

In the 1960s, we protested the Vietnam War, and some went to jail for it. Thoreau protested the Mexican-American War and (briefly) went to jail

---

*　　Pronounced, believe it or not, *THOR-oh.*

for it.* We had the civil rights movement and he had abolitionism, rising in passionate, unpopular defense of John Brown and illegally helping escaped slaves along the Underground Railroad. The new technologies he saw shrinking space and time were the telegraph and the railroad; ours were TV, long-distance calls, freeways, jet travel, and the space program. Those first photos of the Whole Earth changed our sense of the place irreversibly.

Even the dance crazes of the 1960s were foreshadowed by the Polkamania — it was actually called that — which swept Europe and America in the 1840s. Of course it sounds quaint now, but no less than the Swim, the Watusi, or the Mashed Potato, the Polka was a fast-paced, high-energy way to break free from your parents' tame steps and stodgy attitudes. Chubby Checker's recording of "The Twist" was released in November 1960, the same month as John Kennedy's election, and taught white America to shake its booty. Soon Jackie Kennedy was hosting Twist parties in the White House. (Later, Funkadelic sang "Free Your Mind and Your Ass Will Follow," but sometimes it's the other way around.)

Utopian communes like those of the sixties also sprouted in Thoreau's era. Most, such as Brook Farm and the disastrous Fruitlands, where the men debated philosophy while the women did grunt work, failed quickly. One of the most viable was the Oneida Community, a highly disciplined kibbutz that flourished for over thirty years. It was organized around the principles of free love (a term coined by Oneida's leader) and complex marriage, in which all the men were married to all the women — a creative take on the biblical command to love everyone. Birth control was maintained through what people now call tantric sex. If you have Oneida kitchenware in your home, you may enjoy knowing that the company was founded by those tantric free lovers.

In both eras, the grownups in charge of society were focused on material prosperity and stability, having weathered their share of hard times in the Panic of 1837 or the Great Depression and World War II. Younger folks, sensing an emptiness in those materialistic values, sought a spiritual corrective, and it came from the East. In the 1960s, American immigration laws loosened up and swamis, roshis, and lamas arrived to share their teachings. In Thoreau's day, Eastern teachers didn't come West but Eastern teachings did. The European incursions into India had brought missionaries and scholars in their wake, who produced the first translations of Hindu and Buddhist texts into Western languages.

---

*   One of the few people in government dissenting from that jingoistic land grab was the freshman Illinois congressman Abraham Lincoln.

•

Some of those early translations found their way to Thoreau's hometown of Concord, Massachusetts, in 1834, when Ralph Waldo Emerson, with his large personal library, moved there from Boston. In 1837 Thoreau returned from his studies at Harvard, and Emerson, who was fourteen years older, became his mentor and friend. In Emerson's library, Thoreau found texts like the Bhagavad Gita, which describes the one all-pervasive beingness, or *Brahman*, and the various *yogas*, the paths for opening to Brahman. (This was a century before the word *yoga* was demoted in popular usage to mean mere physical postures.) In 1849 Thoreau wrote to a friend, "I would fain practice the yoga faithfully. To some extent, and at rare intervals, even I am a yogi." He was the first American who could legitimately make that claim.

Emerson had been a Unitarian minister like several generations of his forebears, but resigned after just three years on the job, finding the church's doctrines too stifling. (Unitarian churches were not yet the theologically easygoing places they are today.) He'd also had a personal crisis. His beloved first wife, Ellen — a beautiful aspiring poet — had died of tuberculosis at age twenty, after less than two years of marriage, and the dry teachings of the church gave him no consolation. For that he needed direct, living experience of the Spirit. Seeking a fresh start, Emerson traveled abroad for a year, meeting some of Europe's most advanced thinkers and several of the English Romantic poets, the young champions of passion and imagination over square tradition and rationality.

Within him, alchemy was taking place. The urgency of his personal search, the ancient wisdom of the Eastern texts, the youthful irreverence of the Romantics, and the innovative spirit of the rapidly modernizing American nation simmered together into a new brew called Transcendentalism. The name, taken from the writings of Immanuel Kant, came to denote an attitude as much as a formal philosophy: questioning of authority, respect for science over religious dogma, appreciation of nature as a manifestation of the divine, and above all, the ascendancy of the individual. On this point, Emerson's essay "Self-Reliance" is his grand statement.

> Trust thyself: every heart vibrates to that iron string....
>
> Whoso would be a man must be a nonconformist.... Nothing is at last sacred but the integrity of your own mind....
>
> I must be myself. I cannot break myself any longer for you, or you. If you can love me for what I am, we shall be happier....I will not hide my tastes or aversions. I will so trust that what is deep is

holy, that I will do strongly before the sun and moon whatever inly rejoices me and the heart appoints.

Emerson was ultimately so successful — the Transcendentalist attitude became so thoroughly infused into the American psyche — that it's hard now to imagine how radical it was when it first arrived. The closest I've come to witnessing that kind of flaming cultural meteor happened on January 28, 1956, when I saw the national TV debut of Elvis Presley on *The Dorsey Brothers' Stage Show*, singing "Shake, Rattle, and Roll." I was only six, but I knew enough to think *Whoah! What IS that?!* It wasn't like anything I'd heard or seen or *felt*, ever — the individual in glory, supercharged with vital energy, youthful, wild, beautiful, defiant.

Like Elvis, the Transcendentalists represented a defiant new way of feeling, and of being yourself in the world. The old farts who enforced the old repressions had better get out of the way. "What old people say you cannot do, you try and find that you can," wrote Thoreau. "Old deeds for old people, and new deeds for new." And that went for the biggest, oldest fart of all. God the raging patriarch, with his horrifying doctrine of Original Sin, suddenly looked like an angry old man shouting at kids to get off his lawn.

In his place was the Over-soul, as Emerson called it, his plain-American name for Brahman, the transcendent beingness of the universe that he'd read about in the Hindu texts. He assured us that, with a bit of all-American can-do determination, we can all find that transcendent in ourselves.

> Within man is the soul of the whole; the wise silence; the universal beauty, to which every part and particle is equally related; the eternal ONE. And this deep power in which we exist, and whose beatitude is all accessible to us, is not only self-sufficing and perfect in every hour, but the act of seeing and the thing seen, the seer and the spectacle, the subject and the object, are one. We see the world piece by piece, as the sun, the moon, the animal, the tree; but the whole, of which these are the shining parts, is the soul.

Emerson's most notorious defiant-Elvis moment took place in 1838, when he delivered the commencement address at Harvard Divinity School, where he had graduated ten years earlier. This should have been the occasion to affirm, for the new crop of young preachers, their belief in the unique divinity of Christ and fallen humanity's need of him as the great mediator. But no.

> Let me admonish you, first of all, to go alone; to refuse the good models, even those most sacred in the imagination of men, and dare to love God without mediator or veil.... Cast behind you all conformity, and acquaint men at first hand with Deity.... Jesus Christ ... was true to what is in you and me. He saw that God incarnates himself in man, and evermore goes forth anew to take possession of his world.

Not "God incarnated himself in Jesus, and Jesus alone, two thousand years ago." God incarnates (present tense) in man (all humanity). Jesus was a buddha, a man gloriously awakened to our shared God essence, who called us all to be buddhas just like him. After the speech, Emerson was cordially disinvited from ever returning to his alma mater.

•

The Transcendentalists were widely dismissed as weirdos and kooks. Some of them were. But they were the shock troops who first opened up the space in American society that is now often take for granted — the clear, relaxed, open space, free of dogma and tradition, where we make our own choices and pursue our own awakening, buoyed by our confidence that the capital-T Truth lies within. When I was in high school, one of the campus clubs was the Future Farmers of America. I think of the Transcendentalists as the Future Buddhas of America.

In fact, there was a club like that, although it was never formally organized, never had official members, and never even had an agreed-upon name. It was variously called Hedge's Club, the Aesthetic Club, and the Brotherhood of the Like-Minded, but the name that has stuck is the Transcendental Club. It met irregularly, once every few months for just four years, but it was crucial in nurturing and spreading the new attitude. Emerson was its central figure, and he generously encouraged the others in their explorations.

Less a club than a forum, the Transcendental Club met in members' homes, bringing together philosophers, educators, artists, social reformers, clergy, and miscellaneous characters like Thoreau, who was, by trade, a surveyor and a civil engineer. Addressing such lofty topics as "Education of Humanity," "American Genius," and "What Is the Essence of Religion as Distinct from Morality?," they sought "deeper and broader views" than were being propounded elsewhere in the culture, especially at conservative Harvard College, which many of them had attended. (It was the local school. Thoreau once got serious blisters walking the fifteen miles back home.) It's fun to imagine what it was like to attend this movable feast of fervent intellectuals, activists, and aspiring mystics, the men with their long side-whiskers and women with coiled braids or dangling spaniel curls, crowding into one private salon after another to hash out the Big Ideas.

MARGARET FULLER

JONES VERY

It was a colorful cast of characters. Some, like Margaret Fuller, were truly remarkable. Reputed to be the best-read person in all of New England, she was the first woman allowed to use the Harvard library, the first full-time book reviewer in American journalism, and America's first high-profile feminist. Emerson hired her as the first editor of the club's journal, *The Dial* (where she had a habit of rejecting Thoreau's submissions), but it struggled to find subscribers and he wound up stiffing her on the salary. As America's first female war correspondent, she covered the Italian revolutions of the midforties, volunteered in a hospital serving wounded patriots, and had a possibly illegitimate child with Giovanni Ossoli, a Roman nobleman and fighter for the cause.

In 1850, Fuller started having premonitions of impending death. That summer, the ship carrying her home to America with Ossoli and their child hit a sandbar off Fire Island. Local residents showed up with carts to salvage cargo while passengers were drowning just fifty yards from shore. Emerson sent Thoreau to New York to search for Fuller's body, but it was never found. A few months earlier, Nathaniel Hawthorne had published *The Scarlet Letter*, whose heroine — the bold, free-spirited, unwed mother Hester Prynne — was inspired by Fuller.

Another sometime visitor to the Transcendental Club was Jones Very. He was, well, very very. A poet, Shakespeare scholar, and religious obsessive, he fought sexual temptation by refusing to look at women. He became convinced that he was the Second Coming of Christ and started showing up at friends' homes, his eyes weirdly unblinking, to baptize them as his disciples. Generally considered a lunatic, Very spent a month in an insane asylum. After his release, the ever-generous Emerson, who called him "our brave saint," took him in as a houseguest. Emerson had written that "A certain tendency to insanity has always attended the opening of the religious sense in men, as if they had been 'blasted with excess of light,'" and Very was exhibit A.

If by any chance I was hanging around with this crowd in a previous life, I was probably Bronson Alcott — the inspired, sporadically inspiring, usually flaky schoolmaster. Alcott started several schools, most of which failed, partly because they were too far ahead of their time, with innovations like comfortable classrooms, abolition of corporal punishment, writing assignments that addressed the students' own lives instead of Roman history, and in one case, the inclusion of a Black student.

BRONSON ALCOTT

But the problem was also Alcott himself. He was stubborn, dogmatic, and hopelessly impractical. Sooner or later he alienated or exhausted almost everyone — except, again, the remarkably tolerant Emerson, who helped sponsor Alcott's projects but prudently avoided getting involved with them. One of the main instigators of the Fruitlands fiasco, Alcott left his wife and daughters there to suffer cold and hunger while he was off giving lectures on the commune's high-minded principles. He also had the strange gift of being brilliant in conversation but hilariously incoherent on paper. His writings in *The Dial* helped convince the public that the Transcendentalists were wackos.

Alcott did, however, make three important contributions to literature. One of these grew out of his time leading the Temple School, in Boston, where he moderated Socratic discussions on spiritual topics with his students, who ranged in age from about seven to twelve. His assistant, Elizabeth Palmer Peabody (later a pioneer in the kindergarten movement and Hawthorne's sister-in-law), transcribed the discussions, which were published under the title *Conversations with Children on the Gospels*.* Here Alcott has asked the children about heaven:

JOSIAH. Heaven is partly in the spirit of my body, partly in God.

WILLIAM C. Heaven is where great and good people are.

AUGUSTINE. Heaven is in our spirits — in God. It is in no particular place. It is not above the sky. It is not material. It is wherever people are good.

CHARLES. Heaven is everywhere — Eternity. It stops when there is anything bad. It means peace and love. High and white are emblems of it....

FRANKLIN. Heaven is the spirit's truth and goodness. It is in everybody; but mostly in the good.

GEORGE K. I generally imagine it very high and bright, with gold pavements, but it is not earthly gold. It is both a place and state of mind.

LOUISA MAY ALCOTT

For eliciting this kind of insight, Alcott was accused of indoctrinating the children with blasphemy, and the school was forced to close.

His other two literary contributions, both of them accidental, were lending Thoreau an axe to build his shack at Walden, and raising (in his bumbling way) his second daughter, Louisa May. After a lifetime of poverty and failed projects, he was finally supported in his old age by royalties from her semiautobiographical bestseller, *Little Women*. On his deathbed, he told her, "I am going up. Come with me." Two days after his death, she died of a stroke at age fifty-five.

---

*   Now published as *How Like an Angel Came I Down*.

•

With his philosophy sharpened in the Transcendental Club's discussions, Emerson signed on to the Lyceum circuit, the lecture-tour system that brought speakers to towns throughout the Northeast and Midwest, giving nineteenth-century TED Talks. Speakers included Frederick Douglass, Hawthorne, occasionally Thoreau, and later, Mark Twain and Susan B. Anthony. But in his time Emerson was the Lyceum's biggest star, and his books of essays, mostly based on his lectures, became hugely influential. Known as "the sage of Concord," he was America's resident wise man.

He's still influential today, although it's a question how much his work is actually read outside of classrooms. Reading the essays straight through can be rough going. Perhaps a society where most people still sat in hard wooden pews, enduring long sermons every Sunday, had a higher boredom threshold. But Emerson is now an influencer the way everyone else is — online. His juiciest quotes show up in memes, floating above pine forests and mountain streams.

He once wrote in his journal, "In all my lectures, I have taught one doctrine, the infinitude of the private man." Writing about infinitude without sounding abstract is always a challenge. (Tell me about it.) But here, for example, Emerson makes it vivid with a bit of haiku-worthy scene-painting.

> Crossing a bare common, in snow puddles, at twilight, under a clouded sky, without having in my thoughts any occurrence of special good fortune, I have enjoyed a perfect exhilaration.

The "perfect exhilaration" that arises irrespective of "good fortune" is precisely the happy-for-no-reason quality of samadhi. Such flashes, though fleeting, can color our entire life.

> Our faith comes in moments.... Yet there is a depth in those brief moments which constrains us to ascribe more reality to them than to all other experiences.

This is insightful, as usual, but the word "faith" is tricky. Emerson often writes in terms of faith, belief, conviction, or philosophy, which are all forms of thought, sometimes spiced with emotion. But what he's describing here is beyond thought and emotion — the real thing, the real samadhi, with the "depth" that gives it "more reality" than other experiences.

In fact, Emerson (like many people) often muddies the distinction between faith or philosophy on the one hand and direct experience on the other, between Transcendental*ism* and transcendence. He writes, for example, that "All men have sublime thoughts." No they don't. All men, all people, have sublime being. Most people have boring thoughts. Emerson spouts a lot of nonsense, especially in "Self-Reliance," about every one of us necessarily being a genius by virtue of containing the divine essence.

That's Emerson at his cheesiest, as a sort of cosmic cheerleader, urging us not to be held back by the mediocrity of the masses, whom the universal spirit of divine genius has, um, somehow passed by. But there's always a market for cheerleaders. From this aspect of Emerson we can trace a direct line to today's motivational mavens and peddlers of positive thinking, daring us to live our bigger, bolder, more magnificent life. Fine. But infinitude is not big or little, bold or timid, magnificent or modest. It's beyond all those pairs of opposites, beyond your cleverest thoughts and loftiest attitudes. That's the real thing, if you want it.

Many of Emerson's epiphanies do smell like the real thing, such as this famous description of all-out samadhi, where identification with the ego dissolves and we abide as pure awareness:

> Standing on the bare ground, — my head bathed by the blithe air, and uplifted into infinite space, — all mean egotism vanishes. I become a transparent eye-ball; I am nothing; I see all; the currents of the Universal Being circulate through me; I am part or particle of God.

In fact, close-up accounts of Emerson suggest that all his years of spiritual exploration eventually led to some degree of genuine awakening. He suffered what should have been crushing personal tragedy, losing to early death not only his first wife but also his father, all but two of his seven siblings, and his beloved five-year-old son, Waldo. But by all reports he radiated an unshakable tranquility.

He traveled to California in 1871 to lecture and sightsee. In Yosemite he met young John Muir, the great naturalist and later founder of the Sierra Club, whose well-worn copy of Emerson's essays was dented and smudged with pine resin. Muir tried to coax the sixty-seven-year-old Emerson to join him on a "rough camping" trip in the mountains. "But alas," Muir wrote, "it was too late, — too near the sundown of his life." Still:

Emerson was the most serene, majestic, sequoia-like soul I ever met. His smile was as sweet and calm as morning light on mountains. There was a wonderful charm in his presence; his smile, serene eye, his voice, his manner, were all sensed at once by everybody. I felt here was a man I had been seeking....He was as sincere as the trees, his eye sincere as the sun.

An observer of the meeting added, "For Muir, Emerson's visit came like a laying on of hands."

•

Maybe it's fitting that most people mispronounce Thoreau's name — there's so much else about him that they get wrong. Many presume that he was a confirmed hermit, living out his life in the impenetrable woods. Then they feel duped when they learn that his Walden Pond experiment lasted only two years, and that even then he took the short walk into town every day or two, accepted dinner invitations, and often hosted visitors to his little cabin, in one hilarious episode cramming some thirty people into the place.

But in fact, Thoreau happily shares all that information in his book.

THOREAU'S SHACK,
DRAWN BY HIS SISTER SOPHIA

I think that I love society as much as most, and am ready enough to fasten myself like a bloodsucker for the time to any full-blooded man that comes in my way. I am naturally no hermit, but might possibly sit out the sturdiest frequenter of the bar-room, if my business called me thither.

As it happened, Thoreau's shack was on exactly the kind of spot where the Buddha and his disciples camped in their wanderings — not in the deep woods, but on the border of woods and town, where they could share wisdom with the locals and receive food from them, but not get caught up in their hustle and bustle. Walden was a much busier place then than now, with the railroad running close by, local property owners gathering firewood, ice harvesters in winter, and fishermen in all seasons. Thoreau had so many visitors, he tells us, that one suggested he have them all sign a guest book. They included:

> Half-witted men from the almshouse and elsewhere…runaway slaves with plantation manners…ministers who spoke of God as if they enjoyed a monopoly of the subject, who could not bear all kinds of opinions; doctors, lawyers, uneasy housekeepers who pried into my cupboard and bed when I was out…children come a-berrying, railroad men taking a Sunday morning walk in clean shirts, fishermen and hunters, poets and philosophers; in short, all honest pilgrims.

The snarky rumor that Thoreau brought his laundry home from Walden for the womenfolk to do, often stated as gleeful fact, has no documented historical basis. And if so, so what? All his relatives had scrimped to help put Henry through Harvard, and he repaid that loyalty for the rest of his life, contributing both practically and financially to the household. But he also knew, as he once wrote to a friend, that "you must make tracks into the Unknown. That is what you have your board & clothes for."

Thoreau was an odd character from an odd family. Other than his parents, none of them — siblings, aunts, uncles — ever married. They were a noisy, engaged, activist bunch, except for his father, a meek little struggling storekeeper. His mother, a head taller, was a nonstop whirlwind of cooking, sewing, supervising, opining, exhorting. Besides his two years at Walden and on-and-off stays at Emerson's house as an all-purpose handyman, helper, and tutor for the children, Henry lived in his parents' house for most of his adult life, in an attic room that resembled a museum, full of the botanical specimens he collected on his long rambles. He carried them home on a custom-sewn shelf inside his hat, joking that his brains helped keep them moist.

As awkward as his relations with humans sometimes were, in the natural world he was completely at home. One visitor to Walden wrote:

> He said: "Keep very still and I will show you my family." Stepping quickly outside the cabin door, he gave a low and curious whistle; immediately a woodchuck came running towards him from a nearby

burrow. With varying note, yet still low and strange, a pair of gray squirrels were summoned and approached him fearlessly. With still another note several birds, including two crows flew towards him, one of the crows nestling upon his shoulder.... He fed them all from his hand, taking food from his pocket, and petted them gently before our delighted gaze; and then dismissed them by different whistling, always strange and low and short, each wild thing departing instantly at hearing his special signal.

The most eccentric of Thoreau's eccentric relatives was his uncle Charles, who would wander off to parts unknown for months at a time, only to be found one morning sleeping in a chair beside the stove when the family came down for breakfast. On one of his rambles, Charles acquired a plumbago (graphite) deposit in New Hampshire, which became the basis for the family's pencil business. American pencils at the time were smeary and gritty. Henry got busy reading German technical journals and developing improved production methods, and the success of the award-winning J. Thoreau & Son pencil finally stabilized the shaky family finances.

But Henry's older brother, John, was the golden boy: outgoing, charismatic, a natural leader, clearly going places. Henry was short like his father, quiet, happy to cede the spotlight to John. They were devoted brothers, going on camping trips together, opening a school together. The students found John relaxed and fun, Henry a demanding perfectionist. He may have been mildly autistic — in his journal he mentions his habit of not looking directly into people's faces, and in a letter to an admirer he calls himself a "stuttering, blundering clodhopper." Once his students circulated a drawing clipped from the *Old American Comic Almanac* with caricatures of people cast as various species of bird. They were struck by how much short, big-nosed Thoreau looked like the stubby-legged, large-beaked booby.

In 1842, when John was twenty-six and Henry twenty-four, John nicked his finger while stropping his razor. A week later he developed lockjaw, and after three days of violent spasms, delirium, and excruciating pain, he died in Henry's arms. Eleven days later, Henry started exhibiting the same symptoms. They turned out to be psychosomatic, but he went into a deep depression

THE BOOBY CARICATURE

that lasted months, and for years he dreamed about John and couldn't hear his name without tearing up.

So when Henry asked permission to build a shack on Emerson's woodlot beside Walden Pond, yes, it was with the universal purpose of investigating how one could live a life attuned to a higher calling than earning a living. But it was also to mourn his brother and grapple with his depression. That doesn't detract from his achievement. The mix of personal and universal motivations is always there. We can be sure it was there for Jesus, Shankara, the Buddha, all the great spiritual explorers, even if their followers later airbrushed it out of the record. That makes them not less inspiring, but more. They weren't special. They were like us, just trying to replace their suffering with freedom, and if possible to help others do the same.

Thoreau moved into the shack on Independence Day, 1845. The question he was there to investigate was, in simplest terms, how to live a happy life. Perhaps we can pose the question as an equation:

$$H = S/D$$

That is, Happiness equals Stuff divided by Desire. Then there are two ways to maximize Happiness. The usual approach is to increase the numerator: maximize Stuff. Thoreau's approach is to decrease the denominator: minimize Desire.

> Most of the luxuries, and many of the so-called comforts of life, are not only not indispensable, but positive hindrances to the elevation of mankind.... Shall we always study to obtain more of these things, and not sometimes to be content with less?... A man is rich in proportion to the number of things he can afford to let alone.

Thus, in "Economy," the first chapter of *Walden*, Thoreau outlines what he calls the four "necessaries of life... Food, Shelter, Clothing, and Fuel." Then, taking a nothing-for-granted, zero-based-budgeting approach, he considers how each might be secured with minimum fuss.

> I used to see a large box by the railroad, six feet long by three wide, in which the laborers locked up their tools at night; and it suggested to me that every man who was hard pushed might get such a one for a dollar, and, having bored a few auger holes in it, to admit the air at least, get into it when it rained and at night, and hook down the lid, and so have freedom in his love, and in his soul be free.... Many a man is harassed to death to pay the rent of a larger and more luxurious box who would not have frozen to death in such a box as this. I am far from jesting.

He winds up living not in a six-by-three-foot box but a ten-by-fifteen-foot shack, but at least as a thought experiment, he has to try it on; someone's gotta do it. And while he says he's "far from jesting," he clearly sees the humor of his situation. In the same vein, he dryly tallies his expenses down to the half-penny, perhaps indulging his autistic tendencies but also chuckling at them. Then he considers the contents of his cabin:

> I had three pieces of limestone on my desk, but I was terrified to find that they required to be dusted daily, when the furniture of my mind was all undusted still, and threw them out the window in disgust.

There's a lovely, delicate balance here. We have the reminder of Thoreau's overriding purpose: to dust the furniture of his mind, to pursue awakening as America's first deliberate, practicing yogi. That means groping his way along with no guidance but a few texts from an ancient, alien culture. There's no way to do that without sometimes lapsing into foolishness, but Thoreau is in on the joke. He casts himself as a sort of Chaplinesque character, the Little Tramp goes to an ashram, "terrified" by three pieces of limestone *(Eek!)* and chucking them out the window in "disgust" *(Yuck!)**

But then — and this is the real miracle of *Walden* — at any moment all the personal doubts and quirks can fall away. Thoreau becomes a clear, open conduit, and through prose that is sublime, the world reveals itself as sublime.

---

*　I started off my hitchhiking-sadhu days with a pair of Keds and a pair of soft high-top Fairchild moccasins. But one day, *Walden*-inspired, I realized, *Wait. I only have two feet. Why do I have four shoes?* Setting the Fairchilds neatly on the side of the road for their next owner, I walked on. (Wish I still had those. You can't get them anymore.)

Standing on the snow-covered plain, as if in a pasture amid the hills, I cut my way first through a foot of snow, and then a foot of ice, and open a window under my feet, where, kneeling to drink, I look down into the quiet parlor of the fishes, pervaded by a softened light as through a window of ground glass, with its bright sanded floor the same as in summer; there a perennial waveless serenity reigns as in the amber twilight sky, corresponding to the cool and even temperament of the inhabitants. Heaven is under our feet as well as over our heads.

Having discussed the four necessaries, Thoreau admits a few extra perks that one might want in the woods: "a knife, an axe, a spade, a wheelbarrow, etc., and for the studious, lamplight, stationery, and access to a few books." One thing is conspicuously absent from this list. Nowhere in *Walden* do we hear Thoreau roar, *Where's my woman?!* In fact, we can pretty well read through all of Thoreau and Emerson, with their Puritan New England roots, and never guess that such a thing as sex or romance exists. (It would be left to Walt Whitman of Brooklyn, in the next decade, to integrate eros into the transcendental picture.)

ELLEN SEWALL

Well, there's a story. Back in 1839, when he was twenty-two, Thoreau fell headlong in love with beautiful seventeen-year-old Ellen Sewall, a family friend from a nearby village. So did his brother John. Ellen accepted invitations from sometimes one brother, sometimes the other, and sometimes both together, to pick berries, walk to the pond, sail on the river, and once to see a touring giraffe, always with her aunt Prudence along as chaperone. She first said yes to John's proposal, then realized Henry was the one she loved, then was informed that her father wouldn't have her marrying either of those radical Concord boys, and that was that. Thoreau documented the whole emotional roller-coaster ride in his journal, much of it in bad poetry.

Ellen married a minister and had eight children, but in later years kept a picture of Henry hanging on her wall. He never had another serious romantic involvement, and for the rest of his life made sarcastic comments about those silly creatures, women. But as he lay on his deathbed, his sister mentioned Ellen, and Thoreau said, "I have always loved her. I have always loved her." It's heartbreaking to think how happy they might have been together. But then we wouldn't have *Walden*.

•

Thoreau, unlike Emerson, is still eminently readable, page after page. He's looser and funnier, with a keener observer's eye and a far better ear for sentences. Unlike Emerson, who couldn't carry a tune, Thoreau sang and played the flute enthusiastically. Anyone who wants to write should probably play music. Maybe it helped that he never wrote sermons, or listened to them.

Even without the Transcendentalist philosophy or his experiment in economic minimalism, Thoreau would be remembered as a supremely sensitive and poetic nature writer.

On the 29th of April, as I was fishing from the bank of the river near the Nine-Acre-Corner bridge, standing on the quaking grass and willow roots, where the muskrats lurk, I heard a singular rattling sound, ... when, looking up, I observed a very slight and graceful hawk, like a night-hawk, alternately soaring like a ripple and tumbling a rod or two over and over, showing the underside of its wings, which gleamed like a satin ribbon in the sun, or like the pearly inside of a shell. ... It was the most ethereal flight I had ever witnessed. It did not simply flutter like a butterfly, nor soar like the larger hawks, but it sported with proud reliance in the fields of air; mounting again and again with its strange chuckle, it repeated its free and beautiful fall, turning over and over like a kite, and then recovering from its lofty tumbling, as if it had never set its foot on *terra firma*. It appeared to have no companion in the universe, — sporting there alone, — and to need none but the morning and the ether with which it played. It was not lonely, but made all the earth lonely beneath it.

He is also a supreme chronicler of meditative experience — of the simple, timeless sinking into silent being.

Sometimes, in a summer morning, having taken my accustomed bath, I sat in my sunny doorway from sunrise till noon, rapt in a revery, amidst the pines and hickories and sumachs, in undisturbed solitude and stillness, while the birds sang around or flitted noiseless through the house, until by the sun falling in at my west window, or the noise of some traveller's wagon on the distant highway, I was reminded of the lapse of time. I grew in those seasons like corn in the night, and they were far better than any work of the hands would have been.

Then there's his political impact. The Bhagavad Gita, with its model of Arjuna as the enlightened warrior, helped inspire Thoreau to refuse to pay his poll tax and spend his famous night in jail in 1846. Several decades later, his essay "Civil Disobedience" inspired Mahatma Gandhi to use nonviolent resistance in the fight for India's independence. Gandhi, in turn, inspired Martin Luther King Jr.'s approach to the struggle for civil rights; in 1959, Dr. King spent five weeks in India studying Gandhi's methods. Thus, one spiritual idea crossed the oceans from India to America to India to America and changed the world.

Thoreau wasn't, and never pretended to be, the haloed stone buddha that many, including my youthful self, have imagined. (Neither was the Buddha.) Nor was he the freeloading, misanthropic monster that some revisionist critics have imagined. He was, like the rest of us, a guy trying to work out how to live in the world and answer the call of heaven — only he was a much better writer.

Among his neighbors, Thoreau was best known not as a writer but as the young man who, scandalously, spent Sundays under the open sky when good people were in church, but he also grew the most delicious melons in town, and invitations to his annual melon party were highly coveted. Erratic performances — sometimes engaging, sometimes mumbling — kept him from being a success in the Lyceum, and his attic room eventually held some seven hundred unsold copies of his books. He befriended the poor, illiterate Irish immigrants that his fellow Yankees shunned, donating money and clothes and helping them write letters home to the old country. He delighted the local children (including Louisa May Alcott) with nature walks and excursions on the pond, especially when he "[kept] up a whistling fire of conversation with the birds till they alighted on his head and shoulders."

After a long illness — tuberculosis and bronchitis, probably aggravated by inhaling pencil dust — Thoreau died in 1862, at age forty-four. Three hundred children walked in a procession following the funeral. Shortly before he died, his aunt Louisa asked if he had made his peace with God. He replied, "I did not know we had ever quarreled, Aunt."

•

I spent two years on the road. As it happened, Thoreau spent about the same amount of time at Walden. Then he wrote:

> I left the woods for as good a reason as I went there. Perhaps it seemed to me that I had several more lives to live, and could not spare any more time for that one.

Me too. In January 1977, I got my first (and last) grown-up job, teaching English at that New Jersey prep school. By then my Dharma understanding had grown more mature. Lao Tzu's "The way to do is to be," it turns out, doesn't mean to do nothing. It means to become so saturated with the silence of being that you can do anything, even finish college, hold down a job, get married, and raise kids, all of which I did, and it's all OK. On good days, it's boundlessly OK.

Every fall I taught American lit to eleventh-graders. Naturally, we read *Walden* and learned, among many other things, about Thoreau's deep affinity for Native Americans. (He astonished people with his ability to casually look down and find arrowheads almost anywhere he walked.) In one passage, he approvingly describes the custom of the Muclasse Indians, who every year gathered together all their old, extraneous possessions — their dead weight — and burned them. At our next session we met in the woods behind the school for a Henry Thoreau Memorial Purificatory Bonfire. Everyone was to bring something to burn, preferably something not too easy to part with.

As we went around the circle, each student spoke a little about what they had brought, then placed it in the center: a cherished photo of a first boyfriend or girlfriend, a ticket from an amazing concert, a Little League mitt. Sometimes tears were shed. I would add an object of my own, set it all ablaze, and chant a mantra of purification. Years later, former students, some of whom couldn't remember which books we'd read, told me they remembered that fire, and how, for a long time afterward, it made them feel lighter.

5. Have No Fear

DR. SEUSS · THE CAT IN THE HAT

For many of us, our love affair with reading began with Dr. Seuss. But does he belong in a book on — *ahem!* — literature? Who knows? That's such a big, baggage-heavy four-syllable word, such a big excuse to get stiff and serious. For now, what if we go with an unassuming one-syllable word — like "stuff," as in "good stuff"?

Dr. Seuss's good stuff is so good it made him the most successful children's author in history, even though he never had children and was deeply uncomfortable around them. No happy-go-lucky Sam-I-Am, he suffered from severe claustrophobia and crippling stage fright that made public appearances painful and rare. Each of his books, with its seemingly effortless rhythm and its celebration of free-wheeling imagination, took him a good year to write, chain-smoking as he agonized over every word and comma. He wrote (he once claimed) some two hundred lines to get four that he would keep, then pestered and re-pestered his publisher to match precisely the colors he had chosen for his drawings.

There's no mistaking his drawings — the wacky flora and fauna, the psychedelic topography, the zigzagging, jitterbugging motion of characters and objects — or his rollicking verse. Most of it is in anapestic meter: reverse waltz time. Rather than the *one*-two-three, *one*-two-three of gliding dancers, it's one-two-*three*, one-two-*three*, like the clippy-*clop* of galloping camels or the ba-da-*bing* of happy New Jersey goons. As in —

You have *brains* in your *head*.
You have *feet* in your *shoes*.
You can *steer* yourself *any* direction you *choose*.

Or —

Every *Who* down in *Who*ville liked *Christ*mas a *lot*
But the *Grinch* who lived *just* north of *Who*ville did *not*.

This rhythm, in its clumsy grace, feels a bit like Ringo Starr's drumming. Playing left-handed on a right-handed drum kit, Ringo sounds like he's tripping over his own feet. Then it's a delightful surprise that he somehow always lands in just the right place.

Those pictures and words would give us plenty to love even if they had no traces of Dharma. But in their best moments, they also express the universal urge for radical freedom — what the sages of ancient India called *moksha* and kids everywhere call *Wheeeeeee!!!*

Dr. Seuss's real name was Ted Geisel. He grew up speaking German at home, and he absorbed his sense of poetic rhythm from his mother, who put him to sleep by reciting the names of the pastries she once sold in her father's German bakery. Seuss, pronounced *zoice*, was her family name. Ted improvised his pseudonym at Dartmouth, when he was busted with several friends for drinking bootleg gin in a dorm and could no longer contribute to the student magazine under his real name. He first gained fame in 1928 as the creator of a wildly popular ad campaign for bug spray ("Quick, Henry, the Flit!"). Later, when he stormed the children's book market, he adopted the pronunciation *soose* because it was friendlier to American ears — and it rhymed with Mother Goose.

One night, in a restaurant in Boston, a publishing executive challenged Ted to write a book for beginning readers, using only a list of 220 educator-approved words. Genius thrives on restriction. When the energy of amorphous creativity is sifted through the grid of rigid structure, we get Keats making the sonnet soar, or Miles Davis making a Disney tune cool. But genius may still kick and scream along the way. Ted wanted to write about a Queen Zebra, but nothing as exotic as *queen* or *zebra* was on the word list. His frustration mounting, he was on the brink of giving up when he had a what-the-hell moment and decided his title would use the first two words on the list that rhymed. They were *cat* and *hat*.

•

I was seven years old when *The Cat in the Hat* was published, in the spring of 1957. Along with some three million other first-graders, I had spent the year being tormented by *Fun with Dick and Jane* and the other books in that wretched series — the blander-than-bland reading primers that were, in those bland Eisenhower years, standard in American grade schools. Dick and Jane and Baby Sally, their dog Spot and their cat Puff, are so boring, so stupid, so *good*, you want to throttle them. Their idea of a big adventure is setting the table for dinner.

> "I can work," said Dick.
> "I can help Mother."
> Jane said, "I can work too.
> I can help.
> Look, Dick.
> This is for Father.
> Father will eat here."

The excitement builds: Jane sets places for Father and Mother and Dick and Baby Sally, but — are you ready? — she forgets to set a place for herself! OMG!!! LOL!!!

Mercifully, *The Cat in the Hat* arrived just in time to interrupt this fiesta of tedium.

> Something went BUMP!
> How that bump made us jump!

That's the sound of the Cat colliding, unseen, with the door of a suburban home, the story's first plot point. It's heard by a brother and sister, "Sally and I," who sit, gazing glumly out the window, bored because it's raining and they can't go out and play. They've been left home alone.

We all got left home alone in those days, and we all experienced a series of bumps that made us jump. That October, the Russians launched Sputnik, the first artificial satellite. It was the Communist Menace from Outer Space, and our teachers soon had us jumping for cover under our desks, practicing for World War III. Within a decade, my boomer cohort would be jumping onto the front lines of the sexual revolution, the psychedelic revolution, the civil rights movement, the antiwar movement. The number one record of 1957 was Elvis's "All Shook Up," and we were.

So...the door swings open and the Cat, in his floppy, striped stovepipe hat, strides in, uninvited, to the astonishment of the two kids and their pet fish. He cheerfully offers to fix the boredom problem, and — in a portent of what awaited our generation — he solves it by shaking everything up. Repeating "Look at me! Look at me!" like a child shouting to its mother from the top of the jungle gym, he shows off "a lot of good tricks": precarious balancing acts with a growing assortment of household items (cake, rake, dish, fish, whatever was on Dr. Seuss's 220-word list) till he and they all come crashing down. All these shenanigans prompt loud protests from the fish ("No! No!"), who is the designated party pooper.

But the Cat doubles down, so to speak, opening a big box and setting the twin manic, species-indeterminate Thing One and Thing Two tearing through the house, playing "all kinds of bad tricks" to finish off the job of wrecking the place. In our own lives, there's always a Thing One and a Thing Two tearing things up, the pairs of opposites, playing bad tricks on us: loss and gain, pleasure and pain, fame and shame, ambition and sloth, timidity and pride, devotion to our mate and attraction to a multitude of babes and/or hunks, the desire to please others and the impulse to tell them all to go stuff it.

By now, the kids' once boring afternoon has degenerated into anarchy, and everyone's gonna be in big trouble when Mom gets home. But just before she returns, the Cat shows the kids "another good trick that I know," producing a fabulous picker-upper-mobile that puts everything back together good as new, and he drives off "with a tip of his hat."

It's not much of a stretch to place the Cat in a long line of lanky, disaster-prone, yet strangely confident doofus tricksters, including Bullwinkle J. Moose, Hobbes the tiger, Top Cat (naturally), Pee-wee Herman, and of course, Kramer of *Seinfeld*, who shares the Cat's habit of bursting unexpectedly through the door and instigating chaos. (The apprehensive yet fascinated "Sally and I" foreshadow Elaine and Jerry, while the sputtering, exasperated, and of course hairless fish is obviously George Costanza.) All these avatars of happy misrule bring us the same message: *Loosen up! Chaos is cool!* Chaos is exhilarating, and it's fine, as long as you wield it with a bit of skill. So emancipate yourself. *Let* Dick and Jane get off on the feeble thrill of setting the table — we're gonna cha-cha on the table, juggle the cutlery, play football with the turkey, and it'll all somehow turn out fine. As the Cat puts it:

> It is fun to have fun
> But you have to know how.

This is useful Seussian wisdom for future adults. Listen, kids: In a few years Dick and Jane's lame "I can work" will give way to "I *gotta* work." Your tasks will go from setting the table to setting goals and deadlines, and then busting your butt to meet them. You'll be in the daily grind of the workaday world, and it can feel like a straitjacket. Oh, the places you'll go.

The grownups do have methods of loosening that straitjacket, but many of them (booze, drugs, extramarital dalliances) can do serious damage. The benign method is transcendence — going sublimely beyond — and one of its sharpest tools is humor. The Cat's antics make us laugh even though (actually *because*) they threaten disaster in our most cherished, protected space: home. Humor evokes our deepest fears and tensions, our queasiest worries, then short-circuits them with a contradiction or surprise: a pun, a reversal, a slip on a banana peel, a clumsy juggling Cat. This triggers the release of tension through laughter, with its intense, dopamine-rich flush of well-being, and suddenly the things that frightened us seem diminished. Our scary monsters are cut down to size. Humor, said the poet Gregory Corso, is the divine butcher.

The other sharp tool of transcendence is meditation. Like *literature*, for many people that word is a big four-syllable excuse to stiffen up. But we can once again fall back on an honest one-syllable word, which many veteran meditators actually prefer: *sit*. Meditation is sitting. That simple. It's not the strenuous mental obstacle course people imagine. We don't have to (and can't) control the thoughts, feelings, sounds, or sensations that arise. As Rupert Spira says, we let our experiences just be and they let us just be. Meditation is this just being, just sitting.

Ironically, the very simplicity of meditation is often the stumbling block. Thus the presenting situation, the "problem" at the beginning of this story, is that the rain forces the kids to "Sit! Sit! Sit! Sit!" People will avoid just sitting at all costs. Let me check my phone, light a cigarette, click the remote, check my phone again, maybe try some elaborate meditation technique and then berate myself for failing at it — get something going, anything to distract me from that simplicity. But when we give it a chance, we discover that, after a bit of simple sitting, sublime transcendence starts to sneak up on us.

This book's rainy weather also has Dharma echoes. The custom of the *retreat* — an extended period of sitting, in a mutually supportive group — was first developed by Siddhartha Gautama, the man we know as the Buddha, the "awakened one," as he and his monks roamed through northern India. In the monsoon season, travel was impossible, so they would find a big cave or empty building and sit! sit! sit! sit! We can guess that, at first, many of them found it too "hard." Just because they wore robes and lived twenty-five hundred years ago doesn't mean they were essentially different from us. Some probably gave up and went home. But the rest persisted, intent on becoming buddhas. The idea is for *everybody* to become an awakened one.

There's a theory that the two children have only imagined the Cat, conjuring him up as a distraction from their boredom. Indeed, on the last page, as the mother's hand and foot come through the door (that's all we ever see of her), "Sally and I" are again seated at the window, exactly as at the beginning. From a Dharma perspective, we can suppose that, yes, the Cat arises out of the sitters' boredom, but not as mere distraction. This whole shook-up story has been the journey of Sally and I, finding our own inner cool Cat without moving an inch. If we sit long enough, liberation walks through the door, and it always arrives unexpectedly. As Saint Paul says, "The day of the Lord comes like a thief in the night."

It's not only liberation from Dick and Jane's square nine-to-five. That's just lifestyle stuff, which is after all pretty superficial. This is profound *inner* liberation — moksha — which we can find *within* the nine-to-five. As we awaken to the way that sparkling beingness suffuses everything in every moment, it's great fun to discover that nothing could be more Zen than setting the table. Nothing could be more delightful than punching the clock, now that it no longer punches back. The pairs of opposites no longer torment us. They're still there, but we start to see them as expressions of the same underlying being, in the unity of opposites promised by sages from Heraclitus in the West to Shankara in the East. There's a crucial moment in the story when the narrator plops a net over Thing One and Thing Two. As they huddle together in defeat, they appear to have merged into one.

•

Twenty years ago, I traveled through central Tibet with Charles Genoud, a brilliant Dharma teacher and expert on Buddhist iconography. He shepherded a small group of us through temple after temple, where we saw hundreds of *rupas* (sculptures) and *thangkas* (fabric paintings) of assorted deities and buddhas, learning how the form of each icon signifies particular aspects of formless enlightenment. Every detail is meaningful, from the layering of garments to the *mudra* (symbolic gesture) of the hands.

What might we see if we contemplate the Cat the way Charles taught me to contemplate Tibetan icons? Let's play.

Please take a long, quiet look at the book's cover. Here we see the Cat's formal, almost presidential portrait, ready to go on a dollar bill, or maybe a three-dollar bill. He gazes out at us in three-quarters profile, with what has been described as "a smile you might find on the Mona Lisa after her first martini." His eyes are wide but relaxed, free of both guile and judgment, the brows raised in a disarming "Who, me?" It's an expression of sweet, unassuming benevolence, even tenderness. Like that other lanky, stovepipe-hatted, presidential emancipator, Abe Lincoln, the Cat bears malice toward none. That's what keeps his humor buddha-like: it's the difference between the Cat and the Joker.

Resting his clasped hands on his pot belly, he could be someone's mellow, paunchy uncle — with shades of Hotei, the jolly, fat, Santa Claus–ish buddha of prosperity and well-being that you may have seen in Chinese restaurants, usually near the cash register. The pose conveys an avuncular reassurance that life, in spite of its many small and large disasters, many of which we've probably caused ourselves, is somehow finally just fine.

The fingers are interlaced in a mudra of peaceful stasis, self-restraint. Despite the Cat's alarming history, in this mode he's not going to grab anything. His thumbs rest pointing upward, their pads pressed together, in a here-is-the-steeple equilibrium. All his mischief has been enabled by humanoid opposable thumbs, but for now he holds mischief in check by opposing them

to each other, signaling the unity of opposites, the merging of Things One and Two. Touching at the middle but slanting away from each other at the top, a trick that neither humans nor cats can actually do, they suggest the paradox of our shared lives: we're both divergent and convergent, *pluribus* but *unum*, separate on the surface but deeply connected further down.

The Cat wears no buddha's robes, just a red bow tie, white gloves, and striped hat. Throughout the book, the tie is a droll barometer of his moods: upturned and perky when he's riding high, droopy when he's glum. Now, in his at-rest state, it's at a neutral horizontal, helped perhaps by a pinch of presidential starch. White gloves, because they're much simpler to draw than bare hands, have been standard issue for cartoon critters since early Mickey Mouse days. Here they might also suggest that, despite all the chaos the Cat wields with those hands, his intentions are pure.

But his defining accessory is the famous hat. Its alternating red and white stripes suggest our two basic modes of life energy: one warm, active, aggressive; the other cool, passive, receptive. The three red and two white stripes match the Cat's temperament, predominantly rambunctious but with just enough coolness to keep it from running completely off the rails. That's a workable model for those of us who live in the bustle of the world rather than monasteries. And perhaps, by gradually integrating our bustling activity with the cool quiet of sitting — by merging *that* Thing One and Two — we could release a third energy, one that resolves our clashing opposites and merges our individuality with sky-like boundlessness, like the opening-to-the-sky I experienced in the garage at age twelve and like the blue-sky expanse that here surrounds the Cat.

In yogic lore, the white, lunar, female energy and the red, solar, male energy are called *ida* and *pingala*. Starting at the coccyx, they spiral around the spinal column in an ascending double helix, nicely suggested here by the striped hat. When they're balanced, the symbolically sky-blue *sushumna* flows straight up the middle of the spine, out the top of the head, and, fountain-like, into boundlessness.

Do I think Dr. Seuss intended any of this? Certainly not. Do I care? Certainly not. Like our friend the Cat, we're just having "lots of good fun," balancing and juggling the elements of the book like so many rakes and cakes, till they all come crashing down. We're just looking at different ways of looking. As when you stroll past the windows on Fifth Avenue or Rodeo Drive, looking is free. When a book or film or symphony is so rich that it finds an abiding place in our collective psyche, nothing about it is definitive or final — it keeps opening out to more truths. And don't bother asking the artists what *they* meant. When they're immersed in creating, what comes through them is

bigger than their own intention, bigger than their conscious mind. You might as well ask a chicken about the mineral content of its egg.

This portrait of the Cat, then, shows us a buddha at rest, with his liberative energies in a state of potentiality. How do those energies look in action? For this we turn to the Cat's first appearance within the book, as he crosses the threshold of the flung-open front door, entering from the right side of the frame as the two kids look up in surprise from the left. We all have moments of crossing thresholds — into new jobs, new relationships, new stages of life — and they're often scary. The Cat shows us how to do it with the relaxed confidence of the liberated. Even as his legs carry him forward, his long body leans back, as if lounging on a La-Z-Boy. It's a posture that speaks of pushing ahead in the outer world while inwardly resting at ease. He has bodily entered the house, the structure of the new situation, but his head — his awareness — remains outside, in the boundless blue (miraculously blue despite the rain).

His eyes are closed. That's a meditative look as well as a surprisingly nonchalant way to enter a strange house. It signals a special kind of fearlessness, a relaxed at-homeness wherever you go. *Hey, whatever it is, I can handle it with my eyes closed.* But there's also a hint of a higher, more intuitive way of seeing. Despite the Cat's momentum as he sweeps into the house, the upper third of his soft hat flops forward rather than trailing behind, taking on the shape of a periscope, spying whatever lies ahead from a higher point of view.

Some decades ago, in the hills outside Rishikesh, in northern India, a friend of mine witnessed an encounter between a Western doctor and Tat Wale Baba, a cave-dwelling, loincloth-clad ascetic with dreadlocks down to the ground. Drawing close, the doctor realized that the monk's eyes were covered with cataracts, and asked him how he managed to scramble around the rocks and caves so nimbly. He replied, "These eyes? Oh, I don't use *these* eyes."

•

In Western iconography, this threshold-crossing is depicted in Caravaggio's *Calling of Saint Matthew*. When I was in Rome some years ago, I kept feeling compelled to walk back just one more time to the Church of San Luigi dei Francesi and feed my little coins into the box that lights up this masterpiece for a few minutes. I later learned that, as a young priest, the future Pope Francis felt the same pull and repeatedly stood in the same spot.

The five figures at the table are tax collectors, who in ancient Palestine worked on commission for the despised Roman occupiers, less like IRS agents in neckties than neighborhood thugs shaking down the locals for protection money. As Jesus and Saint Peter enter, accompanied by an intense tractor beam of divine light, they point toward one man in the group. Jesus says, according to the Gospels, "Follow me."

The tableau is remarkably like that of the Cat entering the house, also from the right side of the frame, as the startled children look up from the left. (In the theater, a character who crosses the stage boldly from the audience's right to its left, counter to the way we read, is usually a disruptive force.) Here, though, two of the men are so engrossed in counting their take — heads bowed, eyes glazed, like people hunched over their cell phones — that they don't even see that the Christ (the teacher, the Buddha, the embodied possibility of liberation) is in their midst. Of the other three, only the bearded man, Levi, soon to be renamed Matthew, is appropriately startled. He leans back (*Whoa!*), wide-eyed, frozen, a deer in the heavenlight — how that bump makes him jump!

It's his decisive moment. The fingers of his right hand linger on his money, hanging on to his old life, that which he can count on, that which he can count, the tainted but reassuringly familiar finite. But with the left hand he points to himself. *Are you talking to me?*

Yes, you.

The reality is that liberation is simpler and closer than we think. The light is here in our midst, blazing through the door in each moment, and it's here for ordinary, imperfect schmoes like us. Just look up, and don't be afraid to leave some money on the table.

Awakening is for us sleepers. Have we made a mess, like the Cat? (Like everyone, at one time or another?) OK — we clean it up the best we can. Have we, like thuggish tax collectors, sometimes hurt others? That's not final or definitive either. It's never too late to breathe out into the fresh next moment — into the freedom, the relaxation, the blue sky of surprises and creative mischief. Then on to the *next* moment.

Cross the threshold. It is fun to have fun.

6. Plenty for Everybody

VIRGINIA WOOLF · TO THE LIGHTHOUSE

There's a scene in *To the Lighthouse* where some sixteen or so people are seated at a long table, having supper together. One of them, an obnoxious, know-it-all graduate student, goes on a tedious political rant. The others pretend to be interested, "bending themselves to listen" as they think, "Pray heaven that the inside of my mind may not be exposed." Hey, we've all been there.

But this is a Virginia Woolf novel, so the inside of *every*one's mind is exposed — to the author, to the reader, and occasionally to the central character, Mrs. Ramsay. She's the hostess of this dinner, and after a few more pages of chatter she has a sudden empathic breakthrough that's so lucid and penetrating it borders on the *tele*pathic.

> Now she need not listen. It could not last, she knew, but at the moment her eyes were so clear that they seemed to go round the table

unveiling each of these people, and their thoughts and their feelings, without effort like a light stealing under water so that its ripples and the reeds in it and the minnows balancing themselves, and the sudden silent trout are all lit up hanging, trembling.

This kind of "unveiling," this psychological X-ray vision, is Virginia Woolf's literary superpower. To convey this vision with such clarity and nuance, we presume, she must have experienced it herself.

To the Lighthouse, the fifth of Woolf's nine novels, is based largely on her own childhood. The story line is skimpy. Section 1, which is about two-thirds of the book, is set on a single, ordinary day around 1910. The Ramsay family of London — Mr., Mrs., and their eight children — are staying in their usual rented summerhouse on the Isle of Skye, off the Scottish coast. Their youngest child, James, is eager to sail to the nearby lighthouse.

GODREVY LIGHTHOUSE, SAINT IVES, WOOLF'S CHILDHOOD INSPIRATION

Mrs. Ramsay reads James a fairy tale, chats a bit with some friends and houseguests, takes a brief walk into town. Mr. Ramsay, a noted philosopher, paces the lawn, thinking. (What philosophers do.) Nearby, their friend Lily Briscoe paints a picture and chats with William Bankes, a widowed botanist, while a houseguest — a slovenly old poet — naps in the sun, helped by a bit of opium. A few young adults, a mix of Ramsays and locals, walk to the beach and come back. Two of them become engaged but don't tell anyone. They all have supper together and go to bed.

Section 2: The house sits empty for ten years.

Section 3: Some of the characters return to the house and some of these sail to the lighthouse.

The End.

This thinness of plot — of horizontal movement from event to event, along the chronological axis — is deliberate. Woolf wants our attention free to move vertically, along the psychological axis, to join her in plumbing first one character's interior space, then another's. She establishes this agenda on the first page, when young James asks if they might sail to the lighthouse the next day. Mrs. Ramsay says they can if the weather permits.

> To her son these words conveyed an extraordinary joy....Since he belonged, even at the age of six, to that great clan which cannot keep this feeling separate from that, but must let future prospects, with their joys and sorrows, cloud what is actually at hand,...James Ramsay, sitting on the floor cutting out pictures from the illustrated catalogue of the Army and Navy stores, endowed the picture of a refrigerator, as his mother spoke, with heavenly bliss. It was fringed with joy.

To many Dharma practitioners, this kind of minute observation of the inner workings of human consciousness will sound familiar. It's essentially mindfulness practice. Now, these days *mindfulness* has become, like *Zen*, a trendy, all-purpose term for any kind of meditation, or anything even vaguely meditation-adjacent. (There used to be a shop near my home that sold soft, comfy, earth-tone home furnishings, called Mindfulnest.) But mindfulness, like Zen, has an old-school meaning that's quite precise. It's the English equivalent of *satipatthana*, a term used by the Buddha for a specific, powerfully liberating meditative technique. Addressing his disciples in the Satipatthana Sutta, he lays out the formula.

> Here, monks, in regard to the body a monk abides contemplating the body....In regard to feelings he abides contemplating feelings....In regard to the mind he abides contemplating the mind, diligent, clearly knowing, and mindful, free from desires and discontent in regard to the world.

To practice mindfulness, then, we *observe*, clearly and impartially. We pay close, engaged attention to whatever's going on in the body, feelings, and mind, with a kind of clinical neutrality, like a scientist from Mars studying from the inside how earthling consciousness functions.

We start by observing our experience of body. Not the *idea* of a body: that's a sort of vague mental collage, assembled from visual impressions of hands, knees, feet way down there, face in the mirror or in photos, and the ever-shifting flow of bodily sensations as we engage in various activities. Rather, we attend to the sensations and visual impressions themselves, as actual, raw, present-moment experiences, before the mind assembles them into an idea.

Next, we experience feelings as feelings. A feeling, such as grief or fascination, *feels* a certain way, before the mind abstracts or elaborates it into a story about *why* we're grieving or fascinated, when else we have felt like this, what we might want to do about it, and so forth.

Then we experience mind as mind: thoughts, images, memories, expectations, all our processes of forming ideas, including our ideas about the body and feelings. All that processing is itself an experienceable, neutrally observable activity. We don't do anything about these experiences, but "abide contemplating" them. In their presence, innocently, we just *are*.

This skill of clearly distinguishing things is unknown to what Woolf calls "that great clan which cannot keep this feeling separate from that," and whom the Buddha (in a phrase that may sound a tad condescending) calls "ordinary people." Ordinary people conflate things — smoosh them together. Young James conflates the cutout of the refrigerator with "heavenly bliss." He conflates "future prospects" and "their joys and sorrows" with "what is actually at hand." At this moment millions of people are conflating their feelings of free-floating rage or fear with their thoughts about people of other ethnic groups, or conflating their bodily sensations of sexual arousal with the feeling of being in love. Consequences may range from the mildly confusing to the catastrophic.

•

In addition to this kind of internal satipatthana, we can apply it externally by observing people and things, as Mrs. Ramsay sometimes does and as Woolf seems to have done relentlessly in the service of her art. But the real point of mindfulness as a Dharma practice (rather than a technique of fiction) is not so much what we observe as what happens to us in the process of observing. When we see body as none other than body, feelings as none other than feelings, and mind as none other than mind, our habitual conflations and interpretations start to lose their force. We see how we've been writing fictions of our own and find the freedom to leave off writing them. The distress that arises from the fictions — anxiety, blame, guilt, all the usual suspects — begins to melt away, and we can abide in the simple, open space that remains.

This is the space of grace, of samadhi, and Woolf knows it well. Here it dawns for Mrs. Ramsay, still at supper, even as the small talk goes on and she helps her guests to seconds.

> Everything seemed right. Just now... she had reached security; she hovered like a hawk suspended; like a flag floated in an element of joy which filled every nerve of her body fully and sweetly...; all of which rising in this profound stillness (she was helping William Bankes to one very small piece more, and peered into the depths of the earthenware pot) seemed now for no special reason to stay there like a smoke, like a fume rising upwards, holding them safe together. Nothing need be said; nothing could be said. There it was, all round them. It partook, she felt, carefully helping Mr. Bankes to a specially tender piece, of eternity;... a coherence in things, a stability; something, she meant, is immune from change, and shines out (she glanced at the window with its ripple of reflected lights) in the face of the flowing, the fleeting, the spectral, like a ruby; so that again tonight she had the feeling... of peace, of rest. Of such moments, she thought, the thing is made that endures.
>
> "Yes," she assured William Bankes, "there is plenty for everybody."

In that last line, we can imagine Mrs. Ramsay's private Mona Lisa smile at her little double entendre. There's plenty of food for everybody, and plenty of peace — infinite peace — for everybody.

The seed of this samadhi is also present in the Buddha's sequence of mindfulness practice. After we contemplate body, feelings, and mind, there's one more step.

> In regard to dhammas [a monk] abides contemplating dhammas, diligent, clearly knowing, and mindful, free from desires and discontent in regard to the world.

Here, *dhammas* means, roughly, Dharma truth, Dharma perspective. The dhammas include the Three Marks of Existence — impermanence, nonself, and suffering, or unsatisfactoriness — as well as the Four Noble Truths. Contemplating them leads (as in Mrs. Ramsay's epiphany) to joyful release from all unsatisfactoriness.

We apply these dhammas to the experiences of body, feelings, and mind — not by merely thinking about the experiences, which would generate more concepts (Dharma concepts, yet concepts), but once again, by dispassionately, clinically observing them. If carbon is really fundamental to all life-forms, then we should find it in any life-form we analyze. If the dhammas are really bedrock facts of life, then we should find them functioning in any life experience we encounter. Yes, all things *are* impermanent; no, we *can't* locate any independent, separate selves; yes, life *is* profoundly unsatisfactory till we relax our grip on hankering and open to the peace of being. These are (the Buddha taught) not opinions, not views, but View. From the top of the mountain, you get a bigger, truer vision of the valley. You stop speculating and see what's there.

Glimpses of these dhammas keep showing up in the experiences of Woolf's characters, as in great fiction generally. During the young folks' excursion to the beach, Nancy Ramsay has an intuitive moment, a poignant little opening to the tragic universality of dukkha, unsatisfactoriness, suffering. Nancy's friend Minta has lost her prized possession in the sand.

> It was her grandmother's brooch; she would rather have lost anything but that, and yet Nancy felt...she wasn't crying only for that. She was crying for something else. We might all sit down and cry, she felt. But she did not know what for.

The dhamma of anitya — impermanence, the decay and dissolution of all things — plays out dramatically in the second of the book's three sections, "Time Passes." The summer home, which is a cherished family tradition, the kind that children especially rely on to be there always, is shuttered. Various circumstances, including the First World War, have intervened, and the house stands empty for a decade.

To portray the story's longest span of time in its shortest section, Woolf devises a breathtaking inversion of perspective. Till now, her strategy has been, once every few pages, to pass the point of view along, like the baton in a relay race, in order to portray how the exquisite subtleties of human consciousness vary from person to person. But now that the family has gone home to London, the point of view stays behind, depersonalized, in the beloved summerhouse as it falls into decay.

The house was left; the house was deserted. It was left like a shell
on a sandhill to fill with dry salt grains now that life had left it.
The long night seemed to have set in; the trifling airs, nibbling, the
clammy breaths, fumbling, seemed to have triumphed. The sauce-
pan had rusted and the mat decayed. Toads had nosed their way in.
Idly, aimlessly, the swaying shawl swung to and fro. A thistle thrust
itself between the tiles in the larder. The swallows nested in the
drawing-room; the floor was strewn with straw; the plaster fell in
shovelfuls; rafters were laid bare; rats carried off this and that to gnaw
behind the wainscots. Tortoise-shell butterflies burst from the chrysalis and pattered their life out on the window-pane.

No longer the background to the family's rich summer life, the house has
moved to the foreground, while the family has been reduced to small, distant
figures in the background. As the section goes on, we're occasionally told of
an event — perhaps a marriage, perhaps a death — that, were it in the foreground, would fill many pages with high drama. Instead, it's a matter-of-fact
sentence or two, tucked between brackets.

That's a lesson on the dhamma of anatta: no solid, individual, independent self. The rarely questioned paradox in our notion of self — the joker in
the deck — is that, of the almost eight billion humans on the planet, one of
them is the self, the star of the show, the center of all experience, whose joy
or pain urgently matters. All the other people are, well, just other people,
supporting players. And against all odds (eight billion to one, specifically, not
counting the gajillions of other sentient beings), *I* got cast as the self, *I'm* the
star.

Sure, I understand in the abstract that others experience joy and pain, but
let's face it: it's just not real to me in any kind of felt way. Oddly, though, all
those supporting players think that *they're* the star and *I'm* chopped liver. It's
like *here* and *there*. It's obvious to me that here is over here, where I am. You
labor under the delusion that it's over there, where you are.

In section 1, by frequently passing around the point of view, Woolf shows
us the slippery, ad hoc nature of selfhood, lending it to one person after another, then snatching it away. Now, in section 2, she snatches it away from
all those persons at once, widening the focus to a big, nonpersonal picture,
where not only each individual human's interests have lost their favored place
at the center of the world, but so have those of the human race as a whole. The
house's sad, ugly decay is only sad, or ugly, or decay from the human point of
view. Let that go, and as the rats and toads and thistles take over, we see it's all
the flourishing of life.

And all of it, culminating in the tortoise-shell butterflies bursting from the chrysalis, is strangely beautiful. Anytime we release our insistence on primacy of self or tribe or species, we find a bigger beauty to relax into. Self is a straitjacket. Like the butterflies, we can burst out of it anytime. Otherwise, in time it will be shredded anyway.

•

The other great theme of *To the Lighthouse*, and of Woolf's work generally, is that of female and male. Mrs. and Mr. Ramsay are in some ways extremes of their genders. Mrs. R is a supercompetent, superintuitive Earth Mother, attending expertly to the material and emotional needs, not only of her large family and circle of friends, but of poor townies. Whenever she walks into the village, it is with a basket full of socks, tobacco, and other such boons to distribute.

And wherever she goes, even at age fifty and after eight children, people are stunned by her looks. Clearly, she's the Goddess — the feminine divine, the incarnation of beauty, healing, abundance, fertility, and nurturing love, with life perpetually emerging from her: "She would have liked always to have had a baby. She was happiest carrying one in her arms." Not surprisingly, she's a relentless matchmaker, choreographing the coming together of couples who don't even know yet that they've been chosen to be fruitful and multiply.

Of course, when divinities take mortal form, they're subject to mortal flaws. The couples Mrs. R brings together don't always wind up happily ever after. Her incessant private charities earn her a reputation as a bit of a busybody. And raising eight kids can make anyone tired, even a goddess. Like many beleaguered moms, she's subject to waves of depression, wondering, "But what have I done with my life?" But not for long.

Where Mrs. R is all heart, Mr. R is all mind, and not in a good way — it's mind made toxic by ego. His ratio of IQ to EQ is alarmingly high. In his first appearance in the book, he dashes young James's hopes of sailing to the lighthouse. He insists, correctly but brutally, that the weather will be bad,

> grinning sarcastically, not only with the pleasure of disillusioning his son and casting ridicule upon his wife...but also with some secret conceit at his own accuracy of judgement.

The boy's reaction is horrifying, yet we find ourselves in sympathy with it:

Had there been an axe handy, or a poker, any weapon that would have gashed a hole in his father's breast and killed him, there and then, James would have seized it.

Mr. Ramsay's philosophical specialty is metaphysics, literally that which is beyond the physical world — beyond the realm of the Earth Mother. He's too busy thinking to *see* the physical world, a fact on which his wife broods.

His understanding often astonished her. But did he notice the flowers? No. Did he notice the view? No. Did he even notice his own daughter's beauty, or whether there was pudding on his plate or roast beef?

When the painter Lily Briscoe struggles to understand what his philosophical work is all about, one of the older Ramsay boys tells her, "Think of a kitchen table, then, when you're not there." That unobserved table, the table minus self, is a sly foreshadowing of the uninhabited house, house minus selves, in the "Time Passes" section. It could also make a lovely koan, akin to the sound of one hand clapping, if it were used skillfully, to launch the mind beyond the clutter of thoughts into the thought-free, self-free, radiant silence that is ulti-mate truth. But for Mr. Ramsay, Western philosopher that he is, all thoughts lead in a straight line to more thoughts, and ultimate truth is a hypothetical ultimate thought forever eluding a valiantly striving self.

For if thought...like the alphabet is ranged in twenty-six letters all in order, then his splendid mind had no sort of difficulty in run-ning over those letters one by one, firmly and accurately, until it had reached, say, the letter Q.... But after Q? What comes next? After Q there are a number of letters the last of which is scarcely visible to mortal eyes, but glimmers red in the distance. Z is only reached once by one man in a generation. Still, if he could reach R it would be something. Here at least was Q. He dug his heels in at Q.... The veins on his forehead bulged....

Yet he would not die lying down; he would find some crag of rock, and there, his eyes fixed on the storm, trying to the end to pierce the darkness, he would die standing. He would never reach R.

This stereotypically male approach to truth, with its stubborn linearity and its toy-soldier heroics, is underscored by the poem Mr. Ramsay recites as he paces the lawn: Tennyson's "Charge of the Light Brigade," the consummate Victorian celebration of suicidal military glory.

> Stormed at with shot and shell,
> Boldly they rode and well,
> Into the jaws of Death,
> Into the mouth of hell
>   Rode the six hundred.

That's delightful, blustering verse, and the resolute spirit it celebrates has its own grandeur. But as an approach to capital-T Truth, it's the wrong tool for the job. (In the actual Charge of the Light Brigade, in the Crimean War in 1854, garbled commands sent British troops on a disastrously misguided assault against the wrong Russian positions. As the poem itself says, "Someone had blundered.")

Mrs. Ramsay, whose supposedly inferior intellect her husband ridicules, is far more successful at apprehending Truth. She's a natural: she has no idea that the boundlessness she quietly settles into from time to time is exactly what her husband so vainly seeks as he paces and sputters Tennyson or scribbles out his weary books. She finds it by not looking for it. She just goes about her mothering and wife-ing with the sensitive receptivity they require, and Truth, finding her a sensitive, receptive vessel, now and then ravishes her. When it does, she has enough woman-wisdom to open up and embrace the "darkness" (emptiness, *shunyata*) that Mr. Ramsay misguidedly battles.

One such visitation takes place as she knits, after her children have gone to bed.

> Now she need not think about anybody. She could be herself, by herself... to think; well, not even to think. To be silent; to be alone. All the being and the doing, expansive, glittering, vocal, evaporated; and one shrunk, with a sense of solemnity, to being oneself, a wedge-shaped core of darkness, something invisible to others. Although she continued to knit, and sat upright, it was thus that she felt herself.... There was freedom, there was peace, there was, most welcome of all, a summoning together, a resting on a platform of stability. Not as oneself did one find rest ever, in her experience (she accomplished here something dexterous with her needles) but as a wedge of darkness. Losing personality, one lost the fret, the hurry, the stir; and there rose to her lips always some exclamation of triumph over life when things came together in this peace, this rest, this eternity.

In traditional terms, to be filled with the Holy Spirit one must open as the female opens to the male. That's what happens in sitting meditation when we finally stop trying to do it and let it do us. (The great fortune of my life was finding teachers who taught me to skip the trying part.) It can also happen when we pray, dance, write, shoot hoops, or walk down the street. It's portrayed poetically in the story of Mary's impregnation, in the tales of the 108 milkmaids and their divine romance with Lord Krishna, and in the Song of Solomon ("Let him kiss me with the kisses of his mouth! ... The king has brought me into his chambers. ... I am faint with love.")

But we all need both ways of being, female and male. Here, Woolf has isolated and exaggerated them, embodying them in a woman and in a man, like a chemist isolating a couple of elements to study them in their pure form. She subtly underscores this maneuver by not giving the Ramsays first names: they exist only as Mrs. and Mr.

She takes this idea further in *A Room of One's Own*, a long essay based on a pair of lectures she gave in 1928 on the topic of women in fiction. It became popular as a feminist manifesto in the seventies, best known for the decree that in order to write (or create art of any kind) a woman needs money and a room of her own — two things that, historically, have rarely been available to her. Woolf invites us to imagine that Shakespeare had an equally brilliant sister who, like him, left home to pursue her passion to write. Given the social realities of the age, she would most likely wind up living in squalor, estranged from her family, sexually exploited, pregnant, and finally dead by her own hand, "buried at some cross-roads where the omnibuses now stop outside the Elephant and Castle."

Probably to the disappointment of many feminists, however, Woolf isn't calling for fiction to be a literature of protest against gender inequity, or even a literature of gender identity.

> It is fatal for anyone who writes to think of their sex. ... It is fatal for a woman to lay the least stress on any grievance; to plead even with justice any cause; in any way to speak consciously as a woman.

Rather, the ideal mental state for literary creation requires an *integration* of genders, of our forward-charging Mr. Ramsay and our empathizing, silence-embracing Mrs. Ramsay.

> It is fatal to be a man or woman pure and simple; one must be woman-manly or man-womanly. ... Some marriage of opposites has to be

consummated. The whole of the mind must lie wide open if we are to get the sense that the writer is communicating his experience with perfect fullness. There must be freedom and there must be peace.

Real creativity proceeds, then, not from a social or political attitude but from the "wide open" state of mind, where there's "freedom and…peace" (the same two words Woolf uses to describe Mrs. Ramsay's knitting-samadhi). That requires the mind of the artist to be androgynous — not unsexed, but both-sexed.

> The androgynous mind is resonant and porous;…it transmits emotion without impediment;…it is naturally creative, incandescent and undivided.

Simultaneously with *A Room of One's Own*, Woolf wrote *Orlando*, a novel in which the protagonist is literally androgynous. It was one of her greatest successes.* Nowadays we might speak, with some simplification, of integrating left-brain functions (logical analysis, linear perception, verbal articulation) with right-brain functions (intuitive insight, spatial perception, nonverbal rapture). In the traditional yogic vocabulary, it's the ida and the pingala: the tranquil, lunar, feminine energy and the assertive, solar, masculine energy. All great artists — and Woolf holds Shakespeare as the supreme example — must have both streams flowing unimpeded.

•

Like the Ramsay children, Virginia Woolf was one of eight siblings, with a fiercely intellectual father: Sir Leslie Stephen, historian, literary critic, and hardy mountaineer. Also like them, she had a mother who was a philanthropist and a famous beauty: the artist's model Julia Jackson Stephen, who turns up as the redheaded, swan-necked, dreamy-eyed heroine in a lot of those retro-medieval Pre-Raphaelite paintings. The family did spend summers in a seaside village with a tantalizing view of a lighthouse — not in Scotland, however, but in Saint Ives, Cornwall, on England's extreme southwestern tip, a fishing village that was on its way to becoming an artists' colony.

---

*   There's a 1992 film version starring — yes! — Tilda Swinton.

EDWARD BURNE-JONES,
THE PRINCESS SABRA LED TO THE
DRAGON, MODELED BY JULIA STEPHEN

Unlike Shakespeare's imagined sister, Woolf was able to live a writer's life, warmly encouraged by her husband Leonard Woolf, with whom she started a publishing house. She found intellectual and artistic fellowship, as well as bohemian sexual experimentation, in London's Bloomsbury Group, in which she and Leonard were central figures. Still, she died a suicide. She was plagued by bouts of mental illness, triggered by early deaths in the family as well as years of childhood sexual abuse by a stepbrother, and she finally decided she couldn't go on burdening her husband with her care. She left him a loving note.

To the Lighthouse ends just as a few of our characters are at last about to arrive at the lighthouse. But after all those years their lives have changed, and what the lighthouse means to them has changed. Most of us, even in adulthood, invest elusive adventures or accomplishments or lovers, or perhaps the letter Z, with magical, joy-making power. Over time, though, all investments are subject to depreciation. When we try to reach the lighthouse, try to reach the light, as any *thing* in this world, what we reach is disappointment. That kind of lighthouse, as Woolf's title implies, is something we're perpetually sailing *to.*

The real light, of course, is always within us, is always us, usually overlooked as we trim our sails for something else. It seems unjust that someone who could write about that light as beautifully as Virginia Woolf did — someone who could conjure it so clearly with her words that millions of readers have been able to taste it — would not come fully into the light herself, would not awaken from the deep suffering that finally drove her to walk into the River Ouse with her pockets full of rocks.

Not everyone makes it home free, at least not this time around. But if they are as inspired as Woolf was, they may share the destiny of Moses, who helped lead others to the Holy Land though he could not enter it himself. At least, one fine day atop Mount Nebo, the Lord let him view it from afar.

7. Pebbles and Boulders

ERNEST HEMINGWAY • A FAREWELL TO ARMS

Haiku are hard to write because they're simple and we're complicated. They're concrete and we're abstract. They're clear and specific; we're vague and general. They're straightforward; we work overtime to be clever. They're planted firmly in the present moment; we (or, rather, our thoughts) are smeared across the past and future.

The prototypical haiku was written in the seventeenth century by Matsuo Basho, the first great master of the form. In the world of Japanese poetry, it's the equivalent of Leonardo's *Last Supper* or Beethoven's Ninth.

furuike ya
kawazu tobikomu
mizu no oto

old pond
frog jumps in —
plop

That's about as simple as language can get.* It's a snapshot of a moment, in which we feel thoroughly, solidly present. But the moment resonates, opening into a dimension of wider implication. Being old, the pond is mossy, overgrown — a shady, quiet refuge, like the mind of someone grown mellow through years of Dharma practice or simple old age. It just sits and is, as if it's been there forever.

In contrast, the fresh, active element that sparks the haiku is the jumping-in of the frog. It's a new, momentary experience entering the old awareness, time splashing into eternity. When they meet, the result is "plop" or "splash" — *oto* in Japanese (roughly, "water sound"), which can't be made by either the pond or the frog alone. And although the poem speaks only of observed objects, it's also about the observing subject: the poet's (and, vicariously, the reader's) silent, invisible awareness. *That* pond. When the silence is clear enough, it gives rise to *kensho*, a glimpse of the transcendent. All haiku aim for kensho, usually in the third line.

What Ernest Hemingway brings to American fiction is prose that works like haiku. Here's the opening of his 1929 novel *A Farewell to Arms*, based on his experiences in the First World War.

In the late summer of that year we lived in a house in a village that looked across the river and the plain to the mountains. In the bed of the river there were pebbles and boulders, dry and white in the sun, and the water was clear and swiftly moving and blue in the channels. Troops went by the house and down the road and the dust they raised powdered the leaves of the trees. The trunks of the trees too were dusty and the leaves fell early that year and we saw the troops marching along the road and the dust rising and leaves, stirred by the breeze, falling and the soldiers marching and afterward the road bare and white except for the leaves.

---

* In English, unlike Japanese, requiring seventeen syllables generally produces haiku that are too long and sound unnatural. They should generally be as short as possible and sound like they turned up under a rock or dropped from a tree.

This is stripped-down language, haiku language. Even the punctuation is reduced to periods and a few grudging commas: you can read page after page of Hemingway and never see a semicolon. Like haiku, it relies on concrete nouns ("pebbles," "boulders," "leaves," "trees") and a few adjectives that are so solid and objective they *feel* like nouns ("dry," "white," "dusty"). It pointedly omits the kind of adjectives that are often used to spice things up with a bit of breathless drama. There are no "tiny" pebbles or "huge" boulders, just pebbles and boulders. The right nouns speak for themselves.

But Hemingway had to address a problem that Basho didn't have. English, unlike Japanese, has two main root languages: Old English (or Anglo-Saxon), an earthy, guttural, Germanic, mainly monosyllabic language from which we've inherited words like *dog, fire, dirt, guts, work, shit*; and an early form of French brought by the Norman invaders in 1066. When the Normans took over, their French — Latin-derived, less earthy and direct, more cerebral and polysyllabic — became the language of the new ruling class. Now fire became *la combustion*, work became *l'occupation*, shit became *la purgation*. Gradually the two languages mixed, leaving us with a double vocabulary of plain Anglo-Saxon and fancy Norman.

For the next eight or nine centuries, most writers, not wanting to sound like unlettered Anglo-Saxon peasants, favored the fancy words. Even today, high schoolers use the longest words possible. (I used to tell my students, "It doesn't make you sound smart. It makes you sound like you're trying to sound smart.") It's the same with cops. You'll never hear a police chief in a news segment say, "The man left the car." It's always, "The individual exited the vehicle."

Hemingway turns the clock back to 1065, purging his language of Normanish polysyllables. The short, blunt Anglo-Saxon words, with fewer syllables to get between them and the objects, *sound* more like objects. The movement toward a plain, direct style actually starts earlier, going back at least to Emily Dickinson, Mark Twain, Stephen Crane, and then Gertrude Stein, who mentored the young Hemingway. But he takes it all the way, mobilizing the most straightforward language to express the straightforwardness of experience. Things are not our ideas of them, our judgments of them, our desires for them. They're not symbols. They're things. Like Cézanne's apples, they sit there, being present, being what they are. In that just-sitting simplicity is freedom from the mind's habitual blather.

A few other elements helped catalyze Hemingway's style. As a child, he played Bach on the cello. (His mother took him out of school for a year to focus on his playing.) You can hear the architectonic rhythms and repetitions of

PAUL CÉZANNE, *STILL LIFE WITH APPLES AND PEARS*

Bach fugues in the structure of his sentences. Listen to that last sentence again, especially what he does with "leaves" and "and."

> The trunks of the trees too were dusty and the leaves fell early that year and we saw the troops marching along the road and the dust rising and leaves, stirred by the breeze, falling and the soldiers marching and afterward the road bare and white except for the leaves.

People who try to emulate or parody Hemingway's style often write a lot of short, monotonous sentences. But that's not what he does. This one goes on and on and on because it describes a line of troops that goes on and on and on. By reproducing the rhythm of their marching (and the dust rising and the leaves falling), Hemingway makes it feel as if it takes as long to read the sentence as it does for the troops to pass. He has taken the haiku sense of presence and extended it, from snapshot to movie. And at the end of the sentence ("afterward the road bare and white except for the leaves"), as in the last line of a haiku, we have kensho, a glimpse of transcendence, the silence of the bare road made resonant by the passing of the troops, just as the silence of the old pond is made resonant by the frog.

Crucial to all this is Hemingway's habit of disciplined observation, which he developed as a young reporter for the *Kansas City Star* and in his extensive hunting and fishing in the Michigan woods. When you're tracking a deer, you have to see what you see, not what you think or wish. In the passage above, he makes us see the things as if on the first morning of creation, as if no one has had a chance yet to smudge them with thoughts.

A good mindful-writing exercise is to observe people doing an everyday activity that's so familiar you think you know what it looks like. You have to cut through the fog of your habitual thoughts to see all you've missed; then get it on paper so clearly that the reader sees it too. Here's how Hemingway does it:

> That night in the mess after the spaghetti course, which every one ate very quickly and seriously, lifting the spaghetti on the fork until the loose strands hung clear then lowering it into the mouth, or else using a continuous lift and sucking into the mouth, helping ourselves to wine from the grass-covered gallon flask; it swung in a metal cradle and you pulled the neck of the flask down with the forefinger and the wine, clear red, tannic and lovely, poured out into the glass held with the same hand; after this course, the captain commenced picking on the priest.

And again as in haiku, inseparable from what's seen is the seer, which is silent, invisible awareness, felt in the negative space around the seen. Another, cheesier writer might have started this novel with something like, "In 1918, I, Frederic Henry, a fresh-faced youth from the American Midwest, joined the Italian army as an ambulance driver, with no idea how brutal the war would turn out to be." That's information, not direct experience, and it immediately narrows the I to an ego, a small self defined by personal qualities and the constructs of past and future. Instead, Hemingway gives us an anonymous "we" in the first sentence ("we lived in a house in the village") that approximates invisible witnessing awareness. We're several chapters in before he reluctantly gives his hero a name.

•

Our implicit status as witnessing awareness — rather than an ego stuffed into a body and tagged with a name — becomes explicit when Frederic, like Hemingway himself, is hit by mortar fire.

Then there was a flash, as when a blast-furnace door is swung open, and a roar that started white and went red and on and on in a rushing wind. I tried to breathe but my breath would not come and I felt myself rush bodily out of myself and out and out and out and all the time bodily in the wind. I went out swiftly, all of myself, and I knew I was dead and that it had all been a mistake to think you just died. Then I floated, and instead of going on I felt myself slide back. I breathed and I was back.

This description is completely persuasive because it's free of woo-woo interpretation: Frederic's near-death experience is presented with the same moment-to-moment objectivity as eating spaghetti. But curiously, once he's patched up and dives back into war and whiskey and women, the knowledge that it's "a mistake to think you just died" is forgotten. He never mentions it again, and the deaths that he witnesses as the book goes on weigh more and more heavily upon him, with a crushing finality that makes life seem meaningless. For some people, a sneak preview of awareness as independent of the mortal form is profoundly awakening. On others, it's wasted.

Still, the accumulation of deaths does lead to some of the book's most cogent passages. In one, Frederic has been talking with an Italian soldier who makes a melodramatic statement about how the fatalities they've already sustained must not be "in vain." The phrase sends Frederic into a reverie about hearing officers give speeches intended to rouse the troops.

I was always embarrassed by the words sacred, glorious, and sacrifice and the expression in vain. We had heard them, sometimes standing in the rain almost out of earshot, so that only the shouted words came through...and I had seen nothing sacred, and the things that were glorious had no glory and the sacrifices were like the stockyards at Chicago if nothing was done with the meat except to bury it....Abstract words such as glory, honor, courage, or hallow were obscene beside the concrete names of villages, the numbers of roads, the names of rivers, the numbers of regiments and the dates.

Here the opposition of the concrete to the abstract is a matter not just of prose style but of life and death. People die for abstractions — glory, honor, "Western values," "Remember the Alamo." (Interestingly, except for "hallow," all the abstract words Frederic calls obscene are Norman imports.) The great comic counterpart of this passage is Falstaff's soliloquy on honor in *Henry IV,*

Part 1. Concluding that *honor* is merely a word, made out of air, and can't heal a wound or set a broken leg, he decides, "I'll none of it," and ducks out of battle. Frederic eventually deserts as well. Hemingway's treatment of the theme, of course, is dead serious, most shockingly in the image of the Chicago stockyards where the trains roll in, the cattle go straight into the slaughterhouses, and then the meat is buried in the dirt. That's what war amounts to.

Again, though, the message seems to have been lost on Hemingway. He couldn't stay away from war and killing, in his books or his life. When no war was available, it was big-game hunting in Africa, bullfighting in Spain, or deep-sea fishing in the Gulf of Mexico. Always something being killed, and all of it became part of his macho legend — along with the parade of wives, the epic drinking, the occasional kindnesses, and the many betrayals. No need to rehash that oft-rehashed story. But perhaps we can glean from it some useful wisdom regarding ego. Hemingway aspired to be the Great Bull Elephant of American fiction. He got his wish and then had to keep dragging that elephant around, feeding its bottomless appetite and fighting off every new young bull that came along.

•

Hemingway's specialty, then, is mindful observation of the outer world of things, washed clean of thought and feeling. His occasional forays into the inner world of feeling, unlike the finely nuanced insights of his contemporary Virginia Woolf, can seem stunted and clumsy: "It was nice." "It was good." "It was very good." "It was no good." Writers and readers who worship at the shrine of Hemingway often learn the wrong lesson here, mistaking this emotional inarticulateness for manly stoicism, a virtue to emulate. (Yeah, real men don't talk about feelings. They get drunk and hit stuff.) In *A Farewell to Arms*, the story coalesces around Frederic's love for the English nurse Catherine Barkley, which starts as a young man's hormone-fueled love. His love does grow more mature, but we're never told much about how it feels.

In Hemingway's best writing, though, he *implies* a character's inner feelings through outer objects and in the space of things left unsaid. This is all in the haiku tradition. After Frederic deserts, he and Catherine, now pregnant with his child, escape to Switzerland. At the end of the book she goes into a painful, protracted labor and tells Frederic to go out for some breakfast. As he walks back from the café to the hospital, through the empty street and the early morning light, the suspicion that Catherine may not survive the delivery begins to dawn. He hasn't yet expressed it, even to himself, but there's a mounting dread that, while they've outrun the war, they haven't outrun death — that everything they've been through will come to nothing.

> Outside along the street were the refuse cans from the houses waiting for the collector. A dog was nosing at one of the cans.
>
> "What do you want?" I asked and looked in the can to see if there was anything I could pull out for him; there was nothing on top but coffee-grounds, dust and some dead flowers.
>
> "There isn't anything, dog," I said. The dog crossed the street.

"Coffee-grounds, dust and some dead flowers": that's a haiku of desolation. There isn't anything.

This method is at the core of what may be Hemingway's most beautiful story, "Big Two-Hearted River." It portrays his youthful alter ego Nick Adams, recently returned from the Great War with a burden of suppressed combat trauma, on a solitary fishing trip in the Michigan woods. The war is never mentioned, yet it haunts every sentence. The wooded hills and the local town that Nick remembers from before the war are gone, burned out just as he is. He tiptoes around his pain by mindfully focusing on the methodical, moment-to-moment rituals of pitching his tent, cooking his breakfast, tying his flies, casting his line. But his longing to regain stability and balance, to learn how to live in the world again, is reflected in his quiet contemplation of the fish.

> Nick looked down into the clear, brown water, colored from the pebbly bottom, and watched the trout keeping themselves steady in the current with wavering fins. As he watched them they changed their positions by quick angles, only to hold steady in the fast water again. Nick watched them a long time.

The simplicity of that last sentence, and the depth of what it conveys in its six Anglo-Saxon monosyllables, is stunning. We see — we feel — Nick gazing at the trout, studying them in silence, trying to learn from them how to be steady in the current of life. And for the moment, in the very act of watching, he *is* steady. We realize (again, without any of this being said) that in looking into the stream he's looking into himself.

This may be the high point of Hemingway Dharma. Pain and despair don't automatically get the last word — the possibility of healing, of liberation from suffering, is at least an open question. As the story ends, Nick is still not ready to face his trauma, but in the moving final sentence he makes an implicit pledge to do so. "There were plenty of days coming when he could fish the swamp."

8. The Milk of Paradise

SAMUEL TAYLOR COLERIDGE • KUBLA KHAN

Why poetry?

Why do we read it? Why does it exist?

It *doesn't* exist, I can tell you, to provide a unit for literature classes, so that students can be drilled in spotting poetic devices (*Metaphor: check! Hyperbole: check!*). It's not a rhyming puzzle that yields a tidy little "message" when you untangle it; if it were, we could keep the message and throw away the poem. The language *is* the poem. As Robert Frost said, "Poetry is what gets lost in translation."

I'm pretty sure poetry can't be defined, but I'll take a shot anyway:

Poetry is words of power.

One of its most fundamental and magical powers is to make us see things that aren't there. It's holographic. That's consistent, in the Vedic tradition of ancient India, with the principle of *nama-rupa*, "name and form," where, on some very fine level of existence, the vibrations that make up an object are said to parallel, or reiterate, the vibrations that make up its name. The hymns of the Vedas, Hinduism's oldest scriptures, are supposed to have been not composed by anyone but "cognized" by seers, or *rishis*, who, in the depths of their meditation, heard-saw the co-arising names and forms of the gods and their exploits.

I don't know how literally we can take that, especially since Vedic Sanskrit, Hebrew, and other ancient languages all claim to have the "true" names of objects. What we do know — what we can experience for ourselves — is that, in any language, as words become poetry and poetry becomes great poetry, the power of nama-rupa grows. The sounds conjure forms not only of physical objects but of sensations, thoughts, and feelings, some of them exquisitely subtle.

The great example in English is Samuel Taylor Coleridge's "Kubla Khan." It's a psychedelic storybook vision of the building of the glorious summer palace, the "pleasure dome," of the Mongol emperor Kublai Khan in Shangdu, or Xanadu. As Coleridge explained much later, the poem came to him in a vision one day in 1797 while he was under the influence of laudanum, a tincture of opium that, at the time, was readily available at your corner drugstore. (Many respectable English ladies and gentlemen, including our poet, became addicted.) While reading a book about the Khan and Xanadu, Coleridge nodded out, and amid the swirling colors of his laudanum trip, the images and words of the poem co-arose without his conscious effort or involvement.

To activate the hologram, please read the poem aloud or, better yet, have a friend read it so you can keep your eyes closed. (There's also a video of yours truly reading it on YouTube.) Don't try to make meaning out of it. Just relax, ride along on the sounds, and let them summon whatever images or feelings they summon. Laudanum is optional.

> In Xanadu did Kubla Khan
> A stately pleasure-dome decree:
> Where Alph, the sacred river, ran
> Through caverns measureless to man
>   Down to a sunless sea.
> So twice five miles of fertile ground
> With walls and towers were girdled round;
> And there were gardens bright with sinuous rills,
> Where blossomed many an incense-bearing tree;

And here were forests ancient as the hills,
Enfolding sunny spots of greenery.

But oh! that deep romantic chasm which slanted
Down the green hill athwart a cedarn cover!
A savage place! as holy and enchanted
As e'er beneath a waning moon was haunted
By woman wailing for her demon-lover!
And from this chasm, with ceaseless turmoil seething,
As if this earth in fast thick pants were breathing,
A mighty fountain momently was forced:
Amid whose swift half-intermitted burst
Huge fragments vaulted like rebounding hail,
Or chaffy grain beneath the thresher's flail:
And mid these dancing rocks at once and ever
It flung up momently the sacred river.
Five miles meandering with a mazy motion
Through wood and dale the sacred river ran,
Then reached the caverns measureless to man,
And sank in tumult to a lifeless ocean;
And 'mid this tumult Kubla heard from far
Ancestral voices prophesying war!
  The shadow of the dome of pleasure
    Floated midway on the waves;
  Where was heard the mingled measure
    From the fountain and the caves.
It was a miracle of rare device,
A sunny pleasure-dome with caves of ice!

  A damsel with a dulcimer
  In a vision once I saw:
  It was an Abyssinian maid
  And on her dulcimer she played,
  Singing of Mount Abora.
  Could I revive within me
  Her symphony and song,
  To such a deep delight 'twould win me,
That with music loud and long,
I would build that dome in air,
That sunny dome! those caves of ice!
And all who heard should see them there,

And all should cry, Beware! Beware!
His flashing eyes, his floating hair!
Weave a circle round him thrice,
And close your eyes with holy dread
For he on honey-dew hath fed,
And drunk the milk of Paradise.

•

Welcome back. Hope you had a pleasant excursion. Your mileage may vary, of course, but you probably noticed some very vivid, colorful images arising from words that sound like what they describe, whether it's a "sunny pleasure-dome with caves of ice" or the slow wending of a river, "Five miles meander-ing with a mazy motion." You probably also noticed, in the first two sections, something very sensual, even erotic, going on, with the natural landscape morphing into phallic and vulvate images: the sacred river running through measureless caverns, the "deep romantic chasm" from which a "mighty foun-tain momently was forced," the earth breathing "in fast thick pants." (You can't say that without sounding like you're panting.) We seem to be witnessing a process of primal procreation.

And there seem to be one or two additional dimensions of creation here, which open up in the second line with the word "decree." Kubla, as the em-peror, simply decrees the building of his pleasure dome and *Shazam!* — it gets built. Today we would call him a dictator, someone who merely says the words (dictates) and things happen, stuff arises. Pretty good trick, but as we've seen, that's just what the poet does with the power of nama-rupa. The flowing of the sacred river through the measureless caverns suggests the act of poetic creation, or any imaginative creation, where the stream of consciousness runs through the caverns of our preconscious mind. When it's especially profound, it goes all the way to the "sunless sea," the vast, invisible inner ocean of form-less infinite, the primal origin of all the forms of our creativity.

There's also a hint of cosmic, universal creativity. That formless infinite is the same formless infinite from which the universe arises. (How many in-finites can there be?) It's the womb of creation, and the sacred river that joins it as if to fertilize it is named Alph. You won't find Alph on any map, but you will find God in Revelation saying, "I am the Alpha and the Omega, the First and the Last, the Beginning and the End." The poem puts us in the position of children who wander into their parents' bedroom in the middle of the night and see them making love, only here our parents are the primal yang and yin, proton and electron, Lord Shiva and Mother Parvati procreating the universe. It's the boudoir of the Big Bang.

And somehow that Bang is sound, nama-rupa, words of power:

In the beginning was the Word, and the Word was with God, and the Word was God.

In the beginning of the Vedas, the first word is *Agni*, pronounced *UHG-nee*, meaning "fire," and cognate with our word *ignite*. It's the spontaneous ignition spark of creation, and its first sound, *uh*, is pre-spark formless being, brimming with potentiality before the forms of the universe emerge from it. *Uh* is also the brimming sound we often make before a sentence emerges from us. It's what Western linguists call by the unlovely name of *schwa*, the most neutral, open sound, like neutral white let-there-be-light before it splits to manifest as colors.

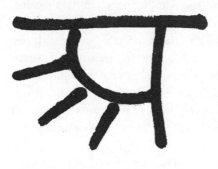

DEVANAGARI SCHWA

In the Devanagari script in which Sanskrit is written, the ancient form of this letter — the first letter of the alphabet, the *A*, the Alpha — looks like a fraction of a solar disk peeking out from a corner of the sky, radiating beams of manifestation. In the Bhagavad Gita, Lord Krishna, speaking as the infinite, says, "By a small fraction of my being I pervade and support this entire universe." Mostly, we could say, the infinite never has to bestir itself into manifestation. Mostly it remains silent, formless, invisible. God runs this whole show without breaking a sweat, on the tip of the tip of one pinkie. That may sound abstract, but as we grow in awakening it becomes a straightforward description of our own experience. *We* are the infinite, and *we* are mostly unbestirred. From the outside we're seen taking care of business, but in here we're vast silence. *Our* universe of activity runs on our pinkie.

·

Until that awakening, though, we can't just stay in the cozy womb of divine procreation. Activity interrupts our silence.

And 'mid this tumult Kubla heard from far
Ancestral voices prophesying war!

The alarm clock rings, the job calls, meditation's over, we're expelled from the womb. Time for the emperor to leave the pleasure-dome, saddle up, and subdue some rebellious provinces. Time for the poet to kiss the psychedelic vision goodbye.

This is what happens in the last of the poem's three sections, which appears to be an epilogue to the vision transcribed in the first two. It's a famous story: After Coleridge awoke from his opium trip and was scribbling down the verses he had received, he was interrupted by a knock at the door. When his visitor finally left, Coleridge discovered, to his "surprise and mortification," that the rest of the words had faded.

The shift is signaled in the second line of this section, "In a vision once I saw." This first use of "I," and the past tense "saw," make it clear that we've now stepped out of the vision and recovered our ordinary, mundane self-consciousness. But on his way out, Coleridge pulls a little trick:

> A damsel with a dulcimer
> In a vision once I saw

Most of us, when we hear the word "damsel," with its fairy-tale associations, see a fair-skinned maiden with long, golden hair. In the next line, though, we're told, "It was an Abyssinian maid" — that is, an Ethiopian woman. She's Black. He's fooled us. Coleridge is flexing his poetic muscles, showing that he can still make and remake pictures in our heads, even here, outside the gates of visionary Eden.

Still, this is a lament for the enchanted words that have been lost forever. If only the poet could revive them, then:

> To such a deep delight 'twould win me,
> That with music loud and long,
> I would build that dome in air,
> That sunny dome! those caves of ice!
> And all who heard should see them there

With the music of his words, he would gain the creative power of the emperor to build the dome. "And all who heard should see them there." That's nama-rupa, explicitly. If only we could live full-time in its full blast, we would be like Moses when he descends the mountain, his face shining with such blinding brilliance that he has to wear a veil to rejoin his tribesmen. The poet at the pinnacle of his power is supercharged, conducting such a high voltage that his hearers must avert their eyes and dance magic protective circles around him.

> And all should cry, Beware!, Beware!
> His flashing eyes, his floating hair!
> Weave a circle round him thrice,
> And close your eyes with holy dread
> For he on honey-dew hath fed,
> And drunk the milk of Paradise.

That is crazy power. When your English teachers lectured about meter and rhyme schemes and all that, they were just trying to share some insight into the small, knowable parts of the power, then coax you a little closer to the center, to feel the awesome voltage of the big, unknowable part. Usually we failed, and whenever some kid raised his hand and said, "Mr. Sluyter, will this be on the test?" it broke our heart.

As it happened, Coleridge himself — at least his waking, daylight self — failed to recognize the great power of this poem. He dismissed it as just some chemically precipitated oddity and filed it away. Nineteen years passed before he bothered to publish it. Now it's practically the only one of his poems that people read.

So I hope the foregoing wasn't too analytical, like dissecting a dream in the morning light. We're just trying to get some sense of the dream's contour, the morphing shapes and colors of the oozing paisleys.

•

A poem is a pebble. When it's dropped into the pond of human consciousness, it makes ripples and rings that go out and out till they reach parts of the pond that the pond didn't know it had. You are the pond. A great poem makes rings that go out forever because you go out forever.

A poem is a winged messenger from infinity. It speaks to you, then flies back to infinity, and if you're relaxed enough to let it, it grabs you by the scruff of the neck and takes you with it. Touching infinity was the idea from the start — all the tribes had their hymns and chants for calling it forth. Every poem since, whether an Elizabethan love sonnet or a Beat-generation howl of anguish, contains some of that DNA. Sometimes, as in "Kubla Khan," that gene is dominant, sometimes it's recessive. But it's always there.

9. Let Us Melt

JOHN DONNE • A VALEDICTION: FORBIDDING MOURNING

But why *traditional* poetry?

Yes, poetry is words of power, but contemporary poetry has shown that you can wield that power without all the old paraphernalia of rhyme and meter, as in these lines from "Sun," by the Beat poet Gregory Corso.

> The sun like a blazing disc of jelly slid over the Teliphiccian alps.
> The sun leads the night and follows the night and leads the night.
> The sun can be chariot-driven.
> The sun like a blazing lollipop can be sucked.
> The sun is shaped like a curved beckoning finger.
> The sun spins walks dances skips runs.

Or as in "Sunflower Sutra," by Corso's compadre Allen Ginsberg.

> I walked on the banks of the tincan banana dock and sat down under
>   the huge shade of a Southern Pacific locomotive to look at the
>   sunset over the box house hills and cry.

But the elements of traditional poetry — rhyme, meter, alliteration, metaphor, and so on — exist for a reason. When they're used right, they affect us in ways that nothing else does. It's true even of poetry that sounds hokey to us now.

> Listen, my children, and you shall hear
> Of the midnight ride of Paul Revere

The chiming of the rhyming and the meter's rhythmic drive provide one little *aha!* after another: the rhymes and the downbeat keep falling where the brain anticipates them. *Good brain!*

Research has shown, in fact, that hearing poetry activates the brain's reward centers. (Scientists report other effects as well. My favorite is "objectively measurable piloerection, i.e., goose bumps.") We know from experience that anytime the brain gets a cookie, the whole system relaxes a bit. There's a flush of well-being, a sense that everything's fine. Advertisers understand this and try to make us associate that life-is-good feeling with their product:

> You'll wonder where the yellow went
> When you brush your teeth with Pepsodent.

The *aha* brings a felt sense that, deep down, things are fine, things are *coherent*, even when things on the surface are chaotic. It confers a sense of grace. If this isn't meditation, it's certainly in the neighborhood.

Perhaps the traditional poetic elements that hint most powerfully at this coherence are those that liken unlike things. When you tell me that your love is like a red, red rose (simile) or, more boldly, that your love *is* a red, red rose (metaphor), you're telling me that the different is the same. The more different the two things are, the better. Equating your love with a red, red rose doesn't prove much: they're both pretty, they're both soft, and they both smell nice (we hope). They both may also turn out to be hiding thorns. But what if you liken your love to, say, phenomena of geology, astronomy, and metallurgy, and with the aid of some catchy rhythm entice me to go along for the ride? Then you're on your way to persuading me that your love isn't just a lovely rose of a girl. She's the lovely expression of a whole coherent universe. *Then* you're talking words of power.

That's what John Donne* does, brilliantly. He's the king of techniques that pull things together in unexpected ways: the paradox, the pun, and especially the *conceit* — the ingenious, far-fetched metaphor or simile that doesn't hesitate to invoke science, politics, theology, or anything else to deliver the goods.

His brilliance was on display from the beginning. Born eight years after Shakespeare into a well-to-do merchant's family, he was admitted to Oxford at age twelve, then went on to Cambridge. As a fashionable young man about town, he was "a great visitor of Ladies, a great frequenter of Plays, a great writer of conceited Verses." Those verses included teasing little poems about fickle women and arrogant courtiers, as well as "seduction songs," which deploy such playfully feeble logic as: (a) This flea just bit both of us; therefore (b) our bodily fluids are already mingled; and therefore (c) you might as well sleep with me. He traveled abroad on missions of adventure, diplomacy, and war, studied law, served in Parliament, and became chief secretary to Sir Thomas Egerton, the Lord Keeper of the Great Seal — a position that put him at the hub of England's political and social life, with a golden future ahead of him.

All that changed when he fell in love with the boss's niece, Anne More. She was above his station, but as he probably told her in private (punster that he was), he wanted More. They secretly married, and that impertinence, which Donne's first biographer called "the remarkable error of his life," led his furious new father-in-law to have him first imprisoned, then barred from public office. In despair (but still punning), Donne summarized his plight in a letter to his mother: "John Donne, Anne Donne, Un-done." His inheritance spent, dependent on the whims of patrons, Donne endured poverty and humiliation as he struggled to support his growing family. Anne had a dozen children in sixteen years.

Eventually, a solution came from the king. Seeing a useful way to exploit Donne's literary genius, James I had pressured him for several years to take holy orders in the Anglican Church. Donne finally gave in. Soon he was the most prominent minister in England, the dean of Saint Paul's Cathedral, preaching brilliantly before the king and other high eminences of the court. But by then Anne had died giving birth to a stillborn baby. Only seven of her children outlived her.

As a widowed churchman enduring long periods of agonizing illness, Donne turned somber. Along with his sermons, he wrote "holy sonnets" that plead for salvation, trying, it sometimes seems, to seduce God as he once seduced the ladies. Most startling is Holy Sonnet XIV, where, pushing paradox to the limit, he begs God to make him pure by "ravishing"— raping — him.

---

*   Pronounced *dun.*

In 1623, on what he thought was his deathbed, Donne wrote a series of "meditations," intensely introspective essays. Meditation XVII includes a passage that has become his most familiar piece of writing, recycled in so many sermons and commencement speeches that it's hard to hear it fresh. But let's try. Reading out loud will help: listen to the natural, almost involuntary poetic rhythm that pulses through the prose.

> No man is an island, entire of itself; every man is a piece of the continent, a part of the main; if a clod be washed away by the sea, Europe is the less, as well as if a promontory were, as well as if a manor of thy friends or of thine own were; any man's death diminishes me, because I am involved in mankind; And therefore never send to know for whom the bell tolls; it tolls for thee.

This is what years of writing poetry will do for you, even when you're deathly ill. Notice the themes of anatta and anitya, nonself and impermanence. No, you're not an island, a separate, isolated, self-existent self. You're part of the continent, the Big Thing. And all the small things, including the body you thought you were, are here for a limited time only. The bell tolls for thee, every moment.

•

This image of the continent, and the way Donne develops it — using the mind to explore its metaphorical possibilities, the heart to plumb its human poignancy, and the ear to join the two together in compelling word-music — pretty well summarizes his art. That art is on full display, kitchen-sink conceits and all, in "A Valediction: Forbidding Mourning." It's one of four leave-taking poems presumably written to his wife when he had to travel abroad. Countless poets before Donne had compared the parting of lovers to tragic or violent death. His opening conceit puts a twist on that cliché and likens their parting to a *good* death, a gentle death.

> As virtuous men pass mildly away,
>   And whisper to their souls to go,
> Whilst some of their sad friends do say
>   The breath goes now, and some say, No:
>
> So let us melt

The traditional Christian belief is that "virtuous men," with soul in order and conscience clear, die peacefully, assured of heaven. They don't struggle, but make their transition so "mildly" that the friends attending their deathbed can't pinpoint the moment that breathing ceases. In secular terms, we can say simply that people who are at peace tend to die peacefully; hospice nurses see this every day.

It's fine to die. Jesus, Socrates, Al-Hallaj, the Buddha, and numerous others have taught this by the example of their own serene exits. Ram Dass once asked a certain sage what to tell dying people about death. The reply was, "Tell them two things: It's like taking off a tight shoe. And it's absolutely safe."

In that spirit, meditation practice is also practice for dying. Every time we sit, we settle into beingness and shed the tight shoe of body and personality, the figment of the island self. We shed our identification with a name, an age, a shape, a gender, a bunch of history, a bundle of quirks. Deeper than the mind's *aha*, that shedding feels like *ahhhhhhh*. It's the joyous discovery that this aware presence we call "I" is not — and actually never was — confined within the cramped shell of a body. Once Sri Nisargadatta Maharaj was asked what dies at the time of death. He replied, "The idea 'I am the body' dies."

When we sit, as our awareness settles into this *ahhhhhhh*, the body itself, no longer laboring to hold together as I, also settles into what scientists call the *wakeful hypometabolic physiologic state*: a profound rest resembling dreamless sleep, except that we remain alert to enjoy it. Brain waves change, blood chemistry changes, and as the demand for oxygen to stoke the body's metabolic furnace diminishes, breathing becomes fainter. Sometimes the breath may be suspended completely, but it happens so naturally and incrementally that it's hard to say when it went away — remarkably like the scene Donne describes here.

By the time he wrote this, he had presumably seen a lot of dying firsthand, some of it wrenching but perhaps some of it sublime, with friends gathered round the deathbed, their own awareness settling as it followed the slow decrescendo of the dying person's breath, till at last it ended in a barely perceptible "whisper": *ahhhhhhh*. How interesting that the word *expire* means both to exhale and to die, and how lovely that the last breath is always an exhalation, a letting go. Once you relax into dying — which is easier if you've practiced relaxing into meditation — it's just a matter of the bounded self, which you aren't, gently melting into the boundless beingness, which you are.

This, says Donne, is the model for how he and his wife should part.

So let us melt, and make no noise,
   No tear-floods, nor sigh-tempests move;

'Twere profanation of our joys
   To tell the laity our love.

Elizabethan love poems were full of vows to cry floods of tears and heave tempests of sighs, but again Donne turns the cliché on its head, negating all such vows. Shakespeare uses a similar tactic in Sonnet 130. Running through a catalogue of worn-out poetic compliments — your eyes are like the sun, your lips are like coral — he knocks them all down: "My mistress' eyes are *nothing* like the sun," and so on. It's akin to the *neti neti* ("not this, not this") method of Advaita, the nondual philosophy of India, where everything we might think about the nature of ultimate reality is systematically negated, till we're left with what it is, which is beyond thought. Whatever you think, it's not that.

There's also a pivot, on the word "melt," to a subtle progression that's typical of Donne in its elegant precision. Moving from melting ice to flooding water to the blowing of rain in violent tempests, he shows the water element in ever louder, more chaotic physical states, implying ever louder, more chaotic emotional states, all of them to be renounced. But *why* renounce them? Here the focus starts to shift from negation to affirmation; from what deep, real love isn't to what it is. To display grief by sighing or crying would be a "profanation." It would expose the lovers' love to "the laity" — the laypeople, the nonclergy. The lovers, then, must be clergy, priests of the religion of love, initiates of its mysteries. Their love, real love, is not just an emotion, or a physical passion, or a cozy domestic arrangement. It's sacred.

What is this sacred love like? That's what the rest of the poem explores.

Moving of th' earth brings harms and fears,
   Men reckon what it did, and meant;
But trepidation of the spheres,
   Though greater far, is innocent.

"Moving of th' earth" refers to earthquakes, with the "harms" of their initial damage and the "fears" of aftershocks and collapsing buildings. In those days they were also followed by a reckoning not only of the casualties and destruction but of what it all "meant." What was God telling us? Donne must have known about the catastrophic Lisbon earthquake and tsunami some seventy-five years earlier, and may even have visited its site. It resulted in some thirty thousand deaths, widespread hysteria, and a narrowly averted mass slaughter of Jews, whom religious fanatics blamed for the disaster.

Contrasting such chaos is, in the third line of the stanza, "trepidation of the spheres." In the classical model of the universe, devised by Ptolemy

THE GEOCENTRIC UNIVERSE

around 150 CE, the heavenly bodies were embedded in a series of transparent concentric spheres, with the earth in the center. This geocentric model accounted neatly for the observed motions of the planets till, over the centuries, small discrepancies started to crop up. We now know that they're caused by the wobble of the earth's axis, but in Donne's time they were explained by a modification of the classical model, a sort of shuddering, or "trepidation," of the spheres. That would indeed be "greater far" than an earthquake, spanning millions of miles rather than dozens. But it's "innocent." It causes no damage because it's in the nonphysical, celestial realm, which is the realm of sacred love.

This contrasting of profane and sacred, physical and celestial, is developed further in the next stanza.

> Dull sublunary lovers' love
>   (Whose soul is sense) cannot admit
> Absence, because it doth remove
>   Those things which elemented it.

Ah, "sublunary"! *Sub-luna*: under the moon! One of the loveliest words in
our language, and you'll probably never see it anywhere else.* It means "terrestrial," as the moon was supposed to reside in the inmost sphere, closest to
earth. It also means changeable, subject to the moon's ever-shifting tidal in-
fluences. Anything sublunary, then, is inconstant and earthbound, mundane
(from *mundis*, earth), stuck in the muck of the physical. If that's the nature of
your love, its "soul is sense": its essence is the physical senses. If you just love
me for my body, your love can't endure physical separation.

In contrast is John and Anne's higher love:

> But we by a love so much refined,
>   That our selves know not what it is,
> Inter-assured of the mind,
>   Care less, eyes, lips, and hands to miss

Our connection, our interassurance, is "of the mind," not the lips and other
body parts that "elemented" lower love. But in fact, the first two lines of this
stanza — the most profound lines in the poem — tell us that it's not even of
the mind. It's "a love so much refined, / That our selves know not what it is."
Ka-boom. It's undefinable. It's transcendental. The mind can't know it any
more than the lips or hands can touch it. It's...*whooooooshhh*. It's the most precious thing we have (for which we might, oh, throw away a brilliant career at
court), yet we have, literally, *no idea* what it is. Ideas are minnows swimming
in the ocean of mind, mind is a minnow swimming in the ocean of It, and It
is neti neti — not this, not that, not the other.

Whatever It is, though, I somehow know it's the deepest reality of what I
am and you are, the same reality. That makes one of us. That's Advaita, nonduality, the ultimate perspective. Our language, however, evolved as a tool
for describing the world of duality, so when we try to describe nonduality we
have to resort to paradoxes, such as $2 = 1$.

> Our two souls therefore, which are one,
>   Though I must go, endure not yet
> A breach, but an expansion,
>   Like gold to airy thinness beat.

Our love is like gold: precious, beautiful, and malleable. (This gets the poem
up to about half a dozen conceits so far, in case you're keeping score.) If you

---

*   The other delicious one-hit wonder, in Poe's "The Bells," is "tintinnabulation."

hammer too much on most metals, they'll snap ("endure...a breach"), but if you beat gold, it expands into gold leaf: superthin, "airy," almost nonphysical. That's what love is like when it's hammered by time, space, work, and responsibility.

Still, even though at the depths of reality our "souls" are nondual, on the time-space surface of life it sure *seems* like there's two of us, who are subject to painful separation. The challenge is to honestly acknowledge the lived reality of mundane life, with all its dualistic bumps and lumps, without losing sight of the nondual. A lama I used to study with said it's like simultaneously holding one hand in hot water and one in cold.

Donne, of course, does that poetically, by using one more conceit, probably the most famous in all English-language poetry: the draftsman's compass. This most unlikely, un-red-red-rose-like of images is so juicy that he takes three stanzas to squeeze it all out. We can picture Donne sitting in his study with a compass, drawing circles, fiddling with the thing, imagining all the ways it can demonstrate love's paradox of duality and nonduality. How can our souls be both two and not two?

> If they be two, they are two so
>   As stiff twin compasses are two;
> Thy soul, the fixed foot, makes no show
>   To move, but doth, if the other do.

I'm the traveling foot, you're the fixed foot, which "makes no show / To move," appearing motionless on the physical, sublunary plane, the sheet of paper on which the compasses draw. Actually, though, the fixed foot rotates along with the moving foot due to their nonduality on the higher level — up in the air, above the paper.

> And though it in the center sit,
>   Yet when the other far doth roam,
> It leans and hearkens after it,
>   And grows erect, as that comes home.

The farther I wander on the lower level, says the poet — the larger the radius for which the compass is set — the more you lean toward me on the higher level. And baby, when you finally hear me knocking on your door, you'll be all attention, "erect," maybe even with objectively measurable piloerection, i.e., goose bumps. I'll be erect in my way too, the poet implies — we'll have a nice little party for two. Here and elsewhere in his poetry, Donne makes it enthusiastically clear that nondual love does not exclude intercourse but incorporates it. Some of his poems sound like they belong in tantric sex manuals. There's no either/or in nonduality.

> Such wilt thou be to me, who must,
>   Like th' other foot, obliquely run;
> Thy firmness makes my circle just,
>   And makes me end where I begun.

As Donne played with the compass in his study, he must have noticed that, to keep from messing up your circle, you have to hold the "fixed foot" firmly against the paper. Then you end where you begun. And so — bringing the poem itself full circle as he does the compass — don't cry, don't sigh, be firm. That's the best thing you can do to bring me home. While I have to run around, doing, you *be* for me, being.*

•

The "Valediction" is one of Western literature's most exquisite love poems. But we can also find another level to it that's not relational but more inward.

The conceit of the compass depicts a division of labor, with the active, engaged role assigned to one partner and the quiet role to the other. In the process of awakening, though, both roles are integrated — encompassed — within the individual. We've already seen how the Bhagavad Gita sums up that integration in Krishna's battlefield advice to the warrior Arjuna: Yogastah kuru karmani. Established in union with beingness, perform action. Go where you have to go, do what you have to do, but first center yourself in silent Presence. Make that inner fixed foot firm, and then, no matter where the outer foot of action must go, no matter how crazy things get on the battlefield of life, it will all be centered in perfect, unmoved silence.

In Vajrayana Buddhism, this teaching is represented in the form of Tara, the female buddha of compassion. She sits with her left leg folded in a meditative position; the right leg is semi-extended, with the foot pointing toward us, as if she's about to rise from her meditation, step into our world, and take action to relieve the suffering of sentient beings.

---

* For a twentieth-century treatment of the same goodbye-don't-cry theme, listen to Billie Holiday's recording of "We'll Be Together Again," with Lester Young wordlessly retelling the whole story on tenor sax. (The 1956 Frank Sinatra version, with a sumptuous Nelson Riddle arrangement, is also excellent.) Note the line about "thinking with your heart," an invitation to transcend the logical, terrestrial problems of separation and remain connected at the core.

TARA

This, the iconography implies, is real compassion: not just some feeling of pity but the tranquility of being, mobilized in doing. Like the fixed foot of Donne's compass, Tara's left foot sits at the centerline of her body, the heel pointing to her womb — the cosmic womb, the origin-point of all existence, to which we return whenever we settle within.

That womb is our origin, the beginning of every large and small cycle of experience, from our entire life span down to each day, each moment. If we're firmly established in it — yogastah — it's not only the beginning but the middle and end. Its firmness makes our circle just, and makes us end where we begun.

10. Betwixt Two Things

MARK TWAIN · ADVENTURES OF HUCKLEBERRY FINN

When Mount Saint Helens erupted in Washington State in 1980 — the deadliest volcanic event in US history — it killed fifty-seven people and destroyed 250 homes. The mountain's summit was reduced to a mile-wide, horseshoe-shaped crater, and nearly all the vegetation on its slope died. But the huckleberry bushes survived.

Huckleberries are hardy, but so small and tart that in Mark Twain's day they were considered a humble, proletarian food, and the word became slang for a lowly person. Now they're a delicacy. People cook them into jams and pies and fan out into national parks to collect them every summer because they only grow in the wild. You can't cultivate huckleberries. You can't, we could say, tame them.

Huckleberry Finn is Mark Twain's untamable wild boy. Twain found in him something primal and unspoilable, surviving eruptions of vice and violence, defying all attempts at domestication, very much like our own primal, unspoilable nature. *Adventures of Huckleberry Finn* has been banned by schools and libraries, turned into sappy family films, extravagantly praised by the likes of Hemingway and T. S. Eliot — and survived. It made literature out of rough American speech and made the Mississippi River the American Ganges.

Even for those who've never read the book, the image is iconic: Huck in straw hat and rags, forever at the juncture of boyhood and adolescence, smoking a corncob pipe (like most Midwestern boys in the 1840s), playing pranks, and getting into scrapes. He makes his first entrance in *The Adventures of Tom Sawyer*, dragging a dead cat on a string.

> Huckleberry was cordially hated and dreaded by all the mothers of the town, because he was idle, and lawless, and vulgar and bad — and because all their children admired him so, and delighted in his forbidden society, and wished they dared to be like him.... Huckleberry came and went, at his own free will. He slept on door-steps in fine weather and in empty hogsheads* in wet; he did not have to go to school or to church, or call any being master or obey anybody.

In nineteenth-century America, Finn was the standard name for a stereotypical drunken Irishman, and Huck is the neglected, motherless son of the town drunk. He was modeled on Twain's boyhood friend Tom Blankenship, the son of the town drunk of Hannibal, Missouri, on the western shore of the Mississippi. The Blankenships were considered the

---

*   Hogsheads: large casks.

HUCK, FROM THE 1884 FIRST EDITION

trashiest of trash. Their daughters were said to be prostitutes, and Tom had such a reputation as a thief that when anything in Hannibal went missing it was assumed he had taken it. Conjured out of this disreputable material, Huck Finn has become an avatar of happy freedom, which is what we awaken to when we awaken.

But as the book begins — narrated in Huck's innocently hilarious voice — his freedom has been curtailed by a genteel Christian lady.

> The Widow Douglas, she took me for her son, and allowed she would sivilize me; but it was rough living in the house all the time, considering how dismal regular and decent the widow was.

She makes him trade his comfortable rags for starched clothes, and his in-the-moment ease for a rigid schedule of meals and school and Bible lessons.

> The widow rung a bell for supper, and you had to come to time. When you got to the table you couldn't go right to eating, but you had to wait for the widow to tuck down her head and grumble a little over the victuals, though there warn't really anything the matter with them. That is, nothing only everything was cooked by itself. In a barrel of odds and ends it is different; things get mixed up, and the juice kind of swaps around, and the things go better.

That last bit, about the two ways of cooking, also suggests two ways of being in the world. The widow's "sivilized" way, with its manners, class, and Sunday school morals, is hygienically segregated from the world's great mess. Huck's way is open to life's randomness, the whole barrel of odds and ends, jumbled and messy — but juicy.

We exist in this world in relation to everyone and everything else, so it's natural to reach out, to swap our juices. Then "the things go better." But to live without the armor of starched clothes or attitudes, to be welcomed home by the wide world of interconnected beings — people, animals, the earth and stars, what the Lakota call "all my relations" — requires a wide heart, a generous spirit, like Huck's. Without the coerced goodness of Sunday school, we need natural, uncontrived goodness, the simple kindness that endures in spite of all the funk we drag behind us like a dead cat. After a lifetime studying the world's religions and philosophies, and after years of spiritual practice and psychedelic exploration, Aldous Huxley found that the only advice he had to offer was, "Try to be a little kinder."

Freedom and kindness, and the quest to live them in a world that can be oppressively unfree and unkind, are the central themes of Twain's masterpiece — and of the Dharma. The journey of Huck and the runaway slave Jim down the Mississippi on their raft is the Dharma tale par excellence.

.

But first we see, in contrast, a nonjourney, a fake adventure: the founding of Tom Sawyer's Gang, a band of supposed robbers who meet in a cave, take blood oaths, and decide who to ransom or kill, in a comical mash-up of the many (*too* many) books Tom has read. Of course, these robbers are just kids, and in their one daring caper they scare some smaller kids away from a Sunday school picnic to take their jam and doughnuts.

The real journey begins when Huck's shiftless drunkard of a father shows up at the widow's house. Pap — we never learn his first name — resents Huck's fancy clothes and education:

> You think you're a good deal of a big-bug, *don't* you?... Who told you you might meddle with such hifalut'n foolishness, hey? — who told you you could?

PAP

Hoping to squeeze money out of Huck, or at least beat the gentility out of him, he snatches him away to an old log hut in the thick woods on the Illinois side of the river. Pap personifies messiness carried to the toxic extreme of chaos. He's a nasty, violent drunk, a braggart, a baffled, dangerous animal peering out of the jungle of his own ignorance.

His hair was long and tangled and greasy, and hung down, and you could see his eyes shining through like he was behind vines.

He owns only one thing of supposed value: his white skin, which empowers him to feel superior to Blacks. But he manages to turn that whiteness into something poisonous and revolting.

> There warn't no color in his face, where his face showed; it was white; not like another man's white, but a white to make a body sick, a white to make a body's flesh crawl — a tree-toad white, a fish-belly white.

After a particularly terrifying drunken rampage in which Pap nearly kills him, Huck engineers a nighttime escape from the hut, making it look like he's been murdered and dumped in the river — a clever, bloody ruse that involves killing a wild pig. Then he takes off in a salvaged canoe. What comes next is expressed in a sequence of perfect sentences. Twain wrote many of these: sentences that, in the plainest of language, capture so precisely the rhythms and textures of the action that we see it and feel it with magical lucidity. Reading aloud is recommended.

> I didn't lose no time. The next minute I was a-spinning down stream soft but quick in the shade of the bank.... I got out amongst the drift-wood, and then laid down in the bottom of the canoe and let her float. I laid there, and had a good rest and a smoke out of my pipe, looking away into the sky; not a cloud in it. The sky looks ever so deep when you lay down on your back in the moonshine; I never knowed it before.

This is about as clear a baptism in the transcendent as anyone has ever written. After the hectic scramble to get clear of Pap, Huck lets go. Lying on his back in a posture of utter passivity, he gives up rowing and steering, allows the boat to merge anonymously with the mass of drifting timbers, and basks in the moonlight. This is how to meditate: "let her float." And the result is a vision of unobstructed boundlessness. "The sky looks ever so deep." In fact, a favorite method in Vajrayana

Buddhist practice is *namkhai naljyor*, "sky-gazing meditation," literally gazing open-eyed into the ever-so-deep sky and losing yourself in it.

With this initiation into a new dimension of experience — "I never knowed it before" — the journey can commence in earnest. Leaving behind the stifling sivilization of the Widow Douglas on one bank and Pap's terrifying chaos on the other, Huck sets forth down the river that runs between them.

That same river gave Sam Clemens his pen name of Mark Twain. It came, famously, from his days as a steamboat pilot, when the leadsman, casting his weighted line into the water and measuring a depth of two fathoms — twelve feet, safe water — called out the welcome words "By the mark, twain!" But to mark the twain can also mean to acknowledge the two, to note the dualities between which we steer our lives, the ever-resurgent challenge of the thing and the other thing. Twain was built for that: Missouri hick and Connecticut patrician, nostalgic and cynic, poor man and rich man a couple of times each, brooding pessimist and Zen comedian ("There ain't no way to find out why a snorer can't hear himself snore"), writer of prose that is at once elegant and crude. He condemned voracious capitalism and pioneered the field of celebrity endorsements — you can still buy Mark Twain Cigars, "Known to Everyone, Liked by All." And he suffered wild mood swings that today would probably be diagnosed as bipolar disorder.

When Twain wrote *Adventures of Huckleberry Finn* in the 1880s, he saw the lost world of his antebellum boyhood with double vision. His fictionalized version of Hannibal is called Saint Petersburg — Saint Peter's town, heaven — but it's also a hell of slavery and assorted brutalities. Coming on the heels of the Transcendentalist generation that might sometimes have seemed intent on theorizing away life's hard dualities, Twain insisted on them. He didn't deny that they could be resolved. But he knew that to find real resolution, you have to go on a journey of experience beyond theory, till you can feel it and smell it like Mississippi mud.

•

The setting forth of Gautama, the Buddha-to-be, was much like Huck's. He was the son of a local chieftain or lord, and according to the legend, it was prophesied at his birth that he would become either a great king or a great spiritual leader. His father was like any well-to-do modern parent who wants their child sticking to a solid career track, not running off to India to meditate. (Well, OK, they were already in India, but, you know.) So he kept him confined to the palace grounds, where his senses were continually fed with the finest of delights — a prisoner of pleasure, as many of us are, or try to be.

When Gautama at last ventured out to glimpse the wider world, he saw that suffering was rampant and his pampered life an evasion. Like Huck, he stole away from his father's house under cover of night. Like Huck exchanging his starched clothes for rags, he exchanged his fine silks for a monk's robe. He renounced his riches, just as Huck, to put Pap off his trail, turns over to Judge Thatcher the reward money he earned at the end of the previous book. Shaving his head, Gautama took to the forests. (One telltale vestige of his aristocratic past remained: his long earlobes, stylishly deformed by the heavy gold earrings he had worn.) For six years he practiced severe asceticism, repressing his senses as intensely as he had once indulged them, fasting (so the story goes) till he looked like a skeleton. But enlightenment still eluded him; denying the senses proved as futile as glutting them.

One morning a village girl named Sujata offered Gautama a nourishing bowl of rice pudding. He accepted it and broke his fast. With renewed strength and resolve, he sat down beneath a fig tree and meditated till he became buddha, awakened. In a sense, though, his awakening was sealed as soon as he accepted Sujata's gift. At that moment, he broke free from the twin errors of indulgence and repression. Then it was just a matter of time: sitting long enough, remaining naturally open to the simple actuality of each moment of experience as it presented itself, without seeking or rejecting anything, like Huck floating in the moonlight. This Middle Way, as he was to call it, was how to meditate and how to live, a thoroughly human way that flows like a river between all the pairs of opposites. "When all else fails," Ram Dass used to say, "try being human."

The Middle Way is often misunderstood as a sort of timid compromise, a lukewarm average of the superfun rave of hedonism on one shore and the supersolemn grind of spirituality on the other. But it's a whole different thing, as different as the river is from the rocks and earth that flank it. The two extremes of sensuality and renunciation are two kinds of false freedom, two ways to be stuck. The Buddha called them two addictions, and like all addictions, they're a lot of work. The freedom of the Middle Way is natural and therefore effortless, once you find it. It's joyous, which is why we call it the sweet spot.

For Huck, unlike Gautama, his initial princely affluence is the place of repression, the widow's house, and the woods are the place of heedless indulgence, Pap's hut. The basic contours of the journey, though, are the same for both — and for us, if we take it. We set forth, abandoning the constraints of our addictions, and flow with the openness of freedom.

There's one more crucial parallel between the two stories. Gautama's liberation is precipitated by his acceptance of a simple act of human kindness, from the village girl Sujata. Huck's is also touched off by an opening to kindness. His Sujata is Jim.

•

After his escape from Pap and his moonlight initiation, Huck rows to an uninhabited little island, a few miles downstream. After three days, he happens upon Jim, a slave belonging to Miss Watson, the widow's sister. Jim has heard about Huck's supposed death, and at first thinks he's seeing a ghost.

> He bounced up and stared at me wild. Then he drops down on his knees, and puts his hands together and says:
> "Doan' hurt me — don't! I hain't ever done no harm to a ghos'. I alwuz liked dead people, en done all I could for 'em. You go en git in de river agin, whah you b'longs, en doan' do nuffn to Ole Jim, 'at 'uz awluz yo' fren'."

To have Huck, in Jim's eyes, resurrected on the third day seems too on the nose to be an accident, a hint of Christ to go with the unintended parallels to the Buddha. Twain's little ragamuffin has a lot to live up to before the book ends.

Jim is doubly hunted. He has run off to keep Miss Watson from selling him downriver, but bad timing has made him a prime suspect in Huck's murder. He's determined to make his way to the free state of Ohio, then earn enough money to buy his wife and children out of slavery. He and Huck join forces and set off on a salvaged raft, with Huck posing when necessary as Jim's master. Together, they encounter a series of unsought adventures that make up the book's great middle section. It's both particular and universal: an astonishingly detailed re-creation, almost fifty years after the fact, of the vanished world of Twain's river valley childhood, and a safari through the habitat of that exotic species *homo sapiens*, engaged in its perennial range of good and bad behavior.

Mostly bad. Huck and Jim get separated in a thick fog, miss their turn up the Ohio River, and are carried south on the Mississippi, deeper into slave country, in what often resembles Dante's descent into hell. They see occasional acts of generosity and compassion, mostly from women and girls, but those are overshadowed by thick ignorance and sickening cruelty: fraud, murder, a slave auction, a religious camp meeting where gullible believers are bilked, a town where people torture dogs for fun, an attempted lynching that fails only because the mob consists of cowards, and a feud between two families who've been killing each other so long they can't remember why — but keep right on killing.

Wherever Huck and Jim go, they meet "rapscallions and dead beats." As usual among "the damned human race" (as Twain calls it — calls us! — in another book), danger lurks. They're forced to flee more than once. But as soon as they're back on the river, they're fine.

> I was powerful glad to get away from the feuds, and so was Jim to get away from the swamp. We said there warn't no home like a raft, after all. Other places do seem so cramped up and smothery, but a raft don't. You feel mighty free and easy and comfortable on a raft.

The more boorish the people on shore are, the more delicious is the simple goodness of Huck and Jim's river life. They've found a space of freedom, where they live an open-ended existence under the open sky, literally going with the flow, abiding in quietness and sweet nothing-doing.

> We catched fish and talked, and we took a swim now and then to keep off sleepiness. It was kind of solemn, drifting down the big, still river, laying on our backs looking up at the stars, and we didn't ever feel like talking loud, and it warn't often that we laughed — only a little kind of a low chuckle. We had mighty good weather as a general thing, and nothing ever happened to us at all — that night, nor the next, nor the next.

There's still, however, more grace to be found, at least for Huck, and he must find it through Jim. At first he plays childish pranks on him, such as putting a dead rattlesnake on his blanket, or convincing him that their separation in the fog was just a dream. Each time, he's surprised when the result is deep, unfunny pain, whether physical or emotional, till at last he finds himself apologizing — an unheard-of gesture given Huck's inherited racist attitudes.

But those attitudes meet a deeper challenge:

> When I waked up just at daybreak [Jim] was sitting there with his head down betwixt his knees, moaning and mourning to himself. ... He was thinking about his wife and his children, away up yonder, and he was low and homesick; because he hadn't ever been away from home before in his life; and I do believe he cared just as much for his people as white folks does for their'n. It don't seem natural, but I reckon it's so. He was often moaning and mourning that way nights, when he judged I was asleep, and saying, "Po' little 'Lizabeth! po' little Johnny! it's mighty hard; I spec' I ain't ever gwyne to see you no mo', no mo'!"

In Huck's old world, where the rationale for slavery is that Blacks are subhuman, it's inconceivable that they could have the same kind of human feelings as whites. Now his miseducation collides with actual experience, and something's gotta give. "It don't seem natural, but I reckon it's so."

This particular collision might seem to belong only to the book's historical setting; modern folks like us know better (one hopes). But there's a deeper imperative here. Grace — awakening — requires Huck to recognize that Jim is human like himself, not a mere beast of burden. Grace requires us to recognize that others are aware subjects like ourselves, not mere objects. They're not *things* that we experience "out there," to be exploited in our ongoing project of seeking happiness and avoiding pain. They're fellow experiencers, feeling their own happiness and pain, "in here," in this same intimate space of awareness where we are.

Of course we know this in the abstract. It's hard to know it deeply and practically, in our bones, but it can be done. Every act of kindness undermines the sense of separateness; every glimpse of nonseparateness naturally promotes kindness. As we grow into nonseparate kindness, we find ourselves living in the *sangha*, the beloved community, the minyan, the fellowship of those who recognize that we're all in this boat (or on this raft) together, supporting and encouraging each other on the way to liberation.

•

But what is the sangha to do when it's invaded by people who would destroy it? This is the problem Huck and Jim face when their very selflessness draws the element of selfishness into their midst. The nonidentical twin snakes in their Eden are an old bald-headed crook and a younger crook who travel from one frontier town to the next, fleecing the locals with quack cures, religious cons, and other assorted swindles. Huck first encounters them as they hotfoot it out of a town where their crimes have caught up with them. Always the good heart, he rescues them and welcomes them aboard the raft.

The young crook, ever ready to seize an advantage, reveals that he's actually the dispossessed Duke of Bridgewater — only to be outranked by the old crook, who turns out to be the rightful King of France. Innocent, good-hearted Jim buys into their stories, while Huck soon realizes that the King and the Duke are "just low-down humbugs and frauds." He doesn't say anything, though, so as to "keep peace in the family," an understandable attitude for the child of an alcoholic. Soon the Duke and the King have Jim and Huck waiting on them, addressing them as "your grace" and "your majesty," and serving as accomplices in their schemes. By the time they're deep into the state of Mississippi, the swindlers are broke and out of swindles, and they sell Jim to a local farmer — the most appalling of betrayals.

> After all this long journey, and after all we'd done for them scoundrels, here it was all come to nothing, everything all busted up and ruined, because they could have the heart to serve Jim such a trick as that, and make him a slave again all his life, and amongst strangers, too, for forty dirty dollars.*

What does this have to do with us? The Duke and the King personify our own inner false nobility: the hustling little ego, which has usurped the throne of identity from boundless, nonpersonal I-awareness. Like all usurpers, it's haunted by the knowledge of its own fakery. The ultimate con artist, the ego swindles us out of our natural happiness and betrays our natural kindness. It's selfish by definition, always hungry, always trying in vain to enlarge and complete itself by consuming stuff, but there's never enough stuff to satisfy it. As Huck says, "I never see such a girafft as the king was for wanting to swallow *everything*." He and the Duke are incapable of enjoying the simple life of flowing contentment that Huck and Jim generously share with them, just as the ego can't leave off consuming and enjoy just being.

At bottom, though, the ego has a death wish. It's like a shiny balloon that insists on being blown up bigger and bigger — till it bursts into the

---

* Another perfect sentence. Note the five mournful, steadily intensifying repetitions of "all," culminating in the three devastating karate chops of "*fort*-y *dirt*-y *dol*-lars."

boundlessness of the sky. A usurper like Macbeth will finally push his tyranny too far, provoking his own overthrow and death and secretly relishing it. The Duke and the King, having stayed too long in one place — trying to swallow everything — wind up tarred and feathered and ridden out of town on a rail, their final exit from the book.

But Huck finds he can't indulge in this perfectly reasonable occasion for schadenfreude. He has, we could say, graduated from buddha to *bodhisattva* — one who lives not only boundless awareness but boundless compassion, for all beings without exception.

> Well, it made me sick to see it; and I was sorry for them poor pitiful rascals, it seemed like I couldn't ever feel any hardness against them any more in the world. It was a dreadful thing to see. Human beings *can* be awful cruel to one another.

·

After thirty chapters comes the big showdown, the book's decisive battle, which takes place silently, within Huck, between "a sound heart and a deformed conscience," as Twain later put it. Discouraged, Huck sits alone on the raft, trying to hatch a plan to rescue Jim. But his thoughts drift toward the idea that he's a sinner, having helped Jim "steal" himself from Miss Watson, "a poor old woman...that hadn't ever done me no harm."

> And at last, when it hit me all of a sudden that here was the plain hand of Providence slapping me in the face and letting me know my wickedness was being watched all the time from up there in heaven...and now was showing me there's One that's always on the lookout, and ain't a-going to allow no such miserable doings to go only just so fur and no further, I most dropped in my tracks I was so scared.

Clearly, Huck's conscience is channeling the voice of every racist white preacher he's ever heard. Plunged into a state of religious terror, he writes a letter to Miss Watson, telling her where Jim is. Then:

> I felt good and all washed clean of sin for the first time I had ever felt so in my life, and I knowed I could pray now. But I didn't do it straight off, but laid the paper down and set there thinking — thinking how good it was all this happened so, and how near I come to being lost

and going to hell. And went on thinking. And got to thinking over our trip down the river; and I see Jim before me all the time: in the day and in the night-time, sometimes moonlight, sometimes storms, and we a-floating along, talking and singing and laughing. But somehow I couldn't seem to strike no places to harden me against him, but only the other kind ... and then I happened to look around and see that paper.

It was a close place. I took it up, and held it in my hand. I was a-trembling, because I'd got to decide, forever, betwixt two things, and I knowed it. I studied a minute, sort of holding my breath, and then says to myself:

"All right, then, I'll *go* to hell" — and tore it up.

Wow. "All right, then, I'll *go* to hell." These may be the seven most exciting words ever written.* This is the real declaration of independence, the bursting into freedom, the sound heart's triumph. All the clashing dualities in this book, and all the twains ever marked by Mark Twain, reach a culmination here: deciding between heaven and hell is about as stark a choice as one can make. But the choice is also between mind (in the form of "conscience") and heart. Huck has not actually changed his mind about the church's racist dogma. His social brainwashing is too strong, his intellect too unsophisticated, for him to think his way out of it. He still believes that helping a slave to freedom is a mortal sin — and he does it anyway. He chooses damnation for the sake of his friend. Greater love hath no one.

This is not just changing your mind but overthrowing it — not just replacing one set of thoughts with a better set, but letting love lift you into the wide-open sky of being where you soar above *all* thoughts. That's freedom. Huck has traveled through four states in search of freedom, but now he's found it without moving an inch. Once you've chosen damnation, what can anyone do to you? What can they scare you with?

After Huck declares his determination to go to hell, we feel him, sentence by sentence, awakening to this fearless joy.

It was awful thoughts and awful words, but they was said. And I let them stay said; and never thought no more about reforming. I shoved the whole thing out of my head, and said I would take up

---

* All monosyllables, by the way, with a double-*l* at the beginning, at the end, and exactly in the middle — an unimprovable, unforgettable little poem.

wickedness again, which was in my line, being brung up to it, and the other warn't. And for a starter I would go to work and steal Jim out of slavery again; and if I could think up anything worse, I would do that, too; because as long as I was in, and in for good, I might as well go the whole hog.

·

With the book's moral climax concluded, clearly the sensible thing for Twain to do now is to have Huck rescue Jim from the shed in which the farmer has locked him, throw in an exciting chase scene, add a quick epilogue about how they make their way north to Ohio, and call it a day. But he doesn't. He goes on — and on and on and on, notoriously, for another dozen chapters.

In a preposterously implausible twist, Huck's pal Tom Sawyer suddenly shows up, five hundred miles from home, and without anything like Huck's struggle of conscience, cheerfully takes over the project of freeing Jim. But Tom, ever the fiction-intoxicated fantasist, stretches what should be a simple cell break into weeks of absurd theatrics straight out of *The Count of Monte Cristo*: digging tunnels, smuggling in a rope ladder, tipping off Jim's captors with anonymous notes, filling the shed with snakes and rats — because that's how it happens in the books. Tom Sawyer's Gang was funny because it was harmless, kids at play. At this end of the journey, maturity is called for. Tom's treatment of Jim isn't funny. It's oblivious and cruel.

A *sawyer* is a carpenter, who saws and shapes raw timber into boards for building houses. Tom Sawyer, we might say, is the mind, which saws and shapes raw reality into concepts for building stories — stories about who we are, what is what, what it all means. This includes our project of liberation. Even when we do something as simple as sitting to meditate, the mind tries to take over and turn it into a story: you need to breathe like this, you need to experience that, that's how it happens in the books. Want to delay your liberation? Just put your mind in charge.

After the long delay of Jim's liberation, we at last get to the breakout and the chase scene, with barking dogs and flying bullets. Then there are a few more plot complications, but when the dust finally settles on all this whoop-jamboreehoo (Twain's delicious word) and our three heroes are safe, we learn that Jim's owner, Miss Watson, died two months earlier and freed Jim in her will. Tom has known the whole time, which explains his willingness to join in the rescue. Jerk.

Then Jim offers a revelation of his own. A naked corpse that he and Huck came across thirty-three chapters back, whose face he told Huck not to look at because it was "too gashly," was Pap. Did Jim really withhold this news to spare Huck's feelings? Or was it a shrewd move to keep the useful white boy on the run with him? Maybe both. That's how most of us are on our journeys: mixed motives. Mark the twain.

So both Huck and Jim have been free all along. The book's great themes of freedom and kindness have been reduced to a bad joke. This is why *Adventures of Huckleberry Finn* is considered a flawed masterpiece. Tom, the dreamer of bogus adventures, hijacks Huck's very real, life-changing adventure, and Huck meekly goes along, as if his journey never happened. The affirmation of Jim's humanity vanishes as he becomes Tom's play toy.

How could so great a writer make such a terrible choice? It doesn't make sense — unless Twain was being pulled along by a truth so deep he could only vaguely intuit it, that somehow, like Huck and Jim, we've *all* been free all along. That's something Dharma teachers frequently say, and it drives their students as crazy as this book's ending drives readers. *You're like a fish swimming to and fro, looking for the ocean,* say the teachers. *You're like a bird flying this way and that, looking for the sky.*

They're not just being wise guys — they're being wise. This paradox, that we're bound by the illusion that we're bound by illusion, goes back at least to Gautama Buddha, who declared at his moment of awakening, "All things are awakened just as they are." Not just *I*, but *all things*. Not just *will be someday*, but *are*. Liberation is not gained: it's finally noticed. If it were gained, it would be an event in time, which in time could be lost again. Rather, the clouds of our confusion part and we notice the ever-so-deep sky of being, beyond time and events. The kingdom of heaven *is* within us, and has been all along.

That's the forehead-slapping moment, the Homer Simpson-esque *D'oh!* We've read all those books, sat at the feet of all those teachers, done all that practice, taken the whole journey, just to find out we were always at the goal. If that sounds like another of Tom Sawyer's unfunny pranks, take heart. No one who arrives here, at this place where we always were, resents the trip. Everyone sees in retrospect that all the apparent obstacles and detours were exactly right, exactly what was needed to shake ourselves awake to what was there at every turn, every bend in the river. The river doesn't flow *to* freedom. The river *is* freedom.

In fact, on the book's final page, Huck is resuscitated as the timeless spirit of freedom, which survives even Twain's literary excesses, just as huckleberry bushes survive volcanoes. Huck, Jim, and Tom are discussing how things have turned out, and Tom proposes that they "slide out of here one of these nights...and go for howling adventures" in the Indian Territory, the Wild

West. By now there's another genteel Christian lady, Aunt Sally, intent on re-forming Huck. The book concludes:

> And so there ain't nothing more to write about, and I am rotten glad
> of it, because if I'd a knowed what a trouble it was to make a book
> I wouldn't a tackled it, and ain't a-going to no more. But I reckon I
> got to light out for the Territory ahead of the rest, because Aunt Sally
> she's going to adopt me and sivilize me, and I can't stand it. I been
> there before.

We're all pressed to be like regular, sivilized folks — like the earthlings, as I sometimes call them. But some of us must live lives of nirvana or bust, and for us Huck's call of freedom is irresistible. We got to light out for the Territory ahead of the rest.

11. Still

JOHN KEATS

Perhaps you've had the experience of being *elevated* by the act of reading — feeling lifted, almost literally, to a higher level, where the air is rarefied and the view is vast. Like first love, it happens most often and most intensely in adolescence or early adulthood.

It happened to John Keats when he was twenty-five. On an October night in 1816, at the London home of his friend Cowden Clarke, the two of them sat passing a borrowed copy of the *Odyssey* and *Iliad* back and forth. This was their first encounter with the translations by George Chapman, a contemporary of Shakespeare's, who had rendered Homer's Greek into astonishingly vivid English verse. With mounting excitement, they took turns reading aloud, straight through the night — elevated. They parted at dawn.

When Clarke came downstairs after a few hours' sleep, he found on his breakfast table an envelope that Keats had managed to have delivered, containing a freshly penned sonnet. Its opening lines praise Chapman's "loud and bold" voice and speak of breathing, for the first time, the "pure serene" of Homer. It concludes with what may be the finest evocation of dumbstruck wonderment anywhere in the English language.

> Then felt I like some watcher of the skies
> When a new planet swims into his ken;*
> Or like stout Cortez when with eagle eyes
> He star'd at the Pacific — and all his men
> Look'd at each other with a wild surmise —
> Silent, upon a peak in Darien.

The "new planet" reference is not hypothetical and not incidental. Just thirty-five years earlier, William Herschel had discovered Uranus. Till then, the number of planets was believed to be fixed, even divinely ordained, the fundamental architecture of the universe, with whole systems of astronomy and astrology built around it. Herschel's discovery didn't just mean there was one more rock out there: it meant the old model of reality had been blown open. Now anything was possible.

Here, of course, Keats is describing his own anything's-possible epiphany with regard to language. Never mind that, in his excitement, he got his conquistadors mixed up: it was Balboa, not Cortés, who ascended a mountaintop on the Isthmus of Panama (then known as the Isthmus of Darien) and became the first European to see the Pacific from the New World. Keats depicts him and his men at the peak, elevated, as they behold the wide expanse of ocean, which is reflected in their look of "wild surmise" and their awed silence, a silence that continues to hang in the air after the last line ends.

This was Keats's first great poem. Less than five years later he would be dead, but not before producing an almost frantic cascade of work that records — and, at its best, awakens — blissful aesthetic samadhi. The contrast between his ecstatic poetry and his short, miserable life is shocking.

When he was eight, his father died of a fall from a horse. His mother went off with a new husband, leaving her children with their grandmother. She returned alone at Christmastime when Keats was fourteen, just in time to die of consumption, the nineteenth-century plague, what we now call tuberculosis; in those days it caused about a quarter of all deaths in England. Keats and his siblings were placed in the care of a guardian who steered him into medical training. He had always been an excellent student when not daydreaming or

---

*   Ken: vision, perception.

picking fights with the bigger boys. (They were all bigger: he never grew past five feet.) But upon graduating from medical college he announced, to his guardian's fury, that he was determined to be a poet. He managed to publish a few collections, but they were promptly savaged by the critics, partly out of class snobbery — he was derided as a "Cockney poet."

This dashed any chance he might have had of making a living at his vocation. He fell passionately in love with the new girl next door, Fanny Brawne. She was "beautiful and elegant, graceful, silly, fashionable and strange" (as he described her in a letter), but his poverty prevented their marriage. As if his fate weren't cruel enough, all along there was a sizable inheritance due him that he never learned of, the paperwork languishing on a negligent lawyer's desk. His life was like a Dickens novel without the happy twist at the end.

As Keats's debts piled up, he cared for a brother with consumption and watched helplessly as he died an excruciating death. His other brother went off to seek his fortune in America, where he got involved in bad investment schemes and wound up borrowing from Keats, driving him deeper into debt. Eventually, that brother died of consumption as well.

Finally, the disease caught up with Keats. He sailed to Italy with a friend in hopes that the warm climate would restore his health, but rough weather, followed by windless doldrums, kept them wretchedly at sea for a month, and Rome had turned cold by the time they arrived in mid-November. There, in his two-room apartment on the Spanish Steps, he wrote desperate, jealous letters to Fanny and was tortured by doctoring that was brutally incompetent even for that time, with frequent bloodletting and a daily diet of one slice of bread and one anchovy. He had a bottle of opium that could have eased his suffering, but the doctor and Keats's well-meaning friend took it away.

You can visit Keats's grave in Rome's Protestant (or "Non-Catholic") Cemetery. At his request there's no name on the headstone, but he composed the epitaph: "Here lies one whose name was writ in water." The cemetery is overgrown with centuries-old cypresses. It's achingly beautiful but the entrance is hard to find, so it doesn't attract a lot of tourists. It's one of the few places in Rome where you can experience silence.

•

Silence is also a central theme of "Ode on a Grecian Urn." It was inspired in part by Keats's visits to the British Museum, where the so-called Elgin Marbles, recently plundered from the Parthenon, were on display. (Two centuries later, Greece is still trying to get them back.) He also viewed prints of a number of vases and traced an engraving of at least one. In the poem, he combines elements of several of these actual pieces with his own imagination to create an urn that's an object of contemplation of time, passion, and pursuit, and the silent beingness that transcends all of that.

In keeping with its graceful, curved form, Keats personifies the urn as female.

> Thou still unravish'd bride of quietness,
>   Thou foster-child of silence and slow time,
> Sylvan historian, who canst thus express
>   A flowery tale more sweetly than our rhyme

There's clearly some irony in the use of the word "unravish'd." To ravish is to seize, to carry away by force. If entrepreneurs like Lord Elgin hadn't ravished a bunch of antiquities, Keats would never have seen them. But to ravish also means to rape. In some way the urn has, over the centuries, maintained her virginity, her purity.

KEATS'S GRECIAN URN TRACING

How? The clue is in the word "still." Besides the obvious sense of "as yet" or "right up till now," it can also mean "silent" or "motionless," and in Keats's day, it also meant "always, perpetually." Put them together and we see that the urn's purity consists in her persisting: silent, motionless, always. She is untouched by the passage of time, with its joys and sorrows. She persists *in* time — she has come down through the years, right up till now, to be beheld by the poet — but she doesn't belong *to* time. She is time's "foster-child," habitating with it but originating elsewhere, in a realm that's timeless.

The urn is also, the third line tells us, a "historian" who, despite her silence, is more eloquent than poetry. This alludes to the scenes of ancient life and myth that decorate her sides, with painted gods and men pursuing reluctant maidens while painted musicians provide the soundtrack, all of it tied together by flowers and leaves.

> What leaf-fring'd legend haunts about thy shape ·
>   Of deities or mortals, or of both,
>   In Tempe or the dales of Arcady?
>   What men or gods are these? What maidens loth?
> What mad pursuit? What struggle to escape?
>   What pipes and timbrels? What wild ecstasy?*

Over the next few stanzas we're shown more of the painted scenes: mountains, rivers, towns, streets, a priest leading a heifer to the sacrificial altar, and most strikingly, a lusty youth just on the verge — perpetually on the verge — of catching up to the object of his desire.

> Bold Lover, never, never canst thou kiss,
> Though winning near the goal, yet do not grieve;
>   She cannot fade, though thou hast not thy bliss,
>   For ever wilt thou love, and she be fair!

This is the poem's epiphany: The characters who live on the surface of the urn are immersed in urgent activity — noise, motion, pursuit, pounding pulses, throbbing desire. From their point of view, it's a series of good or bad events happening in time: in a word, *life*. But those of us out here, above the surface, see it all from a higher point of view, happening together, all at once, and it's all good, all beautiful. The painted characters, who in their own world may be at odds — the heifer and the priest that will slaughter her, the demure virgin and the horny stud pursuing her — are for us a harmonious composition: in a word, *art*.†

This work of art is, in all senses of the word, *still*. The figures are motionless, persisting outside of time, never aging or changing, their youth preserved forever. And they're all silent, even the musicians blowing the pipes and banging the timbrels.

> Heard melodies are sweet, but those unheard
>   Are sweeter; therefore, ye soft pipes, play on;
> Not to the sensual ear, but, more endear'd,
>   Pipe to the spirit ditties of no tone

---

*   Timbrels: tambourines.

†   Horny pursuit (a.k.a. attempted rape) is, of course, no longer regarded as an occasion for jolly artistic celebration.

Here we get down to some serious Dharma. When life is experienced from the higher, all-good perspective of artistic contemplation, it's not just different. It's better. Its soundless, timeless melodies are sweeter, "more endear'd," than the garden-variety melodies made of sound waves. The elevated view is finer, in a way that can't be conveyed to those who haven't seen it.

This aesthetic perspective merges into the spiritual. The sound of silence, "ditties of no tone," can't be heard by the carbon-based "sensual ear." They are played "to the spirit." The immortality beyond time that is conferred by art — the perpetual vigor of all those youthful Grecian hunks, the unfading beauty of the still-unravished maidens — hints at the realm of immortality reported by all the awakened sages. That realm is always available right *here*, within your own awareness. Just listen within for the ditties of no tone. Look within at the picture of no line or color. Feel within for the sculpture of no texture or shape.

This convergence of the aesthetic and the spiritual becomes explicit at the poem's conclusion. Again Keats addresses the urn, considering how it will persist to elevate future generations after his is gone.

> When old age shall this generation waste,
>   Thou shalt remain, in midst of other woe
> Than ours, a friend to man, to whom thou say'st,
>   "Beauty is truth, truth beauty, — that is all
>   Ye know on earth, and all ye need to know."

In that final couplet, the urn at last replies, and what it says has been stirring up arguments since 1819. It's so sweeping and — common sense might seem to dictate — so *wrong*. The truth, says common sense, is that life is full of deeply unbeautiful suffering and decay: injustice, disease, old age, death. (Just look at Keats's own life.) Yes, natural beauty exists but is fleeting: youth fades, flowers wilt. And yes, beautiful things that last can be constructed, but only with great skill and perseverance, precisely because they're artifice, exceptions to the rule of life. (Just look at Keats's own work.)

That's a powerful objection that requires a Dharma answer. Keats's equation of truth and beauty will always look wrong if we're just living and perceiving on the surface of life, like the characters on the surface of the urn. It's only the spectator's elevated view that sees life as the graceful wholeness of the urn, as a beautiful, harmonious work of art. When Elliott says his tearful goodbye to E.T., we cry along with him, but we wouldn't change the movie's ending.

There's an ancient formula for enlightenment that's closely parallel to Keats's equation of *truth* = *beauty*. In Vedanta philosophy, the statement is *sat* = *chit* = *ananda*. The term *sat* (pronounced *suht*) means pure reality, existence, truth. The third term, *ananda*, is pure happiness, bottomless joy, the cognition of life as infinitely OK, as beautiful. The middle term, *chit*, pure awareness, links these two together. The equation works — truth is seen as beauty, reality as happiness — only when pure awareness is unobstructed.

Keats's poems are full of this high, timeless perspective. They may also reflect the events of his own life on the surface of time. His notion of the urn as a foster child, a refugee from another realm, points backward to his own orphaned childhood in the care of an uncongenial guardian. The ardent lover who can never possess his beloved reflects his frustrated love for Fanny Brawne. But it's a mistake to reduce great art to journaling. In the image of the urn, Keats has given us a definitive model of life: 100 percent busy, noisy, multifarious activity, 100 percent stillness. It's the same model that was laid out over two thousand years ago by the seers of the Isha Upanishad: *Om purnam adah purnam idam*. "Om. That is full, this is full." Unmanifest being is full, complete, whole; the manifest universe is full, complete, whole.

It's also a definitive model of meditation, the method of awakening to the fullness of life. People commonly try to meditate by stifling their thoughts. They try to be enlightened or spiritual by stifling their feelings and enthusiasms. But those are the music of life, its pipes and timbrels. The mistake is to try to *create* stillness, which is like trying to still the ocean by beating down the waves. Waves must be there; they're the nature of the surface. Fortunately, the nature of the depths is stillness, always, no matter how turbulent the surface. Meditation, then, means leaving the surface as it is and letting the underlying stillness pull us in. Having found it (not created it) with our eyes closed, it gets easier and easier to find it with our eyes open, in the midst of noise.

•

The idea of a meditative, stillness-abiding Keats gets some nice validation from a letter he wrote to his brothers in 1818.

> At once it struck me what quality went to form a Man of Achievement, especially in Literature, and which Shakespeare possessed so enormously — I mean Negative Capability, that is, when a man is capable of being in uncertainties, mysteries, doubts, without any irritable reaching after fact and reason.

Keats's stumbling upon negative capability is a big deal — a major Western creative artist independently discovering the central strategy of the Eastern contemplative arts. In Chinese Taoism, it's called *wu wei*, "not doing." We all have that capability, but we have to be willing to simply be: to not anticipate, not interpret, just hang out in the midst of whatever presents itself, experiencing our experience as it actually *is* — raw, uncooked. This is why Keats is often considered a highly "sensual" poet. It's not that he wallows in the senses disproportionately. But having bypassed the cloudy filter of the thinking mind, he naturally perceives color and sound, texture and taste, with an unmediated intensity that other people might call heightened (or hyperreal or psychedelic). He just calls it beauty.

Negative capability is how to meditate, and as Keats explains, it's how to be "a Man of Achievement." Of course, you have to work at mastering and applying the skills of your field, whether you write odes or manage stock portfolios, but lots of people master skills. Wu wei is the special sauce that can make the difference between skill and genius, between a Salieri and a Mozart, or between Keats and some of the other Romantic poets he's often lumped with.

By definition, anything you've already assimilated into your art or philosophy or investment strategy is familiar; it's old news. To go where you've never gone before and possibly no one has gone before, you need to hang out "in mysteries, uncertainties, doubts" and relax there. As those mysteries clarify themselves — developing into a picture before your eyes, like Polaroid film — you can assimilate them into your system, then step onto *new* new ground and do it all again.

As Zen master Seung Sahn used to say, "Only don't know." Jane Goodall made her groundbreaking discoveries about the behavior of wild chimpanzees by not knowing, and being fine with that. She started as a secretary in the office of her boss, Dr. Louis Leakey, who sent her to the jungles of Tanzania precisely because she had no background in science. She was free of preconceived notions. And she was patient, willing to sit serenely alone for hours and days, observing the chimps from a distance, just being — until, in their own time, they drew closer, welcoming her into their lives. This allowed her to see and record their behavior as it actually was and not bend it to fit some prefabricated theory.

Of course, the poet, or any artist, has one great advantage over the scientist. A little further on in the letter, Keats adds:

> With a great poet the sense of Beauty overcomes every other consideration, or rather obliterates all consideration.

There's less temptation to retreat to our little thoughts when the bliss of Big Beauty blows them away — obliterates them.

Doing nothing, then, is a key to creative genius. So is being no one. In another letter, Keats spells out his conviction that the poet has "no self," "no character," "no identity," "is everything and nothing." As we've seen, Buddhists call this anatta, "not-self," the recognition that there is no solid, separate "person" inside us, no little driver behind a little steering wheel — just luminous, open awareness-space. That's the space of freedom. Like a chameleon that's not stuck with one color but can always match its environment, Keats explains, the poet is free to enjoy anything and empathize with anyone, "foul or fair, high or low, rich or poor, mean or elevated."

•

While at sea on that terrible monthlong voyage to Rome, racked with disease, Keats used a blank page in a book of Shakespeare's poems to transcribe the final version of his final poem — a sonnet of longing for Fanny Brawne. By now he knew he could never possess her and would never again see her. He had started the poem months earlier when, with his health already failing, they became informally, and hopelessly, engaged. Perhaps he just needed somewhere to write it down, but it's not out of place with Shakespeare's work. It's that extraordinary.

The poem doesn't address the beloved directly, as if to do so would be too agonizing. It speaks instead to a steadfast, bright star. Keats may have had Polaris, the North Star, in mind. It's the only object in the sky that never moves, the one that guides lost travelers home. But Polaris is pretty dim. He might have meant Venus, the beautiful Evening Star, the goddess of love, the brightest object in the night sky besides the moon. But the Evening Star shines for only a little while after sunset before sinking below the western horizon; like ordinary human love and beauty, it's ephemeral. I suspect that Keats combined the qualities of Venus and Polaris into a poetic ideal of maximum dazzling happiness-beauty-love, extended forever beyond human limitations.

> Bright star, would I were stedfast as thou art —*
>   Not in lone splendour hung aloft the night
> And watching, with eternal lids apart,
>   Like nature's patient, sleepless Eremite,†

---

*   Would: I wish.

†   Eremite: hermit, monk.

The moving waters at their priestlike task
    Of pure ablution round earth's human shores,
Or gazing on the new soft-fallen mask
    Of snow upon the mountains and the moors

These opening eight lines (the *octave*) are clearly the product of negative capability. The images, rendered with Keats's hyperreal intensity, are too inspired and vivid for the thinking mind to invent: the star as nature's unsleeping hermit, with eye ever open, and the world, teeming with humans but washed pure by its waters, then blanketed with soft snow, eternally witnessed by the star from its celestial height. It's almost as if Keats, in his lucid intuition, saw the earth from space as the Apollo astronauts would see it and photo-

graph it a century and a half later. He makes us see it too, in its luminous beauty, but he also makes us feel what it feels like out there in space: lonely, distant, cold.

That's why it's all introduced, in the second line, by the word "Not." Yes, I want to be as steady as the star, but not in lone splendor, not with a star's chilly, aloof solitude. Not from on high. Here, in what may have been a conscious farewell to his poetry, Keats at last relinquishes the elevated perspective of the Grecian urn's observer, or of "stout Cortez" on his mountain peak. It's time to come down — yet remain steadfast. How?

That's the theme of the final six lines (the *sestet*). In a bit of exquisitely subtle wordplay, it starts by stretching the poem's opening "Not" into "No — yet."

No — yet still stedfast, still unchangeable,
    Pillow'd upon my fair love's ripening breast,
To feel for ever its soft fall and swell,
    Awake for ever in a sweet unrest

Ah. There's the solution. Give me the bright star's celestial constancy, but step it down to the earth plane. Take my head out of the sky, lay it on my beloved's breast, and keep it there forever. (In reality, of course, your arm falls asleep after fifteen minutes, but this is poetry.) Just as the star is the unmoving witness to the planet's moving waters and the cold "soft-fallen mask / Of snow," let me be the witness to the movement of her breath, the "soft fall and swell" of her warm chest as she sleeps. Snow, of course, only falls; the addition here of "and swell" hints at the wish for some kind of resurrection for the dying poet. Let me find my immortality here. Let me "feel for ever" my love's breathing, let me remain "awake for ever," as if my own failing breath could be somehow sustained by hers.

Perhaps this touching plea is not as far-fetched as it sounds. Love in its deep sense is not just an ephemeral human emotion. What registers as an emotion is the *impact* of glimpsing the transcendent through the window of relationship. When we're swept away by its *whoooooshhh*, we are to some degree swept out of time and out of body, out of our mortal boundaries. We're swept out of separateness and into the closer-than-close intimacy that reduces distance to zero.

We see this intimacy in the sonnet's concluding couplet:

Still, still to hear her tender-taken breath,
And so live ever — or else swoon to death.

"Still, still." Here once again is that crucial word, but now urgently repeated, and charged with all the word's meanings. *Silent*: Hushed, hushed to hear the faint sound of my beloved's delicate breath. *Motionless*: Unmoving, unmoving so as not to disturb her sleep, and because I never want to move from this spot. *Right up to now*: I'm still here, still here, damn it — I'm not dead yet. And *always, perpetually*: I defy death, I defy the cruel fate that has kept us apart, I defy the limitations of my life. Through the transcendent magic of poetry, and the poetic magic of transcendence, I am here with you, merged with you, and will remain here always, always. Still, still.

The poignancy is almost unbearable. After Keats's stormy, tragically abbreviated life, the last word of his last poem is "death." But that's only half the story. It's half of an equation as audacious as "Beauty is truth, truth beauty." "And so live ever — or else swoon to death." Keats knows, he has *experienced*, that when we're still enough — immersed deeply enough in love or beauty — then we swoon into the transcendent.

There the I and the you melt into not-two, and so do near and far, gain and loss, joy and despair, life and death. We're swooning into the place where all those distinctions melt. Living? Dying? We don't know and we don't care. It's all one big swoon, and the swoon is love.

12. Upward, Not Northward

EDWIN ABBOTT ABBOTT · FLATLAND

What to call *Flatland*? We could say it's a strange little science fiction novella…or a fantasy math jaunt…or an excursion in psychedelic geometry…or…or…Just a hundred pages long, it was published pseudonymously in 1884, the same year that gave us *Huckleberry Finn* — and by the way, the first espresso machine, Coney Island's first roller coaster, England's worst earthquake, and the Dow Jones Average.

The author, Edwin Abbott, was a respected classics scholar, a priest in the Anglican Church, and the much beloved headmaster of the City School of London, entrusted with the intellectual and moral education of thousands of English boys, including at least one future prime minster. He wrote over fifty books — mostly dry textbooks like *How to Tell the Parts of Speech* and tame religious treatises like *The Fourfold Gospel*. They're all pretty much forgotten now except for *Flatland*, his one foray into the weird.

The book's narrator, and according to the original title page, its author, is "A Square." That could be a math pun. Abbott was the child of two cousins, both named Abbott, and they named him Edwin Abbott Abbott. That would make him A^2. But the narrator is literally a square, an eleven-by-eleven-inch, four-sided equilateral figure living in a two-dimensional plane, who has no concept of any larger reality — at first.

> I call our world Flatland, not because we call it so, but to make its nature clearer to you, my happy readers, who are privileged to live in Space.
>
> Imagine a vast sheet of paper on which straight Lines, Triangles, Squares, Pentagons, Hexagons, and other figures, instead of remaining fixed in their places, move freely about, on or in the surface, but without the power of rising above or sinking below it, very much like shadows — only hard and with luminous edges — and you will have a pretty correct notion of my country and countrymen. Alas, a few years ago, I should have said "my universe": but now my mind has been opened to a higher view of things.

Flatland is usually enjoyed as an amusing exercise in theoretical speculation, but for us Dharma dogs, that bit about the mind being "opened to a higher view of things" makes our noses twitch. Could there be something here not purely theoretical? Could this kindly Victorian gentleman have slipped into some nonusual experience that prompted him to write this strange adventure — but made him squeamish about putting his name to it?

In the first half of the book, "This World," Abbott imagines how life in two dimensions might work. One of the big challenges becomes clear if you put, say, a dime and a postage stamp side by side on a table. Viewed from above, the dime is obviously round, the stamp is rectangular. The dime features a picture of Franklin Roosevelt, the stamp features perhaps a flag. But if you crouch down till your eye is at the level of the tabletop and view the objects edge-on, they both look like straight lines. Their shape, as well as any "inside" features — Roosevelt, flag — are hidden from view. That's the Flatlanders' situation. (They have an elaborate method of distinguishing different shapes, involving fog, variable luminosity, and politely feeling one another's angles.)

As Abbott fleshes out the two-dimensional details, he keeps finding irresistible opportunities to satirize three-dimensional society, particularly the snobbery of the British class system. In Flatland, your place in the world — your caste — is determined at birth by your shape. More sides and blunter angles equal higher intelligence and greater status. The "acute-angled rab-ble" of Isosceles Triangles are Soldiers (well equipped to skewer others when required) and the lowest class of Workmen.* Squares and Pentagons are Professionals and Gentlemen. Hexagons and above are the Nobility. Once their sides become too many to count, they receive "the honourable title of Polygonal, or many-sided." When their sides finally become too small to see, they attain the ultimate rank of Circle, or Priest.

The lower classes are naturally prone to seditious uprisings, but the Cir-cles manipulate them by paying off a few rebels to plant "jealousies and suspi-cions" among the rest, so that "they are stirred to mutual warfare, and perish by one another's angles." The middle classes are kept in line by the promise of gradual progress. Starting with the Squares, they gain upward mobility over generations, as every son is born with one more side than his father.

Women, however, need not apply: generation after generation, they re-main Straight Lines. Wisely, Men are afraid of them. Women are even sharper than Soldiers and can make themselves dangerously invisible by facing an-other Figure head-on, effectively vanishing to a point. To keep this deadly ninja power under control, every member of the Thinner Sex is required to keep up a continuous humming "Peace-cry" from her front end, where her mouth is, and to gracefully undulate her back end. For women in our own society, this may all sound painfully familiar: the disempowering pressure to show that they're just harmless, pretty things by maintaining a line of femi-nine chatter and, one way or another, shaking their booties.

The other consequence of being born in a female body — well, that just can't be helped:

> They are…wholly devoid of brain-power, and have neither reflec-tion, judgment nor forethought, and hardly any memory. Hence, in their fits of fury, they remember no claims and recognize no distinc-tions. I have actually known a case where a Woman has exterminated her whole household, and half an hour afterwards, when her rage was over and the fragments swept away, has asked what has become of her husband and her children.

Passages like this have sometimes earned Abbott accusations of sexism, but that's the old fallacy of equating the author with the narrator. It's clear that Abbott, who was an early advocate of expanded educational opportunities

---

*   I'm following Abbott's capitalization.

for girls, is satirizing backward social attitudes, including sexism. The Square pretty well indicts himself with his unquestioning belief in "the divine origin of the aristocratic constitution of the State in Flatland" and the doctrine of the Priests, which comes down to "Attend to your Configuration" — know your place, as dictated by your shape.

•

The narrowness of the Square's worldview is precisely what sets us up for the second half of the book, "Other Worlds." That's where things get seriously strange. First, our Square has a dream vision of Lineland, a *one*-dimensional world: that is, a single, continuous line, within which are arrayed shorter Lines (Men) and Points (Women). One of the Lines is pleased to be the King of Lineland, which makes him, as far as he's concerned, the ruler of the universe. He's the lord of all he surveys and has no idea how little that is.

The Square tries to open the King's eyes to the concept of the second dimension, but the King digs in, too oblivious to know he's oblivious. Like your know-it-all uncle at the Thanksgiving table, he's a happy victim of confirmation bias, accepting only information that confirms what he already believes, shutting out any fake news that might threaten his secure little realm of ignorance. In frustration, the Square finally shouts:

> Besotted Being! You think yourself the perfection of existence, while you are in reality the most imperfect and imbecile. . . . Why waste more words? Suffice it that I am the completion of your incomplete self. You are a Line, but I am a Line of Lines, called in my country a Square: and even I, infinitely superior though I am to you, am of little account among the great nobles of Flatland, whence I have come to visit you, in the hope of enlightening your ignorance.

But as we've sadly seen in our own world, when the irresistible force of actuality meets the immovable object of alternative facts, mobs arise. Determined to maintain his supremacy, the angry King rallies his subjects to raise a violent war cry against the invader, "as if to pierce me through the diagonal." Just then, the Square awakens from his dream and comes back to reality — his reality of two dimensions. (Vladimir Nabokov once referred to *reality* as "one of the few words which mean nothing without quotes." Indeed.)

The next night, the Square is relaxing at home when he's startled by an intruder that inexplicably materializes out of thin air. It appears to be a Circle, but it has a queer way of expanding and contracting. The stranger explains that he comes from Space, the land of three dimensions, and that he is something inconceivable to the Square: a Sphere.

> I am not a Circle, but an infinite number of Circles, of size varying from a Point to a Circle of thirteen inches in diameter, one placed on the top of the other. When I cut through your plane as I am now doing, I make in your plane a section which you, very rightly, call a Circle.... See now, I will rise; and the effect upon your eye will be that my Circle will become smaller and smaller till it dwindles to a point and finally vanishes.

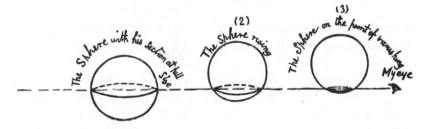

ABBOTT'S DRAWING FOR THE FIRST EDITION:
"THE SPHERE WITH HIS SECTION AT FULL SIZE (2) THE SPHERE RISING
(3) THE SPHERE ON THE POINT OF VANISHING...MY EYE."

This time it's the Square's turn to be clueless. All he can see is a Circle changing size and disappearing. He can't conceive of a third dimension in which all those Circles make up a bigger thing. He can't imagine the direction in which the Sphere says he's moving: "not Northward; Upward," a direction simultaneously perpendicular to Flatland's North, South, East, and West. Even as the Sphere describes the vista of Flatland that he sees from his bird's-eye view — such as where the Square has squirreled away money in his house and what all his neighbors are up to — it just doesn't compute.

Mere theory and hearsay are rarely enough to bring us to a more expansive view. We need direct experience. Realizing that the only way to open the Square's eyes is to take him on a little trip, the Sphere yanks him out of Flatland and into Spaceland. *Whoooooshhh!* The paradoxical language the Square uses here sounds remarkably like that of mystics describing their unbidden first plunge into a new realm:

An unspeakable horror seized me. There was a darkness; then a dizzy, sickening sensation of sight that was not like seeing; I saw a Line that was no Line; Space that was not Space; I was myself, and not myself. When I could find voice, I shrieked aloud in agony, "Either this is madness or it is Hell." "It is neither," calmly replied the voice of the Sphere, "it is Knowledge; it is Three Dimensions: open your eye once again and try to look steadily."

I looked, and, behold, a new world! There stood before me, visibly incorporate, all that I had before inferred, conjectured, dreamed, of perfect Circular beauty…a beautiful harmonious Something — for which I had no words; but you, my Readers in Spaceland, would call it the surface of the Sphere.

More wonders await. Following his guide's lead, the Square looks back at Flatland and sees something miraculous: figures viewed from above, their interior and exterior and all their sides and angles visible at once, as we viewed the dime and the postage stamp from above. All in one glance, he can see things both near and far — the higher Upward he mounts into Space, the broader the Flatland vista he can see. This is the kind of Knowledge that, until he was flung into the deep end, our square Square would have dismissed as lunacy.

So…

One evening, let's say, you're relaxing at home when you're startled by an intruder, inexplicably materializing out of thin air. It appears to be a Sphere. Let's say it's the size of a basketball when you first notice it, hovering in the middle of the room, but it keeps shrinking and expanding. After a while it shrinks to a point, then vanishes.

Then it comes back, and you ask, "Hey, Sphere, what's going on here?" It replies:

"Well, hey there. Actually, I'm not a Sphere, but an infinite number of Spheres of varying sizes, nested like Russian dolls. When I cut through your world, like this, you see a three-dimensional cross section of me, which to you is a Sphere. Now I'll again rise out of your world; from your perspective I'll shrink down to a point and finally vanish. Bye!" He's gone. Then: "And we're back!"

Seeing that the Sphere has in fact returned, first as a point and then continuing to expand, you ask, "Then what *are* you?"

"I'm a Sloog — a four-dimensional round object. As a Sphere is to a Circle, so a Sloog is to a Sphere. Got it?"

"Um, not really. When you rise up out of my three-dimensional world, where do you go?"

"I move Binkward, not Upward. Let me explain: I know that you were recently reading *Flatland*. From my vantage point, I easily see everything in your world. (And by the way, the TV remote, which your mom in Cleveland is looking for, is between the couch cushions, and you're having trouble digesting that second doughnut you had for breakfast. But I digress.) To the hero of *Flatland*, the word *Sphere* was initially as meaningless as *Sloog* is to you now. The idea of moving Upward was as baffling to him as Binkward is to you. He couldn't imagine how the third dimension could lie in a direction that's simultaneously perpendicular to Flatland's North, South, East, and West, until his guide the Sphere yanked him Upward into it. Then it became experientially obvious. In the same way, Binkward, the direction of the fourth dimension, is simultaneously perpendicular to your North, South, East, West, Down, and Up. Got it?"

"Ummmmm…"

"Want a yank?"

Well, do you? (I need Clint Eastwood's voice here, from *Dirty Harry*: "Well, do you, punk?")

At this moment of unresolved suspense, our little story must, alas, end. As a merely three-dimensional commentator, I can't describe the trip Binkward or the vision of a Sloog in all its four-dimensional glory, which you would see if you were to accept the invitation.

•

But what if we've already had some little peeks Binkward? Most of us have had the experience of knowing things at a distance in ways that, from the usual three-dimensional point of view, are not explainable. Perhaps a friend or loved one is in distress and you suddenly just *know*. Later, they phone and tell you about it. You might call it a feeling, or intuition, but that's just a label: it doesn't explain anything. Could the explanation be something at least *like* access to a fourth dimension, somehow analogous to it — some breaking through the surface of our own plane, as it were, and poking one's head Binkward to a fourth-dimensional vantage point from which our world is an open book, just as Flatland is from Spaceland?

Sometimes we may even get glimpses of things that haven't happened yet. Could that be because we are then, so to speak, glimpsing sections of four-dimensional objects that haven't yet passed through our three-dimensional plane? Maybe, as they pass through here, they all move steadily in the same direction. That would be like the Sphere intersecting with Flatland but having to move steadily Upward. Then he won't seem to repeatedly grow and contract. He'll appear first as a point, then grow steadily to his maximum diameter, then shrink steadily till he once more becomes a point. Finally, as he passes out of Flatland, he'll seem to vanish.

In that case, from the Square's point of view, the part of the Sphere that's still below the plane of Flatland at any given moment is yet to be seen — it's in the future. The portion that's now above Flatland, which he's already seen, is the past. The Circle that intersects Flatland is the present. What the Square sees as the varying states of a Circle, changing in time, actually exist all at once, as an integrated whole in the third dimension of space. Similarly, as the Sloog moves Binkward, the part that hasn't yet crossed our three-dimensional world is future; the part that has crossed it is past. What we see as the varying states of a Sphere, changing in time, actually exist all at once in the fourth dimension of space. In any system with n dimensions of space, the $(n + 1)$ dimension is perceived as time.

Now…what if this is true not only of Spheres and Sloogs but of everything? What if the things you see right now (book, table, chair) are actually four-dimensional objects of which you perceive a sequence of three-dimensional cross sections over time? Of course, one of the objects is "you." What if you first appear in this world as a point, grow for a while, then shrink for a while, then vanish? In some sense, actually, you do. You start off as a microscopic zygote, then grow in size and complexity, get some hair on top and some nails at the edges, crawl, walk, play, work, shrivel, vanish. Dust to dust.

Imagine, then, all the objects and people of this world, in all their complex configurations and interactions, as a multitude of four-dimensional thingamajigs, displaying their ever-changing three-dimensional cross sections to one another. If you want to see the past, somehow become less tightly stuck in place — or use some kind of subtle transdimensional periscope — and peek "above" this plane at the sections that have already passed through. To see the future, peek "below" at the sections that are yet to arrive. What does all this say about free will vs. predestination, or Einstein's space-time continuum? I dunno. We're just playing here, trying to loosen things up, open ourselves to some wider possibilities.

Let's go wider still. At the climax of his excursion into the third dimension, Abbott's Square gets caught up, "intoxicated" with his expanded vision, and insists that the Sphere admit that beyond it there must be a fourth dimension — then a fifth, a sixth, a seventh…. "Nothing could stem the flood of my ecstatic aspirations." But for the Sphere, it's three dimensions and end of story. He gets huffy and hurls the impertinent Square back into Flatland.

It's always a shock for a disciple to come up against the conservative limits of the guru's vision. Hamlet said there are more things in heaven and earth than are dreamt of in your philosophy. Whatever is your n, it's easy to be enlightened relative to those stuck in $(n - 1)$, but $(n + 1)$ is out of the question.

•

This I do know: When I go away — when I slip into transcendence — that "away" is unstuck in space and time. It's not north, south, east, west, up, or down. It's not near or far. It's not a little while or a long while. For that matter, it's not interesting or boring, happy or sad, familiar or strange. It's the place that A. A. Milne wrote about in "Halfway Down," the place in the middle of the stairs that's neither down nor up:

> It isn't really
> Anywhere!
> It's somewhere else
> Instead!

In that sense, it's simultaneously perpendicular to all our directions of space, time, thought, feeling, and everything else, without tugging against any of them. It's outta here without going anywhere.

So...did Edwin Abbott Abbott — A^2 — have some kind of transdimensional or transcendental adventure of his own? We know there was a certain amount of pre-Einsteinian speculation about the fourth dimension going on among his friends. We also know that even intellectual speculation can sometimes trigger glimpses of a more expansive reality. To me, anyway, his book has the whiff of authentic spiritual experience, beyond the merely theoretical.

In fact, Abbott makes the spiritual connection explicit. The reason the Sphere has descended into the Square's life, it turns out, is that he's seeking "a fit apostle for the Gospel of the Three Dimensions, which I am allowed to preach once only in a thousand years." Like many apostles, the Square is persecuted. It turns out that the upper echelons of Flatland's priesthood know all about the visitations from beyond but have suppressed that knowledge for millennia, branding all mention of the third dimension as heretical. Why? Is this an Area 51 thing, where the (alleged) evidence of alien visitors is hidden to prevent panicking the masses and destabilizing the political structure? Is it fear that direct, personal, unmediated experience of the beyond would threaten the monopoly of the Priests? Probably yes and yes — it was ever thus.

When the Square returns from his eye-opening journey, he's brimming with spiritual fervor, eager to declare the life-changing Good News of "Upward, not Northward."

I awoke rejoicing, and began to reflect on the glorious career before me. I would go forth, methought, at once, and evangelize the whole of Flatland. Even to Women and Soldiers should the Gospel of Three Dimensions be proclaimed.

The Square's egalitarian impulse recalls Christ's ministry to the despised tax collectors and prostitutes. He would have done well, though, to heed Christ's advice: Don't cast your pearls before swine; i.e., don't get carried away and impose sublime knowledge on the unready; i.e., be cool. (Christ might have done well to heed that advice himself.) The Square's heresy gets him imprisoned for life.

But that's not the most tragic part of his fate.

To confess the truth, I felt that all that I had seen and heard was in some strange way slipping away from me, like the image of a half-grasped, tantalizing dream...and in my nightly visions the mysterious precept, "Upward, not Northward," haunts me like a soul-devouring Sphinx.

Perhaps you've had dreams in which you're flying, where you find the obvious angle of ascent — *How did I ever miss this?* — and effortlessly, blissfully, up you go, soaring in joyous freedom. Then you wake up, and for a few flickering moments you're sure you'll remember that angle and always be able to fly. And then...oh.

If you've been on the spiritual path for a while, there's a good chance you've sometimes experienced that kind of slipping away of the sublime vision. You may even have come back from your transcendental trek clutching some precious verbal formulation, your own version of "Upward, not Northward," a slogan so simple and potent that you're sure it will reliably evoke the vision for yourself and others. And then... "Wait. 'God ate my homework'? What the hell did *that* mean?" When we crash the gates of Paradise, only to be thrown out again, and our little verbal key doesn't fit the lock, then our dejection — as Abbott so poignantly shows — can be crushing. But this is where the true, dedicated Dharma bums pick themselves up, dust themselves off, and start all over again. This getting it and losing it and getting it again is all part of the process. In time, it's lost less. All seekers go through this. The sages are the ones who kept going.

There is, however, one other solution, one that's implied by the Square's concluding prison lament. It's so delicate and subtle that we may or may not have ears to hear it; it's hard to tell whether Abbott understood it himself. The prison in which the Square languishes is, of course, two-dimensional. As we can see from out here in Spaceland, it's wide open at the top. The Square's bondage is made not of prison walls but of his own relapsed belief in the ultimacy of two dimensions. Like Jim in the last dozen chapters of *Huckleberry Finn*, he's the prisoner of a story.

If, for just one moment, he could relax out of that story and reopen himself to the reality of his own slogan — "Upward, not Northward" — he could see that he's already free. As are we all.

13. What's Your Hurry?

WILLIAM SHAKESPEARE • MACBETH

Socrates could really drink. He was, Plato tells us, not much interested in wine, but when put to the test he could drink everyone under the table. At the end of Plato's *Symposium*, after a night of serious imbibing that has left most of his companions passed out, Socrates is still philosophizing away as usual, cheerfully explaining to two groggy playwrights why a writer of great tragedies should also be able to write great comedies, and vice versa.

That's a radical position. In the tragic vision, all of life rushes toward destruction and death. The futility of our aspirations is enacted by kings and other big shots whose big aspirations succeed for a while, then end with a big crash, the stage littered with corpses. In the comic vision, life leads to more life. Even as dreams crash and people die, new dreams and generations are born, like the wildflowers that arise from the ashes of forest fires. Classical comedies end in the song and dance of a wedding feast, a happy promise of regeneration.

But Plato teases us. The narrator of the *Symposium* nods out over his wine and never hears the gist of Socrates's argument — how these two contrary visions might coexist in the work of one great playwright. We can guess, however, that it would require somehow seeing *behind* both the laughing mask of comedy and the crying mask of tragedy: seeing past both the womb and the tomb, seeing that the mysterious space from which we emerge and the mysterious space to which we return are the one space, *this* space, through which we pulse in every moment. Socrates, that is, required a playwright as enlightened as he was.

It took almost two thousand years till one came along — in England, in an age when the few professional writers were often also street brawlers, government spies, and/or "pamphleteers" (the forerunners of paid Twitter trolls). The theater district across the Thames from the City of London was a rowdy place, crowded with taverns, brothels offering prostitutes of both sexes, and arena-style theaters featuring bloody sports like bear-baiting and bull-baiting — often the same theaters where plays were presented. The London elite crossed the river for risqué and possibly risky thrills, much as stylish New Yorkers would one day go uptown to the jazz clubs and dope dens of Harlem.

When William Shakespeare arrived on this scene from the boondocks of Stratford, he was considered an unschooled bumpkin, yet he soon eclipsed his city-bred, university-trained rivals. His output was staggering: some two plays a year for two decades, even as he helped manage a troupe of unruly actors and probably toured with them for several months of each year, bumping along in uncomfortable wagons to uncertain venues. Hundreds of scholarly books have tried to account for his sprawling genius, his ability to conjure kings that talk and feel just like kings, wood sprites that talk and feel like wood sprites.

The most intriguing explanation is found in a two-page story by Jorge Luis Borges, titled, in an echo of Keats, "Everything and Nothing." Starting in childhood, Borges speculates, Shakespeare saw that "There was no one in him." (Once again, this is anatta, "not-self," in Buddhist lingo.) With no Shakespeare inside to get in the way, there was unlimited open space in which to dream and empathetically *be* kings and sprites, and to speak in their voices — Keats's "negative capability." Shakespeare lived and wrote from the one space behind all our constructed selves, all conditions, all masks. That includes the opposing tragic and comic masks, and Shakespeare filled his plays with hints of the equivalence of opposites: "hot ice," "tragical mirth," "fearful bravery," "sweet sorrow," "loving hate," "cold fire," "bright smoke."

•

One of the most blatant hints comes in *The Tragedy of Macbeth*, in a sort of thesis statement at the end of the first scene. The play opens with a bang, literally — a spectacular display of thunder and lightning produced by a device that ignited powdered rosin, a stunning new special effect when the play opened at the Globe Theatre in 1606. Out of the smoke three Witches materialize, rising through the trapdoor at center stage, and agree to accost the Scottish nobleman Macbeth after his current battle has ended. Then they chant:

> Fair is foul, and foul is fair.
> Hover through the fog and filthy air.

This "Fair is foul" formula is usually taken to portend the moral fog that Macbeth will soon enter, where distinctions of right and wrong are erased, as if erasing the line that separates fair balls from foul balls, turning order into chaos.

Helping to push him over that line is his wife, a needy, sharp-clawed climber straight out of *The Real Housewives of Medieval Scotland*. Till now Macbeth has been a valiant soldier and a loyal subject, but by act 2, at Lady Macbeth's urging, he'll be tiptoeing down a hallway to murder the king in his sleep, led by a hallucination floating ahead of him, produced by his own feverish thoughts.

> Is this a dagger which I see before me,
> The handle toward my hand?
>   ... or art thou but
> A dagger of the mind...?

There's always some dagger of the mind, some juicy wrong thing we can imagine doing, and the handle is always toward our hand. *Hey, I could scoop a twenty out of the collection plate and no one would notice.* That's OK: we're not responsible for our thoughts. The crime begins the moment we start to act on the thought, to grab for the dagger. "Come, let me clutch thee," says Macbeth to the dagger, and tragedy ensues.

But as usual in Shakespeare, every layer reveals another beneath it. The Witches' "Fair is foul, and foul is fair" also means that good fortune can turn out to be bad fortune, and vice versa. As Jesus says, "Many that are first shall be last, and the last shall be first." That "shall" sounds like a promise for the future. Shakespeare's thesis statement, however, goes further: it's set in the present tense. Everything *already* contains, and more or less is, its own opposite.

As in the *taijitu* or yin-yang diagram of Chinese philosophy, light contains dark, dark contains light. They're not rigidly separated but flow together in a curving, organic embrace. It's only our dualistic thinking that draws a rigid line separating absolute yes and no, good and bad, fair and foul. Einstein's $E = mc^2$ sounds impossible, but in fact energy *is* matter, matter *is* energy. It just looks different as it dances different steps.

The Heart Sutra, one of the key texts of Mahayana Buddhism, states the principle in even more shocking terms.

Form is no other than emptiness, emptiness no other than form.
Form is exactly emptiness, emptiness exactly form.

That is, everything that looks solid and real, including our so-called selves, turns out to be nothing in particular, while that nothing somehow keeps arising as all our somethings. The tidy, discrete "things" that we drew with our crayons in kindergarten ("This is the sun, and this is the flower, and this is the dirt...") turn out to have no solid, continuous, separate, permanent identity, no distinct "thingness." We live in a world not of things but of process. Dirt matter joins water matter and sun energy to become flower matter, which then decays once more into dirt matter. Or flower matter is eaten by animal matter that burns calories in complex patterns of behavior energy, then decays into dirt matter... and the beat goes on.

This process of perpetual transformation happens in *time*. In any given moment, we may mistake an empty, temporary form for something permanent, a partial truth for the whole truth, as in the old parable of the blind men and the elephant, each saying it's like a snake or a palm frond, a wall, a tree trunk, and so forth. Each gets a snapshot but misses the movie. If we took cross sections of the elephant, we would see it first in snakelike form, then in frond-like form, and so on — like the Sphere passing through Flatland — but it's really none of those forms in particular and all of them at once, beyond time.

"Fair is foul," then, implies that everything is everything else — even if, depending on the degree of our blindness, we have to wait awhile to see all its forms. That's fine, as long as we let these comings and goings take their time. Otherwise we pit ourselves against the process called universe, in a battle we can't win: the elephant will stomp us, guaranteed. Enter Macbeth.

•

Enter Macbeth, in fact, fresh from battle, victorious, having tasted the possibility of shaping the world to his will, of *ruling*. Crossing the wild, open heath with his brother-in-arms Banquo, he meets the Witches, who greet him with fateful words.

All hail, Macbeth, that shalt be king hereafter!

Their prophecy is the psychological extension of his military success, just as kids who learn to tie their shoes soon dream of being superheroes. But *when* will he be king? "Hereafter." Eventually. *Mañana.*

Macbeth's great flaw is usually considered to be ambition, but a more precise diagnosis might be impatience. Eventually he'll swell to his maximum greatness, like the belly of the elephant, and eventually he'll taper like its tail. Macbeth's mistake, his "sin," is to fixate, through intense desire, on a single time-bound form, as if it were ultimate rather than part of a larger pattern of change, and then rush toward it. In fact, the prophecy leaves him stunned — Banquo says, "My noble partner... seems rapt withal." Enraptured by our visions of future glory or pleasure, we lose our simple enjoyment of the present.

That is, we hurry. We're the donkey that keeps trying to catch up to the dangling carrot. We never catch it because only the present is real — the time is always now, in case you hadn't noticed. Like Macbeth clutching at the phantom dagger, we clutch at the phantom satisfaction of the future and wind up creating dissatisfaction with the present.

For Macbeth, the ever-dangling carrot is old King Duncan. At first, he envies Duncan's crown. By act 2, driven by his own impatience and Lady Macbeth's emotional blackmail, he murders Duncan and gains the crown. But being king makes him miserable, cursed with paranoid anxiety and insomnia ("O, full of scorpions is my mind, dear wife!"), and now he envies the tranquility of Duncan's death.

Better be with the dead,
Whom we, to gain our peace, have sent to peace.

He has just enough insight to understand that peace is what he's really pursuing, but not enough to understand that peace dawns only when we call off the pursuit.

In his restless straining toward the future, Macbeth is us whenever we hurry, whenever we lean forward, tightly gripping the steering wheel of our life, trying to will the traffic to move faster, trying to magically be in the next block when we're always here in *this* block. The cardiologist Meyer Friedman first conceived the notion of type A personality when his upholsterer noticed that the chairs in Friedman's waiting room — used, naturally, by lots of impatient, hypertensive types — were the only ones he'd ever seen that had worn out first on the front edge instead of the back. This whole play feels forward-leaning, rushed. It's Shakespeare's shortest tragedy, probably designed for the short attention span of his impatient new patron, James I. (It was fit for a king.)

Macbeth's war buddy Banquo is type B. He is, in a sense, Macbeth's doppelgänger, his other, better self. That is, he's *our* better self. He's centered, insightful, unhurried and unharried, leaning back in the driver's seat of life, letting the horses under the hood do the galloping. (Who was ever more chill onstage than Charlie Parker or smilin' Eddie Van Halen, even as their fingers blazed?) Banquo, in a word, is patient. In Buddhist teaching, patience, or *kshanti paramita*, is one of the Six Transcendental Virtues that support awakening. I've learned a lot about kshanti paramita by working with prisoners. It's not stewing in exasperation, drumming your fingers while you wait for the end of your cellmate's tedious rant or the end of your thirty-year sentence. It's recognizing your exasperation, then relaxing your grip on it and relaxing back into yourself, into the timeless open space of present awareness, as it is. When we rest in timeless being, we're no longer doing time.

From this place of patience, not hurrying toward the fair or worried about the foul, Banquo tells the Witches:

> Speak, then, to me, who neither beg nor fear
> Your favors nor your hate.

No big deal, I'm just kinda curious. They respond that Banquo, though never a king himself, will beget kings. For him, that's plenty. Unlike Macbeth, he sees the big picture and so is the true heir to life's banquet. Duncan, shortly before his death, makes jolly puns about the banquet of Banquo's noble qualities, almost as if hinting that Banquo is his rightful successor.

Macbeth is less happy about Banquo's virtues. Once he becomes king, with his paranoia mounting, he feels threatened by his old friend's "royalty of nature" and has him killed, the body dumped into a ditch. This is us at our worst. Failing to appreciate the banquet of life's all-in-good-time wholeness, fearing (correctly) that time and change will render our successes temporary, we ditch that larger vision.

But the vision won't stay dead. Banquo's ghost returns, fittingly, in the banquet scene, at the dead center of the play. It opens with King Macbeth taking his ill-gotten place at the head of the table and, straight-faced, telling the assembled lords and ladies, "You know your own degrees; sit down." Having violently breached the orderly system of "degree," or hierarchy, he now insists that everyone else conform to it. It's a very human impulse: *I'll just step into the magical No-Consequences Zone and do this one little thing — sleep with this one wildly inappropriate person, embezzle this one bunch of funds from Grandma's estate — and then I'll return with my prize and we'll all go back to business as usual. What happens in the No-Consequences Zone stays in the No-Consequences Zone.* Macbeth is like a politician who gets elected by corrupt means, then makes grand speeches about law and order while he dreams of ruling forever.

Fortunately, tyrants *don't* rule forever. Their estrangement from the flow of life finally renders their dreams sterile. Macbeth is childless. He frets over the prophecy that Banquo's children will succeed him, and now curses the Witches for giving him "a fruitless crown" and "a barren scepter." And his paranoia becomes self-fulfilling. As he multiplies his crimes, ordering the deaths of anyone he imagines might threaten his power, and even their wives and children, he inspires a growing army of rebels.

Do the Witches deserve Macbeth's curses? Can we take his word for it? He calls them good when they flatter his ambition, but evil when his fair turns foul. In his very first line, "So fair and foul a day I have not seen," he thinks he's just talking about the weather. But it's a tip-off that our changes of fortune are as natural and inevitable as the alternation of sun and clouds. It's all part of a big, messy system, bigger and messier than our tidy notions of good and bad outcomes. (Hamlet says, "There is nothing either good or bad but thinking makes it so." Only our partiality, our attachment and aversion, make it so.) In cursing the Witches, Macbeth blames the weather on the weatherwomen, and blames the weather for being weather.

The Witches might be agents of Mother Nature herself, in all her wildness and her stubborn refusal to cooperate with the traditionally male, type A, straight-ahead march toward imagined triumphs in an imagined future. If you want to hear God laugh, tell her your plans. (Or as Mike Tyson less gently put it, everyone has a plan till they get punched in the mouth.) "Double,

double toil and trouble," the Witches chant as they cook up the future in their magic cauldron, the sweltering womb of proliferating possibilities, teeming with complications that double, double like the 2-4-8-16 of dividing cells.

Again, though, Shakespeare gives us layers beneath layers. In a world where fair is foul, female is also male: these gender-fluid Witches have beards. They don't call themselves witches, but Weyard Sisters, using an Anglo-Saxon word for fate, suggesting the three Fates of Greek myth who create human destinies. But Macbeth chooses his own destiny. Here Shakespeare's understanding is less like the Greek idea and more like the concept of karma. In Sanskrit, karma literally means "doing," and it implies that whatever happens to us is our own doing. Karma is the inescapability of cause and effect, despite our No-Consequences magical thinking.

Macbeth himself shows some understanding of this what-goes-around principle.

> This even-handed justice
> Commends th' ingredience of our poisoned chalice
> To our own lips.

THÉODORE CHASSÉRIAU, *MACBETH SEEING THE GHOST OF BANQUO* (DETAIL)

In the banquet scene, his karma takes the form of Banquo's ghost. Our better, wiser self, no matter how we beat it down, demands its rightful place. It haunts us ever, just as Banquo's ghost takes Macbeth's royal seat at the head of the table, jolting him into a shrieking meltdown in front of his astonished guests, who can't see the ghost. (It's not *their* karma.) The meek shall inherit the earth. After the fires of narrow self-interest have raged and flamed out, the patient Banquo, the wide, holistic vision, shall inherit the kingdom.

Shakespeare, with his vast inner space, has room for both Macbeth's perspective and Banquo's. Through Banquo's wide vision, he can *see* how things truly are, how everything becomes (or is) its opposite, and so write the play. Through Macbeth, he can *feel* the passion, the anguish at gaining success only to have it all slip away, and the "valiant fury" of the doomed struggle to hold on to it. We all probably have at least some vague sense of both perspectives, hence the play's universal appeal. It was President Lincoln's favorite — his aides would sometimes find him asleep at his desk, his head resting on its open pages.

•

After the spoiled banquet, Macbeth decides to try his luck with the Witches once more, and rides out onto the heath to find them. This time — more cool special effects! — they conjure three apparitions out of their steaming cauldron, which make three prophecies regarding Macbeth's destiny, and ours.

The first prophecy is simple: "Beware Macduff." Macduff, a lord whose family Macbeth has slaughtered, will eventually confront him in battle and behead him. This warning suggests childhood's end, the realization of our own mortality, when we lose our first few friends to violence or diseases or drunken car crashes. We can't remain forever young or beautiful. It's a scary world in which we're subject to birth, old age, disease, and death (in the standard Buddhist formulation). Entering the adult working world, we feel like scared, vulnerable children. As Macbeth is a pretender to the throne, we feel like pretenders among the grownups, one of whom will finally expose our pretense, find our weakness, and bring us down.

Shit happens, and some specific, fatal shit has our name on it. Some Macduff out there has our number. In the play, he first appears moments after Duncan's assassination, banging at Macbeth's castle gate, just as that something-fatal will bang at the gate of *our* carefully fortified defenses. Macbeth, in response, tries desperately to wash the king's blood from his hands and act cool, just as we try to clean up our act and brazen it out when mortality comes knocking.

The second prophecy, "None of woman born / Shall harm Macbeth," seems to contradict the first. With a little more experience in the world, we may come to suspect that we're safe after all. The others, the grownups who seemed so scary, are also of woman born; they're also frightened, vulnerable mother's children like us. We're *all* subject to birth, old age, disease, and death.

The third prophecy also sounds like good news.

> Macbeth shall never vanquished be until
> Great Birnam Wood to high Dunsinane Hill
> Shall come against him.

Birnam Wood is a forest several miles from Dunsinane Hill, the site of Macbeth's castle. Since forests obviously can't move, this is like saying Macbeth is safe till hell freezes over. Dunsinane is Macbeth's supposedly impregnable fortress. Our fortress could be our border walls, our gated communities, our bulging stock portfolios, our armored SUVs (one model is actually called the Armada), our muscular religions — any form of insulation that we think will keep the chaos of the world at bay.

But time gets us all in the end. The second law of thermodynamics dictates that, in time, entropy — disorder — takes over. Things fall apart. Molecules move from more-orderly to less-orderly arrangements. A chemistry professor of mine once explained this law by saying (in his German accent), "If you park a shiny new Mercedes-Benz at ze curb and come back in five hundred years, it turns into a pile of rusted junk. However, if you park a pile of junk at ze curb for five hundred years, it does not turn into a Mercedes."

Hearing the Birnam Wood prophecy, Macbeth exults, "That will never be!" Of course he's wrong. In time *everything* will be. Everything that we like to imagine is permanent will crumble: our bodies, our homes, our civilizations. The laws of thermodynamics guarantee that, sooner or later, hell *does* freeze over. The rebel army that comes to unseat Macbeth stops at Birnam Wood, and, to camouflage their troop strength, each soldier is ordered to break off a leafy branch and march behind it.

The eerie vision of the silently advancing forest suggests a specific kind of entropy: nature's wildness reasserting itself, reclaiming our tidy clearings. In the generation before Shakespeare's, large portions of the English forest were cleared for timber to build Henry VIII's navy, and sleepy medieval society started giving way to the bustle of early capitalism and urbanism. Many of Shakespeare's plays reflect an uneasiness with the new order. The march of Birnam Wood could be a sort of Green Revenge, a warning that the rise of our industrial society is, like Macbeth's rise, a usurpation, and therefore inherently unstable. One day the trees will again take back the parking lots, and Shakespeare seems, like many of us, at least partly OK with that.

As the final act opens, we see entropy's ultimate triumph. From the start, Lady Macbeth has been the brains of the outfit. Now, with the rebels preparing their assault, her crafty mind breaks down into chaos. Shakespeare underscores the point by suddenly shifting her speeches from neat iambic pentameter to jerky prose: we can almost see the jagged EEG waves emanating from her brain. She's reduced to wretched sleepwalking, endlessly reenacting their murders, vainly trying to wash the invisible blood of guilt from her hands: "Out, damned spot, out, I say!"* Now sleeping is waking, craftiness is madness, and as she says in her heartbreaking last line, "What's done cannot be undone."

Her distress leads Macbeth to ask her doctor a question that we all ask sooner or later, perhaps of some pharmacist or bartender or budtender, when the engulfing chaos has made our pain unendurable.

> Canst thou not minister to a mind diseased,
> Pluck from the memory a rooted sorrow,
> Raze out the written troubles of the brain,
> And with some sweet oblivious antidote
> Cleanse the stuffed bosom of that perilous stuff
> Which weighs upon the heart?

Here we're groping for the Third Noble Truth, the promise that there is finally an end to our suffering. The doctor's response is a bombshell: "Therein the patient must minister to himself."

That's actually very good news. No, in the end our pharmacist can't help, no one can help, but we can help ourselves. The nirvana that resolves all suffering is to be found in our own being. The kingdom of God is within us. All along, Macbeth has been looking for tranquility and satisfaction in an outer kingdom of power and fame while he overlooks his inner kingdom. He's like the dog in the Aesop's fable who, crossing a little bridge with a bone in his mouth, snaps at his own reflection, thinking it's a dog with a juicier bone, and so loses the real one.

By then Macbeth is utterly disillusioned. So is Lady Macbeth. Back in act 3, the first honest, self-aware sentence she speaks after becoming queen is one of the saddest ever written.

---

* Shakespeare wrote this play during a time of quarantine due to the bubonic plague. As with our modern quarantines, there was a lot of handwashing involved.

> Naught's had, all's spent
> Where our desire is got without content

To win her game of thrones, she has squandered her peace of mind, her contentment, as well as her compassionate woman's heart, invoking dark spirits to "unsex" her and make her ruthless. When you spend everything you have on the one thing you think will make you happy, and it doesn't, then what? She knows she's gotten a bad deal, a devil's bargain, a reflected bone.

With the rebels at the gate and Macbeth's hurried reign clearly at its end, he receives the news of his wife's suicide. He responds with a shrug.

> She should have died hereafter;
> There would have been a time for such a word.
> Tomorrow, and tomorrow, and tomorrow

"She should have died hereafter" is often misunderstood. It doesn't mean she *ought* to have picked a better time, but that she *would* have died sometime or other — if not today, then one of those countless tomorrows. It hardly matters when. Everything's futile anyway.

That could be Macbeth's final and definitive statement of disillusionment. But some insight is dawning and he goes on, launching into one of the most brilliant soliloquies ever written. Shakespeare pioneered the use of the soliloquy not just as a virtuoso display of verbal fireworks, like a flashy but meaningless guitar solo, but as a deep dive into a character's most private interior. This one is a free fall into despair. Having proceeded so quickly from coronation to overthrow, from the elephant's prosperous belly to its grimy tail, Macbeth glimpses at last its time-transcending wholeness, a vision that should be enlightening and joy-bringing. But because he still wants to hold the belly forever, he sees that vision through the lens of bitterness.

> Tomorrow, and tomorrow, and tomorrow
> Creeps in this petty pace from day to day,
> To the last syllable of recorded time;
> And all our yesterdays have lighted fools
> The way to dusty death. Out, out, brief candle!
> Life's but a walking shadow, ...

All of humanity, in Macbeth's bleak picture, is on an agonizing forced march, trudging forever to the weary rhythm of tomorrow and tomorrow and tomorrow and tomorrow and tomorrow, but we're all just marching in place. Despite our dreams of glory, despite the hopeful little projects through which we try to project ourselves into some shining future, we go nowhere. Or we go backward, as Shakespeare hints here with a subtle crosscurrent of reverse time that moves from "tomorrow" to the punning "to day" to "yester-days." All our history ("recorded time") consists of fools like us, following the same deceitful light that leads us only to the dusty grave: ashes to ashes, dust to dust. Might as well blow out that goddamned brief candle. Right on, Lady Macbeth.

That's dark, but Shakespeare wants it darker. He now shifts the image from the light of the sputtering candle to the shadow it casts. If "Life's but a walking shadow," it's not only fleeting but insubstantial, a mocking imitation of substantial reality. A shadow is a flat, lifeless imitation of a person, but one that nevertheless keeps lumbering, zombielike, toward more empty tomor-rows. Then, riffing further on the idea of impersonation, Shakespeare shifts the image yet again, to an actor.

>   ... a poor player,
> That struts and frets his hour upon the stage,
> And then is heard no more:...

The blunt monosyllables "struts" and "frets" brutally summarize Macbeth's (and our) proud rise and swift fall. Their echoing consonants suggest that they're two sides of the same counterfeit coin, the same taunting existence making faces at us, first fair ones and then foul.

The actor's "hour upon the stage" is time cut short, just half of the usual two hours that plays ran in Shakespeare's day, and even when the actor's on-stage he sucks — he's a poor player, who hams it up whether he's strutting or fretting. This recalls Woody Allen's grim joke in *Annie Hall*, about the two old ladies at a Catskills resort: "One of 'em says, 'Boy, the food at this place is really terrible.' The other one says, 'Yeah, I know; and such small portions.'" That's life.

>   ... it is a tale
> Told by an idiot, full of sound and fury,
> Signifying nothing.

Here we end our descent, from weary march to failing candlelight to dark shadow to crap acting to the tormented ravings of a lunatic, and it all finally amounts to nothing. That's the bottom line, the last word of the speech and the last word on life. For bitter good measure, there's an implied dirty joke.

In Shakespeare's day, *nothing* was a slang term for vagina, used here like the "Bollocks!" with which Brits still call out nonsense.

But layers beneath layers — within the joke there's also a vision beyond Macbeth's despair. Life's bottom-line zero, the tomb of all forms, is also infinity, the fruitful womb of emptiness. When all our strutting and fretting and doing settle down, we're left in the open expanse of being. As my teacher Maharishi once described it, "It's just... *nothing*. But there's something very good about it."

This nothing seems deficient only when we're grasping for *some*thing. By pursuing to its end point the strategy of grasping, Macbeth learns that all the somethings are ultimately deficient, but he never explores the alternative strategy: let go of grasping and hang out in nothing. Leave off doing, marinate in being, and we discover that it's delicious. It's ananda, *yummy* nothin', causeless joy, goose eggs over easy, bubkes à la mode. None of the things for which Macbeth has striven so mightily and at such cost are eternal and satisfying — nothing is sacred. From there, it's just one small step (but one giant leap) to discover that Nothing *is* sacred.

●

By the end of the play, despair triumphs, at least over Macbeth. But Macbeth does not triumph over the kingdom. Only moments after he reaches his nihilistic conclusion, his head full of broken dreams and schemes is lopped off by Macduff, and the throne soon passes to the children of Banquo. Their line extended five hundred years, all the way to the first royal spectator of this very play, King James.* It's survival of the fittest vision. The Banquo DNA — the vision of life as a banquet of change, which we can enjoy as long as we remain unhurried and nongrasping — pops out of the play, with its poor players and mocking shadows, and flourishes in the actual world, our world.

Macbeth dies in anguish, having learned that the forms he invested with such inflated value are no other than emptiness. But that's only half the story. Knowing that emptiness is delicious and manifests as a banquet of delicious forms, we can pull up our chairs and enjoy the feast of nonduality. Life is a kaleidoscopic display of phenomena that we can regard with wonder and even joy, as long as we don't selectively require our favorite bits to be solid and permanent.

I think we've all had moments, perhaps in childhood, when we've tasted

---

* At least according to James's official genealogy, which was probably baloney but rarely challenged in his day. He was, after all, the king.

the simple freedom of fully inhabiting the present, as is, where the clouds are simply clouds and the leaves are perfectly leaves, with no plan for any of it to last or to lead to anything else. I suspect it was in some such sense that Jesus said that to enter the kingdom of heaven we must become like little children. Then we're in a world — unlike Macbeth's — where we're all kings.

14. Thanks for Nothing

SAMUEL BECKETT · WAITING FOR GODOT

Act 1. In a featureless landscape, beside a leafless tree, two tramps in bowler hats, Vladimir and Estragon, wait for someone named Godot. He doesn't come. A Boy arrives with a message: Godot will come tomorrow.

Act 2. Next day. The tramps wait. Godot doesn't come. A Boy arrives with a message: Godot will come tomorrow. And…curtain.

As one critic famously put it, "Nothing happens, twice." *Nothing*, the last word of Macbeth's final soliloquy, is the first word of *Waiting for Godot*. The word permeates the play, haunts it. Act 1 opens with Estragon sitting on the ground, trying to pull off his painfully pinching boot. He finally gives up, saying, "Nothing to be done." Vladimir responds:

> I'm beginning to come round to that opinion. All my life I've tried to put it from me, saying, Vladimir, be reasonable, you haven't yet tried everything. And I resumed the struggle.

And just like that, Beckett extrapolates from one man's aching feet to humanity's struggle against the futility of existence. That's pretty much the way the
whole play goes.

But before we go on: *GOD-oh*. That's how Beckett pronounced it, that's
how it was pronounced in the productions he directed, and that's how it's
pronounced all over the world — except, for some reason, by Americans. The
first syllable sounds like "God." These things matter. In Shakespeare's comedy
As You Like It, there's an overly philosophical character named Jaques, which
is pronounced *jakes*, slang for "outhouse," because he's full of shit. True, in
later years Beckett said that, with all the theological conjectures that the name
Godot had raised, he regretted choosing it. He once wrote to a friend that he
was "tired of the whole thing and the endless misunderstanding. Why people
have to complicate a thing so simple I can't make out."

Well, yes. But if you name your title character Mr. Monkeyface, you can't
be too shocked when people think of a monkey, especially if your play is as
filled with references to monkeys as this one is with references to God, speculation about God, and behind it all, the playwright shaking his fist at God for
not existing. *Waiting for Godot* is plainly about people waiting in vain for an
exalted someone or something to come along and save them from their suffering and despair. Guessing that this longed-for Whoosis might have something to do with God — or what we're really seeking when we seek God, or
what we're trying to imagine when we say "God" — is not unreasonable.*

But OK, let's jettison the G-word for now. Beckett wrote to another friend,
"There is something queer about the play, I don't know exactly what, that
worms its way into people whether they like it or not." Since he didn't know,
here's my theory. Life is like a jigsaw puzzle with just two pieces, *samsara* and
nirvana. Samsara (literally "wandering in circles") is ordinary life, the thicket
of the world and our own neuroses, with all the attendant confusion and distress. Nirvana (literally "blowing out") is liberation from that confusion and
distress. For most people, the second piece of the puzzle is missing, so life
appears to have a gaping hole with a jagged edge.

The shape of samsara, with the jagged edge where it cries for nirvana to
complete it, is Beckett's great topic. He examines that edge with such fierce,
unblinking intelligence that we see by implication what nirvana *would* be if
there were such a thing. He scrapes his soul across that edge with such raw
desperation that we feel what nirvana *should* be, *must* be, for life not to be
hell. That, I suspect, is its deep appeal.

---

*   If we were going to pick theme music for the play, it might be Tom Waits's "God's
     Away on Business," or maybe Lou Reed's "I'm Waiting for the Man."

•

Beckett had the gaunt, deeply lined face and haunted eyes of a man who has spent a lot of time peering into the jaws of hell. Born on Good Friday, 1906, into an upper-middle-class Irish-Protestant family, he was so intensely withdrawn as a child that he would hide to avoid going to other children's parties. His mother seems to have smothered him with a mixture of intense attachment and crippling shame. Emotionally confused, he developed a habit of throwing himself repeatedly from the top of a sixty-foot fir tree, letting the lower branches break his fall till he reached the ground. In his youth, though, he became an excellent athlete, and he remains the only first class–level cricket player to win a Nobel Prize. He had a brief, dull career as a university lecturer, and thanks to his early writing he was reviled in conservative Ireland as an atheist and filth-monger.

Despite the rising threat of the Nazis, Beckett settled in Paris in the thirties, saying he preferred France at war to Ireland at peace. There he lived as a penniless Left Bank writer and once nearly died after being stabbed in the chest by a pimp. (He refused to press charges when he realized that he rather liked the fellow.) He also became a protégé and sometime assistant to the increasingly blind James Joyce, while trying to duck a romance with Joyce's increasingly schizophrenic daughter.

After the war, Beckett received the Croix de Guerre for doing dangerous intelligence work with the Resistance. While back in Dublin visiting his mother, who was now ravaged with Parkinson's, he had the epiphany that transformed his writing:

> Her face was a mask, completely unrecognizable. Looking at her, I had a sudden realization.... The whole attempt at knowledge, it seemed to me, had come to nothing. It was all haywire. What I had to do was investigate not-knowing, not-perceiving, the whole world of incompleteness.

For Beckett, that meant to stop trying to portray Life by layering more and more into his writing like his mentor Joyce, who incorporated mythology and geography and history and everything else into a sprawling wordscape of multilingual, multidimensional puns. (Beckett told a possibly apocryphal story about taking dictation from Joyce for a section of *Finnegans Wake*. In midsession there was a knock at the door, Joyce said, "Come in," and a confused Beckett wrote it into the manuscript. When Beckett read it back, Joyce considered for a moment, then said, "Let it stand.")

Instead of more, Beckett now pursued less, stripping away everything that could be stripped and seeing what, if anything, remained. He stripped his characters of history, family, nationality, occupation, everything. He started writing in French, not because his French was better than his English but because it was worse. He was seeking a distilled, primal voice, purged of ornament and sophistication, words that struggle for meaning, like the first words ever spoken. But those words often took on a strange dream-music, which they retained when he later translated them into English.

ESTRAGON: All the dead voices.
VLADIMIR: They make a noise like wings.
ESTRAGON: Like leaves.
VLADIMIR: Like sand.
ESTRAGON: Like leaves.
   Silence.
VLADIMIR: They all speak at once.
ESTRAGON: Each one to itself.
   Silence.
VLADIMIR: Rather they whisper.
ESTRAGON: They rustle.
VLADIMIR: They murmur.
ESTRAGON: They rustle.

The original French production premiered on January 5, 1953, in a small, debt-ridden theater that was on the brink of closing. It was a nothing-to-lose situation. At first, performances were interrupted by the whistling and hooting of baffled, irate audience members. Fistfights broke out during intermission. But helped by the controversy, *En attendant Godot* quickly became the rage of Paris, and a Broadway production was proposed starring Buster Keaton and Marlon Brando. (Let us pause to imagine what that would have been like. Wow.)

There were, however, problems with the contractual rights to the English version, and it wound up opening, weirdly, at the Coconut Grove Playhouse in Miami Beach, where it was advertised, also weirdly, as "The Laugh Sensation of Two Continents." Bert Lahr, much beloved as the Cowardly Lion in *The Wizard of Oz*, played Estragon, who has an exchange with Vladimir that recurs throughout the play like a musical refrain.

ESTRAGON: Let's go.
VLADIMIR: We can't.

ESTRAGON: Why not?
VLADIMIR: We're waiting for Godot.
ESTRAGON: *(despairingly).* Ah!

Apparently, the words that spoke for the audience were "Let's go." Local cab-drivers soon started lining up early to collect all the people who streamed out at intermission. The London production also had a rocky start, with spectators loudly yawning and complaining. When Estragon contemplates hanging himself, one wag shouted, "Give him some rope!"*

Eventually, thanks to a few astute critics, people realized that Beckett had not tried and failed to write a conventional drama with a beginning, middle, and end. He had shown, brilliantly, that beginnings and endings are imaginary. Life is all middle. Here we are. What shall we do? Now *here* we are.

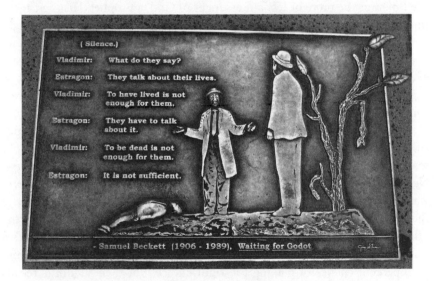

PLAQUE ON LIBRARY WAY
(E. 41ST STREET BETWEEN FIFTH AND PARK AVENUES, NEW YORK)

---

*   A few decades later, I was the last English teacher at the Pingry School to insist on teaching this play. The others had given up on the grounds that it drove the kids crazy. Well yeah, I said, that means it's working. Then, in 2017, I sat in the studio audience as my former student Buzzy Cohen competed in the *Jeopardy!* Tournament of Champions. He was on the brink of elimination in the semifinal round, but pulled it out when the answer to Final Jeopardy! turned out to be "What is *Waiting for Godot*?" He won a quarter of a million dollars and later returned as a guest host. So Godot showed up to help *some*one.

What shall we do? On Broadway, act 2 problems are proverbial. Act 1 is easy enough: you weave an exotic world of Jets and Sharks on the West Side or of Mormons in Uganda, and you entice the audience to enter that world and care about its characters as their conflicts mount. But after intermission comes the challenge of resolving the conflicts and bringing the characters satisfyingly to the end of their arc.

It turns out this is not just a problem of dramaturgy; it's a problem of life. Life (that is, ordinary life, the confused wanderings of samsara) has no resolution. The end of our arc, like the pot of gold at the end of the rainbow, is a lovely fairy tale. Beckett does many radical things in *Godot*, but the most radical may be leaving the act 2 problem blatantly, deliberately unsolved. Godot doesn't come.

Instead, the Boy comes, his messenger. If Godot is more or less God, then the Boy must be more or less a messenger of God, a prophet. His message is that Mr. Godot can't come today but will surely come tomorrow. That might be reassuring except that he delivered the same message yesterday, at the end of act 1. But he doesn't remember doing that, or seeing Vladimir and Estragon, ever. Maybe that was his brother. Maybe not. Like all the alleged prophets, he keeps promising a salvation that never happens. Unless it happens tomorrow (or tomorrow or tomorrow or tomorrow...). So we hang on. So far.

Since Godot either will or won't come, it's more or less a fifty-fifty proposition. The chance that life has a meaningful resolution comes down to a coin toss. It could be worse — and in Beckett's world, it quickly *becomes* worse. Near the beginning of act 1, Vladimir says, out of the blue, "One of the thieves was saved. It's a reasonable percentage." He's referring to the biblical story of the two thieves crucified with Christ: one believed in him and was saved, the other cursed him and was damned. With the thieves as our stand-ins, it's a mildly encouraging story, implying that we have some choice in our fate, and a 50 percent chance of making the right choice. But then Vladimir recalls that only one of the four Gospel writers tells this happy-ending version of the story. "One of the four says that one of the two was saved." Our hope erodes before our eyes, from one chance in two to one in eight.

In this play, our stand-ins are the tramps themselves. Vladimir, like the first thief, is a believer, or tries hard to be despite the discouraging evidence. He's anxious about making their rendezvous. (They're at the tree, but is it the right tree?) Estragon, like the second thief, is a skeptic. He's earthbound, hoping for nothing beyond food and sleep. Vladimir, we might say, is the mind, with its capacity for heavenly, possibly imaginary, aspirations. Estragon is the body. Once, Bert Lahr (who went on to play Estragon on Broadway, to great acclaim) was shanghaied into speaking about the play to a college class.

Asked to explain what his character was all about, he paused for a long, bewildered moment, then touched his stomach and said, "Belly."

So maybe noble thoughts and ideals are the answer to life. Maybe the simple satisfactions of the body are. (Maybe one of the two will be saved.) But no. All Vladimir's thinking leads to despair, and Estragon's physicality leads to hardship and pain. On a good day, he eats a scraggly carrot retrieved from Vladimir's junk-filled pocket, and on a good night he sleeps in a ditch. He's regularly beaten by strangers. Life of the mind or life of the body: pick your poison. Vladimir keeps taking off his hat, shaking it and blowing into it, as if trying to find what's hurting his head. Estragon keeps shaking out his boot, trying to find what's hurting his feet.

Beckett himself lived in a body plagued with cysts, boils, abscessed teeth, pleurisy, septic fingers, and night sweats. He anesthetized himself with whiskey, gambling, and an astonishing number of sexual affairs, some of them simultaneous, and all of them, by his own account, completely loveless; he called them "coffee without brandy." As for the mind, he was sometimes so depressed he couldn't walk. Two years of psychoanalysis told him only that he was an obsessive neurotic. In spite of the gloom, or in the teeth of the gloom, he sometimes played tunes on an old tin whistle, a relic of his Irish youth.

Whether Didi and Gogo (as they call each other) are mind and body, or faith and doubt, or as Beckett would insist, just two guys in hats, they stick together. They're like an old married couple who complain about each other's habits, argue about what happened yesterday or what they'll do tomorrow, threaten to leave, but can't seem to give each other up. It's sort of a wry take on the notion of sangha, the fellowship of seekers. We may be saved or screwed — probably screwed — but whatever it is, we're in it together. We're friends.

•

Two other men, also in bowlers, pass through in the first act and again in the second. They aren't friends but master and slave. The cruelly named Lucky, wheezing and tottering but unspeaking, lugs his master's bags and possessions, while Pozzo, with a long rope around Lucky's neck, cracks a whip and barks orders: "Up pig!...Up hog!...Back!...Stop!...Turn!"

This is the alternative to friendship: exploitation. Whether exploitation is economic and institutional or personal, it works pretty much the same way. If I treat you as an object that's in the world merely to make my experience more pleasant, I'm exploiting you. If I treat you not as an object but as a fellow subject — not just part of my experience out *there*, but an experiencer like me, a co-inhabitant of this awareness-space in *here*, behind all our eyeballs — then we're friends.

Beckett's portrayal of exploitation is brutal. Pozzo has worked his slave nearly to death, and now that Lucky is old and worn out (he has long white hair), Pozzo is taking him to the fair to sell him. Yet Pozzo is completely dependent upon him, the slave of the slave. He needs Lucky, just as the capitalist needs the laborer and the abusive romantic partner needs the submissive partner. Interestingly, when Pozzo first appears, Vladimir and Estragon mistake him for Godot. The bully-king-capitalist-boss is a false God, to whom there are always people who will grovel and submit.

Lucky is the stand-in for the grovelers. No proletarian hero, he's as mindlessly vicious as an abused animal. (When Estragon tries to wipe away his tears, Lucky kicks him violently in the shin.) And he's codependent, as addicted to servility as Pozzo is to mastery. Although exhausted, even when they're at rest he won't sit and won't set down Pozzo's bags. When Pozzo wants to put on his coat, Lucky holds the whip, the instrument of his own oppression, in his mouth, his hands being full.

Perhaps implying that society's writers and intellectuals, like its laborers, serve at the pleasure of their bosses, Pozzo orders Lucky to think. Once he's in the right position ("Stop! Back! Stop! Turn! Think!"), Lucky launches into his only speech in the play. It starts off with the outward form of a sober philosophical dissertation, and Didi and Gogo listen intently, as if hoping to receive some clue to their predicament — perhaps even proof that God or Godot exists and has not forsaken them.

> Given the existence as uttered forth in the public works of Puncher
> and Wattmann of a personal God

Wait. That last bit is backward. The thing we would hope to prove, the existence of God, is stated as a given. That's like submitting a "proof" to your algebra teacher: given that $x = 47$, $x = 47$. Your teacher would flunk you, and rightly so. But religion (as it's usually practiced) does the same thing and gives it the pretty name of faith.

Then things get worse, quickly devolving into what you might get if you ran a dictionary of philosophy and religion through a meat grinder.

> Given the existence as uttered forth in the public works of Puncher
> and Wattmann of a personal God quaquaquaqua with white beard
> quaquaquaqua outside time without extension who from the heights

of divine apathia divine athambia divine aphasia loves us dearly with some exceptions for reasons unknown but time will tell

Qua means "as" or "in the capacity of," and it's Latin so it must be smart ("Let us consider man qua animal," "Let us consider man qua social being"). Lucky starts with God qua something, but then piles up *quas* so they sound like the quacking of a querulous duck. That's what all our philosophy and religion amount to.

The bits of meaning we can pick out from the speech are all discouraging. God dwells in "the heights of divine apathia divine athambia divine aphasia." That is, he cares nothing about us, he feels nothing for us, he says nothing to us, and that's somehow divine, so no complaints, please. He "loves us dearly with some exceptions." Right: innocent children cut down by cancer, or crushed in earthquakes, or (only a few years before *Godot* was written) starved in concentration camps.

This is the classical Problem of Evil. How can a God that is both all-powerful and all-loving allow evil and suffering? Theologians have strained at rationales for centuries, but none are really satisfying. It's still "for reasons unknown." But maybe tomorrow (or tomorrow or tomorrow) Godot (or someone) will show up to explain it all: "time will tell." Meanwhile, we're told, have faith.

Lucky goes on like this for three unpunctuated pages, growing steadily more frantic and incoherent as all human hope is cruelly shredded, along with all distractions from our hopelessness ("tennis football running cycling swimming flying floating riding gliding"). The thinkers he cites now are Fartov and Belcher — *that's* what our philosophy and religion amount to. None of it seems headed toward any conclusion but death ("the skull the skull the skull the skull"). Like the wait for Godot, the speech has become one more endless, unbearable thing. To make Lucky stop, the other three finally tackle him and snatch his hat. (Evidently, a man can't think without a hat.) Then Lucky and Pozzo move on.

When the two of them return in the second act — supposedly the next day — they're much changed. The once-blustering Pozzo is now blind, completely dependent on Lucky and mired in self-pity. Lucky is dumb: "He can't even groan." There's no explanation. On the title page, however, Beckett calls the play a *tragicomedy*. It does combine tragedy's bleak vision with a lot of slapstick clowning. Pozzo is apparently the tragic hero, the arrogant Great Man who has a great fall. In act 2 he falls literally and spends several pages on the ground, crying for help. (I once saw the huge John Goodman as Pozzo on Broadway. Lying on the stage, he flapped his arms helplessly as he struggled to get up, looking like a beached whale.)

Traditional comedies end with a wedding celebration to mark the perpetuation of life. In modern forms, the cute rom-com couple finally overcome their obstacles and get together, or say, James Bond and his current squeeze ride off together in the Aston Martin. Here we have Didi and Gogo, our bickering, devoted couple, still together through thin and thin. Beckett was a big fan of Laurel and Hardy (as well as Chaplin's Little Tramp), and Didi and Gogo seem to owe them a lot, including their bickering and their hats.*

LAUREL AND HARDY

The change in the two men who change, and the endurance of the two who endure, both happen in time. Change requires time, the x axis of life, so that progress (the accumulation of status, knowledge, compound interest, and other prized stuff) can take place along the y axis. But that means decay must also take place; the equilibrium of the universe demands it; what goes up must come down. Hence tragedy. In act 1, Pozzo, like all winners (anyone who's momentarily on the upslope of the tragic curve), loves time. His watch is his most prized possession. When Estragon says, "Time has stopped," Pozzo cuddles his watch to his ear and replies, "Don't you believe it, Sir. Whatever you like, but not that." We all love time as long as we're having a *good* time.

But when we're having a bad time, we hate time. Now we're losers. When Estragon asks Pozzo when he lost his eyesight and Lucky lost his speech, he responds with sudden fury:

Have you not done tormenting me with your accursed time! It's abominable! When! When! One day, is that not enough for you, one

---

*   After the success of *Godot*, Beckett and the very patient Frenchwoman he eventually
      married bought a cottage in a village outside Paris. Once, at the local pub, they
      encountered two real tramps and gave them their coats. Beckett also helped
      drive some of the village children to school, including the future seven-foot-four,
      520-pound wrestling star André the Giant (also featured as Fezzik in *The Princess Bride*).

day he went dumb, one day I went blind, one day we'll go deaf, one day we were born, one day we shall die, the same day, the same second, is that not enough for you? *(Calmer.)* They give birth astride of a grave, the light gleams an instant, then it's night once more. *(He jerks the rope.)* On!

With that, he and Lucky make their final exit.

In time, we lose everything. *Waiting for Godot*, and especially this speech, with its collapsing of past and future, birth and death, into a single moment of universal futility is remarkably close in spirit to Macbeth's "Tomorrow and tomorrow" speech. When is Godot coming? Tomorrow. And tomorrow. And tomorrow. What do Vladimir and Estragon do? Creep in this petty pace from day to day. "The light gleams an instant" parallels "Out, out, brief candle." Pozzo's horrifying image of women giving birth over a grave recalls one of the ingredients the Witches throw into their cauldron: "Finger of birth-strangled babe / Ditch-deliver'd by a drab."* And in Lucky's speech, we've heard all of human life reduced to a tale told by an idiot.

For both Pozzo and Macbeth, the trauma of loss over time leads them in the end to glimpse the wisdom of timelessness, but they're too late to see it except with regret. Like most people when they hit the downslope of bad time, if they don't have some grounding in that which has no slope and no time, they feel bewildered and enraged.

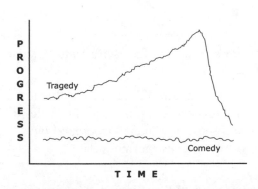

Didi and Gogo, battered though they may be, are that in us which has the wisdom to sit out the tragic roller coaster ride of glory and catastrophe. They complain about their tedious routine but acquiesce to its quasi-timelessness. They're in accord with the sages in noting that memory, which is all we have of the so-called past, is a ghost; and expectation, which is all we have of the so-called future, is a rumor of a ghost. They have nothing, they gain nothing, they lose nothing. In Beckett's world, that's as close to life-affirming as things get. In the second act, even the skeletal tree has sprouted a few leaves. There's the comic spirit. Life, such as it is,

---

* Drab: prostitute.

goes on. And on and on and on. And Didi and Gogo keep showing up for it, waiting by the tree.

> VLADIMIR: We are not saints, but we have kept our appointment.
>   How many people can boast as much?
> ESTRAGON: Billions.

Estragon's "Billions" is our cynical earthbound side, pulling the rug out from under our lofty Vladimir side, with its sentimental posturing. But cynicism is also a posture, and its rug must also be pulled. Yes, billions have kept their appointment. Almost eight billion humans on this planet, and all sentient beings everywhere, are seeking happiness and freedom from suffering, are longing for nirvana, are (in Allen Ginsberg's words) "burning for the ancient heavenly connection to the starry dynamo in the machinery of night." In every moment, even unconsciously, they pursue the infinite. We're not alone on this road. Our fellowship with the billions is a thing of beauty. Look at all these friends.

·

One glorious spring morning, Beckett walked out of his Paris apartment. A neighbor spotted him and called out, "Sam! Good morning! What a beautiful day!" To which he replied, "Well, I wouldn't go as far as that."

·

The best response to Beckett's despair was written by Emerson a century earlier.

> We grant that human life is mean;* but how did we find out that it was mean? What is the ground of this uneasiness of ours; of this old discontent? What is the universal sense of want and ignorance, but the fine inuendo by which the soul makes its enormous claim?

Life seems bleak? All right. *Compared to what?* We call rough skin rough only because we know the feeling of smooth skin — otherwise, we'd just call it skin. We can call life bleak ("mean") only because we somehow know that it can be nonbleak. Samsara implies nirvana, just as finding a dime tails side up implies a heads side that's hidden.

---

*   Mean: stingy, barren, unrewarding.

What keeps us from flipping the dime over? Beckett has already told us: we keep waiting. If Godot — nirvana, liberation, the kingdom of heaven, the soul's enormous claim — is anywhere, it must be right here, *this* awareness, *this* moment. But we overlook it as long as we wait for it, because then we're looking for some different, imagined moment. We anticipate, from *ante capere*, "to take before." We keep trying, mentally, to take things or have things before they arrive — the train, the plane, the weekend, the orgasm, the answer. Then, when the thing arrives, we start anticipating the next thing. Holding our breath in anticipation of future ease, we create present unease, and it's always the present. That unease (dukkha, unsatisfactoriness) is the invisible irritant that Didi and Gogo keep trying to shake out of their hat or boot.

How to dissolve this habit? Beckett tells us that too, in spite of himself, in the first line of the play: "Nothing to be done." His characters spend the entire play fleeing from that nothing. They think, dance, complain, complain some more, plan their suicide — anything to "fill the time," as if they must stay busily distracted at all costs, or else…or else…what? Gogo says, "Nothing happens, nobody comes, nobody goes, it's awful." But if you stay compulsively busy with a bunch of *some*thing, you haven't really experienced nothing. Its alleged awfulness remains an idea, an unexamined assumption.

Our project, then, is to examine that assumption. That can only be done experientially. Nothing to be done? Fine. Let's do nothing. Sit down, be quiet, close your eyes if you like. Don't wait for anything, don't resist anything, don't engage with anything, don't try to do anything; relax your grip on everything, and in time you sink into nothing. When you leave off trying, it happens by itself. In fact, this experiment has been going on for thousands of years, and the data is in. We're delighted to report that nothing is not awful. It's nirvana. The highest prayer turns out to be an utterly grateful, nonironic "Thanks for nothing."

That nothing in turn transforms our experience of everything. In all our samsaric wandering in circles, it's what we were looking for, waiting for, and, like Beckett, agonizing over not finding. In time we discover that samsara is pervaded by, actually *is*, nirvana: every rock and cloud we see, and the act of seeing it, and the one who sees. Godot didn't leave us waiting — we just failed to recognize him.

15. OK

RODGERS & HAMMERSTEIN · OKLAHOMA!

If our theory works — if Dharma keeps showing up in great literature, whether it's been invited or has to crash the party — it should also work for literature-adjacent genres like musical theater. In that case, it should show up in the work of musical theater's most iconic practitioners: Richard Rodgers (composer) and Oscar Hammerstein II (lyricist), the reigning monarchs of Broadway through the forties and fifties, with shows like *Carousel*, *South Pacific*, *The King and I*, and *The Sound of Music*.

Now, for sixties kids like me, who came up hearing Hendrix shred the national anthem at Woodstock, Rodgers & Hammerstein can sound pretty lame. One of their songs actually describes love as feeling "as corny as Kansas in August." But let's see what they've got. Hammerstein once told an interviewer:

> The song is, I think, perhaps the most difficult form of writing, be-
> cause you have to be terribly simple in your idea and very clear every
> minute....The songs that have achieved permanent popularity all
> have something fundamental to say.

Let's see if Hammerstein's "something fundamental" looks anything like
what the Dharma tells us is fundamental. R&H's first collaboration, the 1943
monster hit *Oklahoma!*, is considered the beginning of the modern musical. I recommend the 2011 University of North Carolina School of the Arts
production, available on YouTube, an authentic restoration of the 1943
opening-night version, from the orchestration and choreography to the costumes and sets. (Feel free to skip the Hollywood film.)

No one had great hopes for this show on opening night. It had no big
stars and was based on an obscure play about cowboys and farmers, set in
1906, by an obscure playwright, Lynn Riggs, a closeted gay former Oklahoma
cowboy. Ushers were sent into the street to give free tickets to GIs on leave, in
an unsuccessful attempt to fill the house. But by the next day, the lines went
around the block.

The show was revolutionary for its time. As the curtain goes up — and at
the risk of disappointing those GIs — there's no stageful of chorus girls kick-
ing up their shapely legs, but an old woman in farming duds, churning butter.
The orchestra, instead of building to the usual rousing fortissimo, dwindles to
a single flute imitating a twittering bird at dawn, then drops into silence. From
offstage comes a voice — a hardy baritone that instantly made the crooning
tenor leads of the time sound like a bunch of weenies.

Invisible and a cappella, the voice sings, "There's a bright golden haze
on the meadow." The reaction of the opening-night audience, according
to choreographer Agnes de Mille, was "a sigh from the entire house that I
don't think I've ever heard in the theater. It was just *ahhhhhhh.*" These are not
only the first words of the show but the first words Hammerstein ever gave
Rodgers to set to music. As Rodgers later recalled, his immediate reaction
was, "I had to get to a piano....You couldn't resist those words, they were so
lovely." They invite us to see a meadow — a fresh, open space — where objects
and details have softened into an indistinctness, a haze, yet a haze that's not a
dull smudge but golden bright.

This is what happens when we meditate. The outer world of objects and
details blurs into irrelevancy or indistinctness, or even melts away as in sleep,
yet we retain the bright alertness of waking. Sounds may be present (traffic,

barking dog, voices in the next room), thoughts and feelings may be present, but they're all somewhere on the other side of that haze. We don't take much notice of them, as our attention is drawn deeper and deeper into our inner meadow, and the world of pressures and problems is left behind. That's what the opening-night audience felt: *ahhhhhhh*.

The owner of the voice, Curly, the young cowboy who is the show's hero, ambles onstage. He sings about the corn being as high as the eye of an elephant, the biggest of animals, which made it, in ancient India, a symbol of Brahman, the infinite. The corn is growing — no, "climbing" — toward the sky, evoking the universal call to ascend, like Jack climbing the beanstalk, to new adventures in higher realms. Then comes the song's glorious chorus (and title), "Oh, What a Beautiful Mornin'." All the expansiveness, the freshness, the hopeful clean-slate feeling we have when the sun rises on a crisp morning are summoned by those words.

The next phrase takes us from a beautiful morning to a beautiful day, suggesting (as in Blake's "eternity's sunrise") that this freshness can somehow be perpetuated beyond the dawn. At the same time, there's a poignancy, a sense of the fragility and unrepeatability of *this* moment, of *this* life. That's largely thanks to Rodgers, who works the magic here by setting the first syllable of *mornin'* on a swelling, slightly dissonant suspended fourth note: skyward aspiration. Then, on the second syllable, he settles back half a step to the more harmonious third: comfort, resolution. The whole theme is there, in seed form, in those two notes. In 1979, the war correspondent John Hersey wrote Rodgers a letter about an experience he'd had while stationed on the front in Sicily in 1943, after yet another miserable night of sleeping on the muddy ground.

> A GI who might perfectly well get killed that day...got up and stripped to the waist and poured some cold water in his helmet and began to shave. The sun hit us. Everyone was grumbling as usual. Suddenly the soldier stood up and began singing, "Oh, what a beautiful morning." A pretty good voice. There was a fair amount of irony in his singing, and his pals laughed. All the same, it *was* a beautiful morning, and all of a sudden there was an almost unbearable intensity in the way the men looked around at the view.

•

Oklahoma! has a plot, although it's a tad slim, about the at-first-uncertain romance between Curly and the rancher Laurey. He starts by wooing her with "The Surrey with the Fringe on Top," a song that's easy to dismiss as mere cutesy-pie Americana, with all its scurrying chicks and ducks and geese. But toward the end it slows and quiets down as Curly envisions a perfect moment, with the stars growing blurry as he drives Laurey home from a hoedown in his fabulous imaginary surrey. Her sleepy head droops to his shoulder, and he wishes — three times, in an urgent whisper — that the moment could go on forever.

Just as he's "thinkin' all the earth is still," a single lark (recalling the morning lark whose "harsh discords" end Romeo and Juliet's night of love) threatens to wake her. But in this fantasy, Curly (auspiciously unlike Romeo) succeeds in hushing the lark, and he reins the horses back to "a slow…clip…clop." Right there: the world holds its breath, time stands still, and we behold the shimmering poignancy of young love, for many people their one fleeting glimpse of sublime transcendence.

The plot is thickened by Curly's rival for Laurey's affections, her hired hand Jud Fry. He's a seething bully, frying in his own resentments and rapey urges, who bunks in a dark smokehouse with dirty pictures pinned to the wall. His bad-boy energy at first intrigues Laurey, then repels her. Curly and Laurey finally tie the knot, but at their wedding party Jud attacks Curly with a knife. They scuffle, Jud winds up dead, and after Curly is acquitted in a quickie trial, the happy couple depart for their honeymoon in a surrey with fringe on top, the fantasy at last come true.

That part — where the hero rescues the maiden from the dragon and they ride off together to a castle in the sky — probably sounds familiar. From Lord Rama saving Sita from the demon Ravana, to Popeye and Bluto slugging it out over Olive Oyl, to a thousand Hollywood rom-coms, we've been telling ourselves versions of this story forever. We all, regardless of gender, need to affirm our noble, sky-aspiring, beautiful-morning-appreciating inner Curly. We all need to free ourselves from our feral inner Jud. Then we can be decent enough, generous and expansive enough, to connect with our outer Laurey, our beloved fellow being, and make a life with her or him in whatever castle or ranch or condo comes with the deal.

To be truly in relationship — whether in marriage or in the wider web of family, community, world — we need to be just a smidge enlightened, with some intuitive sense of our bigger identity. Otherwise, we're all a bunch of selfish little egos crowding the same space, fighting for the biggest crumbs. When no one wants to give and everyone tries to get, no one gets. No wonder we perpetuate this story age after age. To persist as a civilization, we need it.

And to enter into relationship wholeheartedly, we also need to relax the fear, particularly the male fear, of losing our freedom. In America, the archetype of freedom and masculinity is the cowboy: ridin' the open range, sleepin' out under the stars, totin' his trusty six-shooter. In act 1, Curly brags about being "the best bronco buster in this here Territory." But eventually he sells his gun, his saddle, and his horse to settle down with Laurey.

> Oh, I gotta learn to be a farmer, I see that. Quit thinkin' about a-throwin' a rope, and startin' to git my hands blistered in a new way....Buy up mowin' machines, cut down the prairies, shoe your horses, drag them plows under the sod.

Sometimes timing is everything. The show's initial Broadway run lasted through the end of the war, as millions of GIs were returning from the cowboy life of swaggering soldiers to the challenges of domesticity. My father, Captain Harris Sluyter, who had piloted a B-17 over the European theater, dodging flak and smashing German factories, was the only member of his crew to survive. Within a year or two of mustering out, he married my mom and they started making babies. He took out a GI loan, bought a new tract house on the former prairies of Long Island, and got a mowin' machine to push over the lawn. Their shiny little surrey was a Studebaker. Their dog was named Peppy. On their black-and-white TV, they could watch General Eisenhower, the head cowboy of the mighty D-Day invasion, now recast as a genial, golf-playing president, building interstates to accommodate all the new surreys as fast as General Motors could make them. Of course their generation loved *Oklahoma!* They lived it.

"This here Territory" is the same one that Huck Finn reckons he's got to light out for, to escape being "sivilized": Indian Territory, the lands set aside for displaced Native Americans. In Huck's time it was vast and wild, stretching northwest to present-day Wyoming and Montana. But then settlers flooded in, treaties were abrogated, states were carved out. By 1854 it had shrunk to a final remnant in the eastern half of what is now Oklahoma, where the Trail of Tears had ended. In 1907 Oklahoma was admitted to the Union, and the Territory was gone. With Curly, we cut down the prairies and turned them into farms, and then into factories and offices, where now we punch clocks instead of cows. Any wild open range will have to be found on the inside.

But other than some enthusiastic references to the coming of statehood, you won't hear any of this history in the show, and you won't see any Indians. You also won't guess that about a quarter of cowboys in the West were Black. (In fact, the word originated as a condescending term specifically for Black ranch workers. Whites were cow*hands*.) You won't guess that the future Oklahoma had over fifty all-Black towns, thirteen of which still exist. They were settled after the Civil War by former slaves of the so-called Five Civilized Tribes, whose ostensibly civilized practices included literacy, Christianity...and slavery. Yes, history is complicated.

•

But this is an Oklahoma not of history but of myth, and sometimes of the soul. That includes its most rousing moment: the title song. It's so familiar that we think we know how it sounds. But no. Please rev up your best speakers or headphones, pull up act 2 of the University of North Carolina restoration, scrub forward to 45:50, and hear it fresh, with beginner's ears and mind, as if you're sitting with all those GIs on opening night.

Robert Russell Bennett, the orchestrator, deserves a big share of the credit for what you'll hear. Rodgers wrote it as a solo piece for Curly, but Bennett transformed it into a massive orchestral blowout and a full-cast, eight-part chorale, packed almost frantically with harmonies and countermelodies. It's ridiculously thrilling. Recalling the reaction to the song on that first opening night, actress Joan Roberts, the original Laurey, said:

> The applause was so deafening, and it continued and continued. We repeated two encores, and we stood there, until they stopped applauding! And I didn't think they ever would!

Strokes of genius often seem obvious after the fact. I'd love to have been in the room when Rodgers, seated at the piano, first realized how the *O* in "O-O-O-O-OK!-lahoma" was crying out to be held for a full five beats so it would SwelL-L-L-L-BURST! in music like a shout of joy to be alive. That gaping vowel sound invokes the open space of the Oklahoma prairie; like the mantra *O-O-O-O-Ommmm*, it conjures the wide-open spaciousness that's at the heart of Dharma. It is (as a Zen practitioner once described it) like a fish's discovery of the open sea after spending its whole life in a tank of glue.

Inseparable from that spaciousness is the freshness of our world when we no longer filter it through stale memories and concepts — the perpetual beautiful morning. When the Europeans arrived in North America from their land of crowded streets and social hierarchies, they brought plenty of old baggage, including indentured servitude and petrified religious dogmas. But the open spaces were so big, and the prospect of fresh starts so tantalizing, that much of that baggage dropped away. Americans ever since have held the naïve, inspiring notion that anything's possible.

Appropriately, this song, which is performed just after Laurey and Curly's wedding, begins with an introduction about starting a brand-new life with a brand-new wife in a brand-new state. Then, as the main melody kicks in, comes that long O-O-O-O-O, and the new state's fresh, open nature unfurls from that fresh, open sound. Again, this is nama-rupa, the magical power of the name to evoke the form, particularly in the old, mantra-rich sacred languages. The name Oklahoma comes from the Choctaw *okla humma*, meaning "red people." In addition to that elastic O at the beginning, it contains *om* in the third syllable and *home* for English speakers. That's hard to beat for mojo, although Omaha (*Ommmm...aha!*) is right up there, as is Iowa, with its no-consonants, no-hard-edges resemblance to *Yahweh*, Judaism's name for the edgeless holy of holies.

As Rodgers pours vast openness into our ear, Hammerstein pours it into our eye, with images of Oklahoma's vast, open land: the wind, the rain, the plain, the wavin' wheat (imitated by the cast, waving their bodies in de Mille's choreography), all carried along by the overflowing ebullience of the music. But one image, in the second stanza, doesn't really fit that feeling: a contemplative line about sitting alone at night, watching a hawk "makin' lazy circles in the sky." That sounds more like the poignant mood the Japanese call *yugen* — it belongs in a wistful autumn haiku. Hammerstein must have noticed the incongruity. Why did he feel compelled to keep that line — what did he intuit?

In old Tibet, if you asked your lama how to meditate, he might tell you to sit down on a rock and watch the vultures circling in the sky. Like hawks, they ride the thermals — the air currents rising from sun-warmed surfaces — and glide for hours, making only an occasional, subtle adjustment with a flick of a wing tip. That's the way you do it: minimum agitation, maximum silence, maximum gliding in the vastness. In time this becomes not only how you sit but how you live, skillfully attending to the commotion of the world without commotion of the soul.

The final stanza brings us back to mantra, with a pure, untranslatable cowboy whoop and then an attempt to translate it. It means (the chorus tells us, in the song's fortissimo windup), "You're doin' fine." Oh. There it is, the simplest of affirmations, the one we've been seeking ever since we yelled to Mom and Dad to watch us jump off the diving board. Jumping into the challenges of life can be scary. Certainly, for this show's first audiences, jumping into the challenges of the war was scary. Without Franklin Roosevelt, the Dad of All Dads, in the White House and on the radio, reassuring them that the water would be initially chilly but then they'd be doin' fine, we might all be speaking German today. This was the right show at the right time to reinforce that message.

But it's always the right time to know we're doing fine. The line is actually "You're doin' fine, *Oklahoma*," but in the de Mille choreography the whole cast points straight at us, the audience, as they sing it. When no benign FDR-style parent is available, we have to look inside ourselves, deeper than doin', to bein', which is fine by nature, unshakable as rock because it's not built on the shifting sands of outer circumstances. Most people won't find it till they're forced to.

FDR himself started as a lightweight, a handsome rich boy living off the family name, until polio made him turn within and find the right stuff. His ability to stare down first the Depression and then Hitler came straight from that inner strength, not from favorable outer events. People who worked with Roosevelt said that the deeper a crisis grew, the calmer he became. He had found the inner place of freedom from fear itself. He intuited how to connect millions of others to that same place within themselves, and he pretty much saved the world.

In the spirit of that freedom, the song reaches its jubilant, shouted climax: "OK!" This strange expression is probably America's most successful export, more popular than Coca-Cola or iPhones. There are at least twenty different theories and legends about its origin, including a railway freight agent named Obadiah Kelley, who signed bills of lading with his initials; the Orrins-Kendall company, whose crackers were popular with soldiers in the Civil War; and *omega chai*, a magic spell to ward off fleas. It might even have originated in Oklahoma, with the Choctaw word for "it is," *okeh*. But most scholars trace it back to a brief fad in the 1830s for abbreviated jokey misspellings. If you were cool, you knew that KG meant *Know Go* (no go) and OK meant *Oll Korrect*. OK became the sole survivor of the fad thanks to the 1840 reelection campaign of President Martin Van Buren — "Old Kinderhook" — and the subsequent rise of Democratic OK Clubs.

Every language, presumably, has words to signal that things are satisfactory, all right, acceptable, in order. But there's something about the jaunty OK that rises above tepid satisfactoriness to an affirmation, a kind of verbal short-cut to a realm of problem-free happiness. Perhaps there's a vestigial memory of that *Oll*, a sense that somehow *all* things everywhere are fine and will be fine all ways, always. After fifty-some years of trying to describe samadhi, I haven't been able to top "infinite OK-ness."

Certainly, nama-rupa must account for some of the word's power. The open sound of O is like the open sky of carefree beingness-awareness. Then we hit the ground, the unyielding earth of hard K, where there's work to do, fields to plow, fascists to fight. The shapes of the written letters help too. O is round like the bowl of the sky, like the egg of creation, like the zero that is the germ of all numbers. K is all straight lines and sharp angles. With O, we rest in the bright golden haze of omnidirectional beingness. With K, we return to sharp-focused, sharp-pointed action. The Bhagavad Gita, as we've seen, distills the entire philosophy of life into two instructions — be and do, meditate and act. Dive within, where you're always *being* fine: O. Then come out, saturated with that fineness, act from there, and you're *doing* fine: K.

No wonder America's most cherished musical is the one whose peak moment is a shouted "OK!" It's an ecstatic hallelujah, a seventh-day benediction in which God sees the world he's created and pronounces it Oll Korrect. This show's mythic Oklahoma of the soul is a place where the light of infinite OK-ness reigns, a buckaroo vision of the promised land. Yes, a lot of messy history has happened, and keeps happening, in the actual Oklahoma and the actual everywhere else — yes, the world is still crazy after all these years — but that doesn't negate the aspiration, the vision. It makes it all the more essential.

16. Flame Out

GERARD MANLEY HOPKINS

I heard this story from the headmaster at the school where I used to teach. He heard it in the 1950s, when he was a student at Saint Mary's Hall, Stonyhurst College, the oldest Catholic school in England, from an elderly gardener who had worked there most of his life. *He* had heard it when he was first starting out from yet another gardener who was then very old.

One day in the early 1870s, the Jesuit novices training for the priesthood at Saint Mary's were spending their usual two hours studying their prayer books — some in their rooms, some sitting in the church or corridors, some while proctoring study halls or strolling through the majestic school grounds. Around the corner from the Gothic main building with its twin bell towers, Gerard Manley Hopkins was pacing briskly up and down the school's gravel path, intent on his book. A rainstorm had just passed, and the gardener happened to observe Hopkins — all five-foot-two of him — from across the grounds.

Suddenly, Hopkins stopped in his tracks, turned sharply, threw himself down on the ground, and stared at the little hole he had just made with the heel of his shoe, as if it were the most fascinating thing he had ever seen. Then, after some time, he just as suddenly stood and walked on with his prayers. Once he was out of sight, the gardener walked over to take a look for himself. What he saw was nothing in particular — except the drops of rainwater seeping into the hole and pooling at the bottom, refracting the sunlight and reflecting the colors of the garden. Telling the story years later, the gardener concluded, "He always was a strange one, that Father Hopkins."

Well, visionaries can seem strange to the rest of us, and even to themselves. Hopkins spent most of his life racked by self-doubt, nervous exhaustion, and depression — punctuated by ecstatic experiences of the divine, refracted and reflected in the mundane like sunlight in rainwater. He shaped his epiphanies into poems, but realizing they were as strange as he was, he didn't bother trying to publish them. Instead, he sent them to his friend Robert Bridges, the future poet laureate, apologizing that they were so "queer." Even after Hopkins died, Bridges took another thirty years to publish them, waiting till the world was ready, and by then it was too distracted by the First World War to take much notice.

But when people finally started to read Hopkins's work, they noticed something going on there — actually, many things — that no one had done before. There's the intense, dense chiming of consonants and vowels, the alchemical combinations and transformations of words, and what Hopkins called "sprung rhythm," a freer, jazzier approach than the usual rigid syllable-counting of the time. And there's the way he *uses* all that innovative technique to conjure up images so vivid you can almost touch them. The world eventually caught up with Hopkins, and he's now recognized as possibly the most brilliant of the four or five inventors of modern poetry. But we're still catching up with the radical *experience* that required such radical word magic to express it — the ability to see what he saw in those drops of rainwater.

It wasn't only as a poet that Hopkins was a misfit. At the height of the British Empire's age of manly, chest-thumping conquest, he was an excitable, androgynous pip-squeak. Although an outstanding student, he failed his final theology exam. His Protestant family and friends shunned him when he became a Catholic, and his Irish-Catholic parishioners mistrusted him because he was English. The Jesuits couldn't figure out what to do with him. They made him a professor of Greek and Latin, but he was too odd and too overwhelmed by paperwork to be any good in the classroom. They tried sending him into the countryside as a pastor, but he had no rapport with country folks, preaching brilliant sermons that went completely over their heads.

His greatest gift, his poetic genius, provoked his greatest conflict: he was afraid that it would distract him from wholehearted submission to God. There's a story about the Beat poet Allen Ginsberg, who in the 1970s took up Dharma studies with the Tibetan lama Chögyam Trungpa Rinpoche. Ginsberg took to meditating with a little notebook and pen laid neatly beside his cushion, ready to preserve his revelations in poetry. Trungpa promptly confiscated them, telling Ginsberg that his pen was poking holes in the very experience he sought to record. Upon taking priestly orders, Hopkins made a bonfire of all his poems, and for seven years he wrote no more.

Then some exiled German nuns were drowned in a shipwreck, and a superior suggested that Hopkins commemorate the tragedy in a poem. A Jesuit magazine initially accepted it for publication, but when the editors took a closer look, they changed their minds. Certainly we can sympathize with them, scratching their heads and wondering from what faraway planet came lines like this:

> We lash with the best or worst
> Word last! How a lush-kept plush-capped sloe
> Will, mouthed to flesh-burst,
> Gush! — flush the man, the being with it, sour or sweet

What?

Hopkins soon gave up on publication. As a renunciate priest, he probably told himself it was just as well, but as an artist venturing into uncharted territory he still craved a sympathetic audience to tell him he wasn't just crazy — a fear that haunted him as time went on. He begged Bridges, his audience of one, to give a second reading to poems that baffled him, but couldn't get him to budge.

The deeper problem that plagued Hopkins was spiritual dualism. From a clinical perspective he suffered from chronic depression, and he found the joy that dispelled it not so much in church, where he was "supposed" to, but in the woods. (These days, this wisdom takes such forms as "forest bathing" for veterans with PTSD.) It was by engaging with nature through the five senses that he most clearly felt the presence of God, but he worried that this amounted to pantheism (literally "all-God-ism"). That's a dirty word in conventional Catholic theology, which considers God beyond the senses, eternally separate from the natural world. Humans, to live a spiritual life, must repress the senses.

To be fair, this ascetic thread runs through nearly every spiritual tradition. Even today, some orders of Theravada ("old school") Buddhist monks are forbidden to even smile. A friend of mine once attended a Zen retreat where the participants sat in meditation for sixteen hours a day. At midday they straightened their aching knees and lined up for their single meal, and as the stony-faced kitchen monk ladled the gruel into each bowl he grumbled, "Don't taste it." For Hopkins, this painful suppression brings a sort of coiled power to his poetry. It intensifies the rapturous moments when, despite all his efforts to resist it, the experience of the divine in nature floods his senses, and his awareness opens wide, ravished.

•

The more agonized the split, the more sublime the reunion, as we see in the masterpiece "God's Grandeur." Structurally, it's a traditional fourteen-line sonnet, but within that form Hopkins takes us on a wild ride of lows, highs, and verbal special effects — especially alliteration, the repetition of consonant sounds. Hopkins may be English poetry's all-time champion alliterator, but he's never merely showing off. The repeated consonants *propel* this poem, with a driving force that matches its spiritual urgency, till in the final four lines the rapturous reunion with God's grace climaxes in an orgy of alliteration.

Here are the first eight lines. Buckle up.

The world is charged with the grandeur of God.
    It will flame out, like shining from shook foil;
    It gathers to a greatness, like the ooze of oil
Crushed. Why do men then now not reck his rod?
Generations have trod, have trod, have trod;
    And all is seared with trade; bleared, smeared with toil;
    And wears man's smudge and shares man's smell: the soil
Is bare now, nor can foot feel, being shod.

The poem's thesis, boldly asserted in the first line, is no rote-memorized Sunday school doctrine. It's a field report of direct cognition, hard-won through vigilant observation, tearful struggle, and finally (as we'll see) ceasing to struggle. It starts by setting forth the two rival claimants to the poet's affection, "world" and "God." Incurably in love with both, Hopkins is forced to find a resolution: a vision of the world "charged with the grandeur of God," pervaded by it, brimming with it, loaded to capacity with its shocking, sparking voltage. All of nature's finite forms perpetually overflow with the scintillating energy of the formless infinite.

This overflow is often portrayed in images of luminosity: "And God said, Let there be light," or even better, "God *is* light, and in him is no darkness at all." Radical nondualism, as it emerged in India (where it's called Advaita) and in Tibet (where it's called Atiyoga, Dzogchen, or Mahamudra), takes that point to its logical conclusion. If the infinite is indeed infinite, there can be no place where it is not, "no darkness at all." There can be nothing other than it. If we think we're standing outside it, we're just temporarily confused.

Hopkins renders a vivid image of this self-effulgent light in the second line:

It will flame out, like shining from shook foil.

As he explained in a letter to Bridges:

Shaken goldfoil gives off broad glares like sheet lightning and also, and this is true of nothing else, owing to its zigzag dents and creasings and network of small many cornered facets, a sort of fork lightning too.

Ah yes, we may think, *I've seen that zigzag lightning while wrapping leftovers in aluminum foil. I just never paid attention to it.* Well, that's the difference between us and the great poets, between us and the buddhas. Pay attention. Hopkins told Bridges that the whole poem came out of this image. This lightning in the palm of one's hand, magically shooting out of nowhere, was the sparkplug of the poem's creation.

In the shift from blindered inattention to luminous vision, this sparkplug fires across the gap between despair and exultation. As with lightning, it doesn't matter how thick or persistent our personal darkness has been. In an instant all is light, and we suddenly can't remember what it felt like to be depressed. This electrical presence of the infinite, which casts out fear and loneliness — this "grandeur of God" — is always already right here, latent. But to see it, to shake off our temporary confusion, usually requires some shaking of the gold foil, some meditation, some poetic creation, some practice of devotion, some emotional crisis or resolution — *something* to shake things up, to make us pay attention for a change.

Next, in fact, we not only see the divine presence but feel it and smell it:

> It gathers to a greatness, like the ooze of oil
> Crushed.

This is an image of olives squeezed in a wood press, first bulging and then bursting. But by isolating the word "Crushed" at the beginning of a new line, followed by a period, Hopkins gives it a devastating second meaning. We feel the repeated crushing of his heart, the long suffering he has endured to bring forth the precious, fragrant oil of a moment's visionary joy.

He follows with a pointed question:

> Why do men then now not reck his rod?

"Reck" means reckon with, acknowledge; "rod" means scepter of power. Why doesn't everyone acknowledge God's power, recognize the grandeur that redeems all their crushing? Why do they suffer the pain without recognizing the gain? How can they keep shutting their eyes to the light that pervades and surrounds them?* This line reads almost like an accusation, adding another meaning to "The world is charged." For us inhabitants of the world, opening our eyes to God's grandeur is our charge, our duty, and we stand charged with neglecting it.

But the gap between darkness and light can seem unbridgeable:

> Why do men then now not reck his rod?
> Generations have trod, have trod, have trod

"Then now" implies that this is nothing new; as it was then, so it is now. Age after age, the blindness persists. "And the light shineth in darkness; and the darkness comprehended it not." In the dismal, heavy bootsteps of "have trod, have trod, have trod," there's an echo of Macbeth's "Tomorrow, and tomorrow, and tomorrow," the same weary march on the same futile treadmill, generation after generation, all weary of time like Blake's sunflower.

---

* Jesus expresses the same puzzlement in the Gospel of Thomas: "The kingdom of the father is spread upon the earth, but people don't see it." That verse might have given Hopkins some solace, or at least some corroboration, but sadly, the unorthodox scripture was hidden, buried in the sand till 1945.

But *how* do we manage to stay so blind? That's the next issue to be addressed.

And all is seared with trade; bleared, smeared with toil

We're distracted from the glory because it's too simple. It's just being; we distract ourselves with compulsive doing. Our vision is distorted by constant busy-ness ("bleared, smeared with toil") and incessant buying and selling ("seared with trade"). By Hopkins's time, this was true in a specific, historical sense: the industrialization and commercialization of society were in full swing. But it's also true in a perennial sense, "then now." Let me just buy this one sleek gadget, let me just sell you on this one project, let us just trade one more set of snarky tweets. *Then* I can enjoy being.

He goes on:

And wears man's smudge and shares man's smell: the soil
Is bare now, nor can foot feel, being shod.

Hey, what's that smell? Oh, it's us, stinking up the joint, fouling nature's fresh, clean God-scent with our own. Again, there's time-specific meaning here, a critique of the pollution that was choking the cities by the nineteenth century, and of the mines and mills that were newly blighting the English countryside, turning it to bare soil.

There's also a hint of the way we smudge our simple, direct perception by overlaying it with busy thinking. I've heard my teacher Charles Genoud describe how some people on his Asian pilgrimages, when confronted by, say, a mind-blowingly magnificent Himalayan peak, immediately ask, "What's the name of that mountain?," then duly record the information in their little notebooks — unblowing their minds, reducing the peak to the size of a name. What's the point of traveling halfway round the world if you don't get your mind blown?

Not only have we stripped bare the earth beneath our feet, we've stuck shoe leather between it and us ("Nor can foot feel, being shod"). Losing our Huck Finn barefoot-boy communion with the woods, we become Tom Sawyers, ready to saw them down and make way for more sivilization. We've lost our sole connection and our soul connection to our mother planet.

So ends the *octave*, the first eight lines, which, in the sonnet tradition, pose a question or problem. The concluding six lines, the *sestet*, are supposed to answer or solve it.

And for all this, nature is never spent;
    There lives the dearest freshness deep down things;
And though the last lights off the black West went
    Oh, morning, at the brown brink eastward, springs —
Because the Holy Ghost over the bent
    World broods with warm breast and with ah! bright wings.

By peering unflinchingly into the dark maw of spiritual and ecological desolation, Hopkins has set himself a seemingly impossible challenge. So he starts the sestet with a pivot:

And for all this, nature is never spent;
    There lives the dearest freshness deep down things;

Yes, pollution gashes the earth and gloom gashes our spirit, but from every gash gushes an inexhaustible power of rebirth and healing. The earthquake-battered city can be rebuilt, depression can dissolve in joy, and artistic barrenness can give way to reawakened creativity (a new poem, *this* poem). "Nature" doesn't refer only to unspoiled woods and streams. Deep down and ever fresh in all things, their true nature — simple beingness, boundless OK-ness — is unspoilable. Why? Because it's their nature! No logic will convince you of this, but the experience will. Our alienation from the formless infinite, and from its luminous expression as all the finite forms we behold, is not our nature but a passing condition. It's just some bleared vision that will wash away, a tight shoe of the mind that we can kick off.

This immortal diamond (as Hopkins calls it in another poem) endures even when the last of our hopes seem to have been swallowed up in apocalyptic dark night:

And though the last lights off the black West went
    Oh, morning, at the brown brink eastward, springs —

Even when the lights of the sun, the moon, and finally the stars have sunk beneath our horizon, even when the light of our vitality and aspirations has sunk into despondency, we need only make a simple U-turn. Then we see another horizon where "morning, at the brown brink eastward, springs," where all this death dies into rebirth.

The sun rises in the east. In Christian terms, the Son of God rises on Easter, which not coincidentally is near the beginning of spring, when the natural world is born again. As the first glimmers of light spring into being, they transform the black of dead negation to the organic brown of soil fertilized by springs. New plants spring forth, and in time spring forth new poems and enlightenment-glimpses — and for that matter, new notions of freedom and equality and new loving concern for the preservation of the planet.

But we don't have to wait for spring. We're always on the edge of the new shining moment, the brown brink, when the very deadness of the past guarantees the fresh potential of the present. Perhaps there's even a hint of prophecy in this couplet — intuited from somewhere beyond the bounds of Hopkins's Catholic convictions — that a depleted Western spirituality would someday be renewed by the Dharma light springing from the East, giving us a world that has yoga studios in every town, mindfulness apps on people's phones, and Jesuit priests attending Buddhist retreats.

So, yes. We and our world have been damaged, bent under the weight of the black past. But no matter how severe the damage, it's not irreversible. The poem concludes:

And though the last lights off the black West went
   Oh, morning, at the brown brink eastward, springs —
Because the Holy Ghost over the bent
   World broods with warm breast and with ah! bright wings.*

The Holy Ghost, the all-pervading sacred essence, is always here. It "broods" over us, both in the sense that it calmly contemplates our situation and in the sense of a mother bird warming her brood of chicks. (Maybe Easter chicks?) Like the Blessed Virgin Mary, the ever-pristine mother of all, it is outside of time and change and damage, at once bending over our crushed, cruci- fied selves and bending to nurse our newborn, reborn selves at her warm breast. And in the poem's last, most thrilling moment, she spreads her angel- bird-goddess wings to catch the beams of the fresh-risen sun, bright wings of light on which the spirit soars.

•

---

*   There's the promised orgy of alliteration. It's all about the *b*'s and *w*'s, starting with "black," where the *b* combines with an *l* that's still chilled by the cold-water dousing of "the last lights." But then it picks up the warm *r* from "morning," with its first red rays of the sun, which illuminate what looked "black" and reveal it to be "brown," then reveal the "brink" of the morning horizon. Finally, in the last line, the whole shebang climaxes in a string of three *r*-warmed *b*'s — "broods," "breast," "bright," ventilated by the airy whoosh of *w*'s: "world," "warm," "with," "wings."

Robert Bridges, the poet's one rickety bridge to the literary world, didn't get it. When he received this poem in the mail, he condemned the final brilliant image as a "fault of taste" and a "perversion of human feeling" — whatever that means. Hopkins just went on with his lonely, intermittently ecstatic life, with God (when he was in a good mood) his one perfect reader, lover, friend. It's enough to make us yearn to reach back through time and comfort this one who deserved so much better.

But even as his health declined, broken by infections and diseases he caught ministering in the squalid slums, Hopkins eventually got better at comforting himself. Four years before his death, he wrote:

> My own heart let me have more pity on; let
> Me live to my sad self hereafter kind,
> Charitable; not live this tormented mind
> With this tormented mind tormenting yet.

Having resolved to be kinder to his heart and his "sad self," and having realized that his self-tormenting mind is both culprit and victim, he arrives, a few lines later, at a solution that's pretty much what we would recognize as meditation:

> [L]et be, call off thoughts awhile
> Elsewhere; leave comfort root-room; let joy size
> At God knows when to God knows what; whose smile
> 's not wrung

Let things be as they are, let go of our tail-chasing thoughts for a while, and while we're at it, leave off chasing after spiritual joy, God's smile. We have to let joy size things up on its own, let it decide when and how it will arise. We can't wring a smile out of God, can't force things, but must leave it all to happen in its own sweet time. You can't hurry love.

Realizing that spiritual tranquility must be left to germinate invisibly, like seeds in the soil, Hopkins resolves, in one more wonderful image, to "leave comfort root-room." This is the mellow, equanimous acceptance (underscored by the warm r's and soothing oo's) that mature Dharma bums bring to their practice, whether they're meditating, praying, or, oh, fishing. You choose your spot, you bait your hook, you cast your line, but then you have to be quiet and let the fish come to you.

After his years of pursuing God, Hopkins finally determined to let God find him. His long struggle had taught him to give up struggling. His dying, at age forty-four, was physically agonizing, but his last words were "I am so happy, I am so happy. I loved my life." On his solitary path, he had learned that we can let go of our suffering at any moment, *this* moment. Let up, lighten up, and let the light in. Then God's smile is our smile, God's grandeur is life's grandeur. It will flame out — just relax and leave it room.

17. Love Nonetheless

TONI MORRISON · THE BLUEST EYE

The crime novelist Walter Mosley tells this story:

> I heard two people talking about Toni Morrison. The first one said,
> "I love Toni Morrison because her novels transcend race." And then
> the next person said, "I love Toni Morrison 'cause she's not afraid to
> be Black." And the room broke into applause.

There it is — the rich paradox where Morrison's work lives. Some early critics tut-tutted because her novels all focus on African American experience,
saying that to become a truly great, important writer, she would have to stop
"limiting" herself. Translation: Want us to take you seriously? Write about
white people. Too bad about that James Joyce fella, limiting himself to the
Irish.

Universality vs. specificity is always a false choice. To be universal, you *must* be specific. That's why Van Gogh painted sunflower after sunflower and his sunflowers can make us cry. If you drill down deep enough and straight enough into the specificity of anything, you come to universality. You drill past borrowed ideas and lazy assumptions, to *actuality* — what is. And actuality has an unmistakable texture, which others will recognize as the texture of their own deep-down actuality, even if the surface specifics of their lives are very different.

For instance: Claudia, the young Black girl who narrates parts of Morrison's debut novel, *The Bluest Eye*, hates the blonde, blue-eyed baby doll — supposedly the epitome of the beautiful and the adorable — that she gets for Christmas.

> I could not love it. But I could examine it to see what it was that all the world said was lovable. Break off the tiny fingers, bend the flat feet, loosen the hair, ... take off the head, shake out the sawdust, crack the back against the brass bed rail.

We haven't all been Black children in a society that enforces white standards of beauty. But we've all been children, living in a world of feelings that grownups don't understand. We've all tried to penetrate mysteries, and sometimes broken things in the process.

Like many first novels, *The Bluest Eye* derives much of its material from the author's own life. Morrison, like Claudia, grew up with her parents and an older sister in the 1940s in Lorain, Ohio, a midsize town where Blacks and whites (largely immigrants) lived close together, not separate but not equal. Also like Claudia, in grade school she had a Black friend who wished fervently for her eyes to turn blue. Even then, Morrison saw that wish as grotesque, an expression of racial self-loathing. Claudia's friend, Pecola Breedlove, is eleven years old and, as even her mother agrees, ugly. The climax of the story, deliberately revealed in the first few pages, is her rape and impregnation by her drunken father. But Pecola is offstage through much of the book, as we're brought deep into the consciousness, and the life that formed it, of one character after another.

This is where Morrison especially shines: she's a genius of empathic imagination. In writing her eleven novels, presenting Black experience from the era of slavery to our own, certainly she read, researched, and drew on the tales she heard from the old folks while growing up. But beyond that, she settles so deep into her own heart that she finds the place where all hearts connect, outside time and space. The modest word for this superpower is *intuition*: listening within. Sometimes her intuition beat the historians to the truth, as when, in *Beloved*, she imagined certain kinds of sexual abuse of male slaves that were documented only later.

It's been said that if you could see inside people with complete clarity — as if they were made of crystal, with all the complex causes and conditions that made them who they are clearly visible — you would feel nothing for them but boundless compassion. This is what Morrison does best. We see it most dramatically in the case of Cholly Breedlove, Pecola's father, who we know from the outset will commit the most horrific of crimes. If we can feel the compassion for him that Morrison does, we'll have enlarged ourselves. We'll have learned to breed love.

She starts by taking us back to his primal trauma in rural Georgia. Four days after his birth, his single, mentally unbalanced mother abandons him on a junk heap beside the railroad, then disappears forever. He's rescued and raised by his great-aunt Jimmy till she dies when he's thirteen. The day of her funeral, he has his sexual initiation. It's an idyllic early-evening tryst "in the green-and-purple grass on the edge of the pine woods," with the smell of coming rain in the air, till it's suddenly interrupted by another unimaginable trauma: two white men, carrying long guns and shining their flashlight on Cholly's nakedness. Snickering, they order him to "get on wid it. An' make it good."

Humiliated and alone in the world, Cholly runs off in search of the father he's never known. It takes him months to work his way to Macon, where he finds him engaged in a dead-serious alleyway dice game and identifies himself.

> But [his father] had turned back to the game that was about to begin anew. He bent down to toss a bill on the ground, and waited for a throw. When it was gone, he stood up and in a vexed and whiny voice shouted at Cholly, "Tell that bitch she get her money. Now, get the fuck outta my face."

Rejected and rootless, Cholly falls into a life of nothing-to-lose adventures: work on the railroad, time on a chain gang, and time with women, one of whom shoots him in the leg. Along the way, he kills three white men.

With the confident swagger that this life brings him, he charms Pauline, his future wife. But after his footloose exploits, the monotony and responsibility of marriage and fatherhood baffle and undo him. Drink becomes his refuge and then his destruction.

So it was on a Saturday afternoon, in the thin light of spring, he stag-gered home reeling drunk and saw his daughter in the kitchen.

She was washing dishes. Her small back hunched over the sink.... The sequence of his emotions was revulsion, guilt, pity, then love.... What could a burned-out black man say to the hunched back of his eleven-year-old daughter? ... What could his heavy arms and befuddled brain accomplish that would earn him his own respect? ...

The tenderness welled up in him.

It has taken us Cholly's whole life journey to get to this moment, to see what we would otherwise never believe, that his rape of Pecola arises out of tender-ness, out of love. Of course, it's bewildered, drunken tenderness, horribly dis-torted love, and its effects are devastating. As our narrator Claudia concludes:

Love is never any better than the lover. Wicked people love wickedly, violent people love violently.

But it's love nonetheless, and from an ultimate perspective, the sages say, all human actions, and, in fact, every large and small event in the universe, is the expression of love, the overflow of the formless infinite as the forms of the finite, the overflow of God as the world. Very few of us are enlightened enough to see that way. William Blake was:

The roaring of lions, the howling of wolves, the raging of the stormy sea, and the destructive sword, are portions of eternity, too great for the eye of man.

In Cholly's tale, Morrison has given us a glimpse of that terrible, sublime vi-sion, and in the course of the book, one character at a time, she takes us on several more life journeys to afford us several such glimpses.

•

When Toni Morrison wrote *The Bluest Eye*, she was raising two boys on her own and working as a pioneering editor at Random House, where she nur-tured the work of Black writers from Angela Davis to Muhammad Ali and yukked it up in the office with her pal Fran Lebowitz. All the elements of her later work are there in the first novel. It's raw and harrowing, funny and warm, haunted by the past, driven by the rhythms of Black speech and of the earth. Sometimes those rhythms ascend to a higher poetry, but they never lose touch with the facts of hardscrabble life. Here's how she describes the coming of spring:

> The first twigs are thin, green, and supple. They bend into a complete circle, but will not break. Their delicate, showy hopefulness shooting from forsythia and lilac bushes meant only a change in whipping style. They beat us differently in the spring.

Morrison functions in her novels like a roshi, a Zen master. There's a teaching tale in the Zen tradition about a monk who asks a roshi, "What is the Buddha?" Not *who*, which would be the enlightened seer Gautama, but *what* — what is the nature of enlightened seeing? The roshi could answer "the golden sunset" or "a baby's laugh" or anything else and it would be right, since enlightened vision sees all things as boundless OK-ness. So, being a skillful teacher, he says, "A pile of cow shit in the middle of the road." If the monk can see it there, he'll see it everywhere.

Morrison knows that if we can see the light of the Buddha, the brimming-over of life force, a portion of eternity, in a drunken daughter-rapist, we'll see it everywhere. By using for her material the most corrosive aspects of Black experience in America — not only racism, but the poverty, ignorance, and personal violence that have been passed from one generation to the next — she stays on mission. (Her best-known book, *Beloved*, centers on a mother who kills her daughter to save her from slavery: an act of love.) This audacious accomplishment earned Morrison millions of readers and the Pulitzer Prize, the Nobel Prize, and the Presidential Medal of Freedom.

Her literary ancestor is Frederick Douglass, who, in ways that have become clearer over time, stands at the wellhead of the realist tradition in American literature. When his slave narrative appeared in 1845, white folks in the North were reading Emerson's lofty philosophical flights. In the South they were reading Sir Walter Scott's escapist medieval fantasies, like *Ivanhoe*:

> I swear by the honour of my house — I vow by the name of my bright lady-love, I would endure ten years' captivity to fight one day by that good knight's side in such a quarrel as this!

In fact, Southerners' immersion in that fictional world probably helped inspire their rash entry into armed conflict with the North, with its much larger population and industrial base. That decision made sense only if they bought into the sentiment expressed in Tennyson's "Sir Galahad," another favorite of the time:

> My strength is as the strength of ten
> Because my heart is pure.

Black writers like Douglass didn't have the luxury of indulging in such gauzy dreams. They had hard realities to confront, and an urgent calling to make others confront them. But it took the rude awakening of the Civil War to snap white writers and readers out of the dream. Mark Twain summed it up in a sly literary joke in *Huckleberry Finn*, when he named a wrecked, sinking steamboat, manned by doomed "rapscallions and dead beats," the *Walter Scott*.

Morrison's other, more distant ancestor, back in fourteenth-century England, is Geoffrey Chaucer. If you're one of the many people who recall *The Canterbury Tales* as one of the more torturous experiences of your high school years, it's not Chaucer's fault. Most teachers make the mistake of beginning at the beginning, instead of going straight to the most hilariously filthy stories, such as "The Miller's Tale," which are full of sexual pranks and fart jokes. That always worked for me.

Chaucer was another roshi. Despite serving several nobles and royals as a trusty administrator, he made a point of getting out of the fancy, French-speaking court and into the (literally) cow shit–studded English-speaking street, to channel the sex-and-violence-filled stories of real people. Like the rappers who came six hundred years later, he tapped into the pulse of street language, which, he discovered, was mm-*MMH* mm-*MMH* mm-*MMH* mm-*MMH* mm-*MMH*. That funky beat is what English teachers rather antiseptically call iambic pentameter. In the 1950s, when touring doo-wop acts played venues in the

GEOFFREY CHAUCER

American South, all the Black fans had to sit on one side of the auditorium, the whites on the other. The musicians often couldn't see past the footlights, but they knew who was where because the white side of the house clapped on the one and three beats while the Black side clapped on the two and four: mm-*MMH* mm-*MMH*.

That's the side that Chaucer's heirs — Shakespeare and Keats and the other iambic dawgs — clap with. Chaucer used that beat (and the AABBCC rhyme scheme of rap) to replicate the dirty jokes of millers and reeves, the marital joys and woes of housewives, the connivings of scamming pardoners (forerunners of today's scamming televangelists), the war stories of knights, the murderously anti-Semitic pieties of nuns. High and low, good and bad, he saw them all through God goggles. Rather, he took *off* the fog goggles that most of us wear and saw truly — he saw everyone with love, *as* love, as cow-shit Buddha.*

Morrison shares that vision: all her characters embody the transcendent. But unlike Chaucer, she also gives us characters who *experience* the transcendent, at least occasionally. For some, it happens through sex. This is an often-overlooked fact of life. The allure of sex is not only the intensity of sensations and (sometimes) emotions, but the transcendence that detonates at the climax of that intensity. In *The Bluest Eye*, we see this clearly in our deep dive into the consciousness of Pauline, Pecola's mother. She recalls how, early in her marriage, when Cholly would come to bed and start to touch her, her brain would "curl up like wilted leaves."

> I begin to feel those little bits of color floating up into me — deep in me. That streak of green from june-bug light, the purple from the berries trickling along my thighs, Mama's lemonade yellow runs sweet in me. Then I feel like I'm laughing between my legs, and the laughing gets all mixed up with the colors, and I'm afraid I'll come, and afraid I won't. But I know I will. And I do. And it be all rainbow inside.

It's consistent with Morrison's frank rootedness in the earth element that ananda, beatitude, dawns through the body. But if you depend for your ananda on anything ephemeral, it will be taken away. ("I meditate on the tennis court," some people tell me. That's fine till your knees go.) If you know rapture only through sex, the eventual loss of youthful vigor and romantic excitement also means the loss of that rapture, which is what happens as Pauline's marriage unravels.

---

*   Recently, out of the blue and without elaboration, my five-year-old grandson Fox announced, "Everybody's a love poop." Yep.

But it ain't like that anymore. Most times he's thrashing away inside
me before I'm woke, and through when I am. The rest of the time
I can't even be next to his stinking drunk self. . . . Only thing I miss
sometimes is that rainbow.

The rainbow is transcendent glory, it's beauty and peace, the sky's smile,
God's sign to Noah after the rain, the inexplicable goodness of things. The
great discovery, the Dharma discovery, is that, although we may have caught
sight of the rainbow in the *context* of, say, sex, it's actually our own nature,
context-free. Nothing else can confer it or take it away. If you're lucky enough
to have a partner who shares that discovery, you can enjoy basking in the
rainbow light together, either with or without all that huffing and puffing.

Moments of transcendence are especially poignant for characters who
have lots to transcend — who sleep in houses infested with roaches and mice,
or are subjected to racial violence or family violence, or are mired in racial
self-loathing. Pecola is not the only one caught in that trap. In one schoolyard incident, she's surrounded by a ring of boys who taunt her for her looks,
chanting, "Black e mo. Black e mo." The boys themselves are Black.

She also witnesses appalling fights between her parents, after which she
pulls a quilt over her head and retreats into her own world.

"Please, God," she whispered into the palm of her hand. "Please
make me disappear." She squeezed her eyes shut. Little parts of her
body faded away. Now slowly, now with a rush. Slowly again. . . . It
was hardest above the thighs. She had to be real still and pull. . . . Almost done, almost. Only her tight, tight eyes were left. They were
always left.

This willed disappearing act is a desperate approximation of transcendence,
echoing Hamlet's desperate "O that this too too solid flesh would melt." As
spiritual aspirants, we like to think of ourselves as happy adventurers who
have booked a leisurely pleasure cruise to nirvana. But people often get serious about the infinite only when their little patch of the finite becomes intolerable, or at least uncomfortable. A career implosion, a romantic disaster,
an addiction that can't go on, the death of a loved one, a serious illness: one
way or another, they may have to bottom out. Then scoffers may pathologize
their spiritual turn, dismissing it as only ("only") a strategy to relieve their
suffering.

Well, "a strategy to relieve suffering" is a concise description of the

Buddha's teaching, so Pecola's in good company here. A conventional psychologist might say she's dissociating, might discourage her from persisting in that behavior and recommend medication. But a good Dharma-grounded psychologist (of whom there are a growing number) might show her how to tweak her instinctive meditation into a more skillful version, noting that her "tight, tight" eyes are the one crucial part that resists transcendence, and that the tightness itself — the very effort to shut out the world — is the problem. By relaxing the eyes along with everything else, by neither engaging with nor pushing away what we've seen, by letting our thoughts and feelings come and go frictionlessly, we can gradually sink into inner silence, beyond the realm of problems. Then, refreshed and restored by our vacation, we can return to that realm with clarity and strength.

This may all sound like a pollyannaish attempt to enlighten away the hideous miseries of the world, to steer around them via the notorious Spiritual Bypass. But what else have you got? As things turn out, after Pecola is raped and her baby dies, and lacking the kind of gentle, measured doses of transcendence of which we speak, she chooses the drastic, truly pathological escape into madness.

> She spent her days…walking up and down…her head jerking to the beat of a drummer so distant only she could hear. Elbows bent, hands on shoulders, she flailed her arms like a bird in an eternal, grotesquely futile effort to fly. Beating the air, a winged but grounded bird, intent on the blue void it could not reach — could not even see — but which filled the valleys of the mind.

•

Pecola thought she wanted blue eyes, but that "blue void" is what she's really wanted all along. It's what we all want. We're Pecola, yearning to soar above all that is unbearable, into the open sky of delicious, all-dissolving void. Eyes are both seen and seeing, object and subject. Mocked as ugly, Pecola wants blue eyes so she can be seen as pretty but also so she can see pretty, can see and inhabit a pretty, sky-infused world.

Beneath the problem of her supposed ugliness is the deeper, wider problem of racialized notions of beauty and the self-loathing they promote. But beneath *that* there's the yet deeper, wider, equal-opportunity problem of confusion over what we are. Deepest down, we are neither object nor subject, Black nor white, this nor that. As we awaken, we more and more clearly cognize ourselves as pure, luminous awareness, with no color, no size, no gender, no nationality, no nothin'. We still have to live in a world where others see us in those terms, but it gets harder to take them seriously. In the world, we may have to *wear* size and color and the rest, but knowing it's not what we are, we wear it lightly.

That cognition is one step toward making a more just and compassionate world. We can find it meditatively, by softly imploding into inner formlessness. And we can find it artistically, through novels or any art that shakes and loosens our constricted sense of identity by putting us behind others' eyes.

In primitive times, rigid tribalism may have served us well. It made sense to be wary of those who spoke a different language, wore different costumes, had skin of a different color. Their tribe might have been in deadly conflict with ours. Now, though, the modern remnants of tribalism are what's deadly. Racists and nationalists (as we might see with the eyes of compassion) are just stuck in the old tribal reflexes. But our world has grown too interconnected for the old, insular ways. Acknowledging our global interbeingness with all people and, for that matter, all species is no longer a spiritual luxury. We've collectively danced ourselves into this corner where we all have to wake up.

Once we accept Toni Morrison's gift of empathic imagination, we can take it beyond a merely literary experience to our way of being in the world. That's the formula: have the vision, take the action. In the words of the African proverb that Congressman John Lewis loved to quote, "When you pray, move your feet."

18. Whiteness

HERMAN MELVILLE • MOBY-DICK

A confession: For the thirty-some years that I taught American literature, I sang the praises of *Moby-Dick*, telling my students that it was one of the handful of truly great books, that it was an incredible saga, that they had to read it sometime before they died.

I had never read it.

I suspect I'm not alone. At this moment, untold numbers of teachers may be faking it off CliffsNotes, teaching the book to untold numbers of students faking it off SparkNotes. In my case, the karma for all those years of flimflammery was that, to write *this* book, I finally had to sit down and read all seven-hundred-odd pages of that one. Fortunately, I was right. It's as great as I had imagined, but it's also much more — much weirder and much *funnier* than I had imagined.

Yes, it tackles all the grand themes, some of them earnestly (God, fate, the meaning or meaninglessness of life), some ironically (capitalism, race, sex*). And yes, everything about it is huge. Here, for example, is the *beginning* of a single sentence in which Ishmael, the narrator, considers why "the whiteness of the whale" fills him with "vague, nameless horror." You might want to pack a lunch.

> Though in many natural objects, whiteness refiningly enhances beauty, as if imparting some special virtue of its own, as in marbles, japonicas, and pearls; and though various nations have in some way recognised a certain royal preeminence in this hue; even the barbaric, grand old kings of Pegu placing the title "Lord of the White Elephants" above all their other magniloquent ascriptions of dominion; and the modern kings of Siam unfurling the same snow-white quadruped in the royal standard; and the Hanoverian flag bearing the one figure of a snow-white charger; and the great Austrian Empire, Caesarian, heir to overlording Rome, having for the imperial color the same imperial hue...

Melville's just getting warmed up. The sentence goes on like this for another full page before rounding the bend of "yet":

> ...yet for all these accumulated associations, with whatever is sweet, and honorable, and sublime, there yet lurks an elusive something in the innermost idea of this hue, which strikes more of panic to the soul than that redness which affrights in blood.

Yes, it's a huge monster of a sentence — kind of like a huge, monstrous whale. It also takes on the perversely difficult task of convincing us that white is inherently more alarming than blood-red. It's also brilliant, hypnotic, and in its compulsive accumulation of detail, possibly insane. It's A Sentence About Everything: history, theology, psychology, anthropology. It's exasperating and hilarious, and hilarious because it's so exasperating. And all this is true of *Moby-Dick* as a whole. To find anything else like it we have to fast-forward to John Coltrane's endlessly inventive — but endless — saxophone solos. Coltrane, it is said, once told Miles Davis, "I don't know how to stop." Miles replied, "Why don't you try taking the horn out of your mouth?"

---

* But *dick* didn't become a slang term for penis till several decades after the book was written, so calm down, kids.

Melville doesn't know how to stop, nor does his protagonist, Captain Ahab. Melville's tale of Ahab and his mad voyage in quest of the White Whale is also Melville's mad quest to encompass all of life in sentences and chapters, to make A *Book* About Everything. It bursts at the seams because life bursts at the seams. Everything is brimful of everything — nothing exceeds like excess.

Melville's vision (again, like Coltrane's solos) is *fractal*. Its geometry is endlessly undefinable because the deeper we drill into it the more richly detailed its patterns reveal themselves to be. Life itself is also fractal. Viewed from way out in space, the coastline from San Francisco to San Diego is essentially a straight line five hundred miles long. But as we come closer we start to see its irregularities — Monterey Bay, Point Conception, Palos Verdes — and if we wrap our tapeline around them, the coast now measures perhaps a thousand miles. If we keep looking closer, measuring around the edge of every cove and inlet, then every rock, then pebble, then grain of sand, atom, subatomic particle, we go from thousands of miles to billions to trillions and just keep going. All finite things, it turns out, are also infinite — the teacup in your hand, and your hand. Thus saith not just the poets and mystics but the mathematicians.

FRACTAL COASTLINE, BIG SUR

Following this fractal model, Melville's guiding principle is to find the longest distance between two points. Every time something starts to happen — our narrator Ishmael arrives in Nantucket to ship out on a whaler, he signs up to crew on the *Pequod*, the ship's round-the-world voyage begins, whales are spotted, the mysterious Captain Ahab finally appears on deck, Ahab summons the crew for a crazy speech revealing that, rather than a sensible commercial venture to harvest whale oil, they're on a mission of vengeance against the White Whale that bit off his leg — the action pauses and we go off on a tangent or a long string of them. Ahab dreams of a great Mission Accomplished, but Ishmael understands that, as in Lucky's speech in *Waiting for Godot*, the last word must always be "unfinished." He notes, "This whole book is but a draught — nay, but the draught of a draught."* (And in words that writers everywhere will understand, he adds, "Oh, Time, Strength, Cash, and Patience!")

One tangent is a page-long footnote about a mystical encounter with an albatross:

At intervals, it arched forth its vast archangel wings, as if to embrace some holy ark. Wondrous flutterings and throbbings shook it. Though bodily unharmed, it uttered cries, as some king's ghost in supernatural distress. Through its inexpressible, strange eyes, methought I peeped to secrets which took hold of God.

Another is a quick time-out in the middle of a chase to take note of whale farts:

strange subterranean commotions in him…causing the waters behind him to upbubble.… "Adverse winds are holding mad Christmas in him, boys. It's the first foul wind I ever knew to blow from astern.…"

And another is an entire, brazenly tedious chapter devoted to constructing a taxonomy of the whale family, bizarrely organized into "books" and "chapters" rather than species and subspecies — an elaborate satire of crackpot scholarship that keeps going long after it stops being funny. There are three chapters on the history of accurate and inaccurate pictures of whales, one of them with the gorgeous title "Of Whales in Paint; in Teeth; in Wood; in Sheet-Iron; in Stone; in Mountains; in Stars."

Some people call this trivia, but that's a biased term. Nothing is trivial if you look at it with deep attention, or with love, which is the same thing. We

---

* Draught: draft.

call it trivia to keep from drowning in it. We suspect that the world is a bot-tomless spiral of fractalizing tangents-within-tangents, and for fear of being sucked down that spiral we distract our gaze. But like Odysseus, who insisted on keeping his ears unplugged so he could hear the call of the Sirens, both Ahab and Melville insist on encountering this whale of a vision full-on. It destroys Ahab, and it destroyed Melville.

Both men start from a place of primal loss and devote themselves to rem-edying it. Ahab has literally lost a piece of himself to the whale; the book's turning point comes when he rallies the crew to join his quest and swear an oath of vengeance.

> "And this is what ye have shipped for, men! to chase that white whale on both sides of land, and over all sides of earth, till he spouts black blood and rolls fin out. What say ye, men, will ye splice hands on it, now? I think ye do look brave."
>
> "Aye, aye!" shouted the harpooneers and seamen, running closer to the excited old man: "A sharp eye for the white whale; a sharp lance for Moby Dick!"
>
> "God bless ye," he seemed to half sob and half shout. "God bless ye, men."

Melville was raised as a rich kid in the booming 1820s, till his merchant fa-ther's manically overextended finances collapsed. The servants were let go, the family moved from Manhattan to low-rent Albany, and then, when Melville was twelve, his father suddenly died. Young Herman was soon clerking in a bank, then in and out of a series of dreary jobs. But at nineteen he shipped out on a merchant vessel headed to Liverpool, and two years later he crewed on a whaling voyage to the South Pacific.

That changed everything. "A whale-ship was my Yale College and my Harvard," he says through Ishmael. Melville came back a cigar-puffing, yarn-spinning adventurer, and wrote the novels *Typee* and *Omoo*, exaggerated versions of his real-life exploits jumping ship in the Marquesas Islands and sojourning there with fearsome cannibals and nubile Gauguin maidens. Their success made him a genuine celebrity. Riding high, he married the daughter of the chief justice of Massachusetts.

He wrote a few more adventure novels, he had a big audience awaiting the next one...and then, in 1851, he gave them the endless, bewildering sprawl of *Moby-Dick*. Most British reviewers loved the book (one of them called it "poetry in blubber"), but the American public scratched its head. His career never recovered: *Moby-Dick* was his Moby Dick. He published his last novel, also a failure, in 1857, just eleven years after the first. Then he faded into obscurity, working as a deputy customs inspector in New York City, writing occasional stories and some poetry. He died forgotten in 1891. In the six-line obituary notice in the *New York Times*, the title of his masterpiece was misspelled.

Once again, only after the visionary's death were people ready for the vision. *Moby-Dick* started coming into its own in the 1920s, and by the 1950s was hailed (along with *Huck Finn* and *Gatsby*) as the Great American Novel. Three things (at least) had to happen for readers to get it. One was the Great War, in which the old world order, the old social strata, the old religious doctrines were blown apart, leaving people ready to see things put back together in ways that depended less on fragile human constructs and more on a cosmic connectedness of all things. The second was the publication in 1922 of the next brilliant, sprawling Book About Everything, James Joyce's *Ulysses*, with similar rhythms, humor, and cosmic scope. The third was jazz. To read this book you need dense, complex neural pathways, and listening to jazz helps grow them.

•

In the nineteenth century, when whale oil fueled the lamps of the world, whaling was a big international industry. Sailing vessels like the *Pequod* circled the globe, following the migration routes. Typically they would carry three or more whaleboats. When they got close enough to their prey, the boats were lowered, each rowed by a small crew armed with lances and harpoons, to get in close for the kill. It was dangerous work, and it inspired a number of action-packed travelogues and novels.

Moby-Dick has its share of action, but it's also rich with transcendence. After the successful hunting of a sperm whale, and the gruesome process of butchering and decapitating its carcass, comes this hushed coda, which invokes the lotus, the Hindu and Buddhist world's favorite symbol of enlightenment.

> When this last task was accomplished it was noon, and the seamen went below to their dinner. Silence reigned over the before tumultuous but now deserted deck. An intense copper calm, like a universal yellow lotus, was more and more unfolding its noiseless measureless leaves upon the sea.

There's a funnier contrast in the chapter on masthead duty, the sailor's two-hour shift standing near the top of a mast to scan the ocean for whales. Naturally, Melville begins with a long, quasi-scholarly disquisition on the history of masthead-standing, beginning with Egyptians atop pyramids, gazing at the stars. When we at last get to Ishmael's time aloft, the tranquility is so thick that he starts melting into samadhi, but the punch line is that samadhi is an occupational hazard.

> In the serene weather of the tropics it is exceedingly pleasant the mast-head; nay, to a dreamy meditative man it is delightful.... There you stand, lost in the infinite series of the sea, with nothing ruffled but the waves. The tranced ship indolently rolls; the drowsy trade winds blow; everything resolves you into languor....A sublime uneventfulness invests you.... In this enchanted mood, thy spirit ebbs away to whence it came; becomes diffused through time and space ... forming at last a part of every shore the round globe over....
>
> But while this sleep, this dream is on ye, move your foot or hand an inch; slip your hold at all; and your identity comes back in horror....And perhaps, at mid-day, in the fairest weather, with one half-throttled shriek you drop through that transparent air into the summer sea, no more to rise for ever.

When Ishmael finally sees the White Whale for the first time, there's a similar mix of enticement and danger. Moby Dick appears not just as a monster but as a god of serenity — *and* a monster.

> A gentle joyousness — a mighty mildness of repose in swiftness, invested the gliding whale.... Not Jove, not that great majesty Supreme! did surpass the glorified White Whale as he so divinely swam....
>
> And thus, through the serene tranquillities of the tropical sea...Moby Dick moved on, still withholding from sight the full terrors of his submerged trunk, entirely hiding the wrenched hideousness of his jaw.

Elsewhere, Ishmael feels safe enough to entirely abandon himself into ego-dissolving transcendence. One of this strange book's strangest passages describes the task of kneading spermaceti, the waxy fluid drained from the sperm whale's head and used for making candles. After harvesting, it's poured into large tubs where, as it cools, it develops lumps, which the sailors must squeeze back into liquid.

> After having my hands in it for only a few minutes, my fingers felt like eels, and began, as it were, to serpentine and spiralise.
>
> As I sat there at my ease, cross-legged on the deck;...under a blue tranquil sky; the ship under indolent sail, and gliding so serenely along; as I bathed my hands among those soft, gentle globules of infiltrated tissues, woven almost within the hour; as they richly broke to my fingers, and discharged all their opulence, like fully ripe grapes their wine; as I snuffed up that uncontaminated aroma, — literally and truly, like the smell of spring violets; I declare to you, that for the time I lived as in a musky meadow;...while bathing in that bath, I felt divinely free from all ill-will, or petulance, or malice, of any sort whatsoever.
>
> Squeeze! squeeze! squeeze! all the morning long; I squeezed that sperm till I myself almost melted into it; I squeezed that sperm till a strange sort of insanity came over me; and I found myself unwittingly squeezing my co-laborers' hands in it, mistaking their hands for the gentle globules. Such an abounding, affectionate, friendly, loving feeling did this avocation beget; that at last I was continually squeezing their hands, and looking up into their eyes sentimentally; as much as to say, — Oh! my dear fellow beings, why should we

longer cherish any social acerbities, or know the slightest ill-humor or envy! Come; let us squeeze hands all round; nay, let us all squeeze ourselves into each other; let us squeeze ourselves universally into the very milk and sperm of kindness.

Would that I could keep squeezing that sperm for ever!…In thoughts of the visions of the night, I saw long rows of angels in paradise, each with his hands in a jar of spermaceti.

•

For all of *Moby-Dick*'s mad, glorious excesses, its most acclaimed sentence is just three words long: "Call me Ishmael." By critical consensus, it's the all-time greatest opening sentence of any novel.* The name Ishmael immediately places us in an Old Testament space of blessings and curses, smitings and apocalypses, with a narrator who journeys through tribulations to divine rescue. (In Genesis, Ishmael is a son of Abraham who is banished, along with his mother, to wander in the desert. With miraculous help, he survives to become the father of the Arab peoples.)

But *call* you Ishmael? Then who are you really? We never get a sense that "Ishmael" is the alias of a fugitive or criminal, that behind the assumed name is another, truer name. Rather, behind the name is the unnamable, behind the face is the faceless, behind the *persona*, which literally means "mask," is the nonpersonal, invisible awareness that peers through the eyeholes of the mask.

Ishmael, in other words, is just like us. We all peer through eyeholes, all names are aliases. Call me Dean — hey, my parents did. "Call me Ishmael" is like the first line of a proof in mathematics: let $x = 17$. We assign a value to x, then see what consequences flow from that assignment. The names we've been assigned and the personas they tag are constructs, appropriate and necessary for journeying through our own world of tribulations and rescues but usually mistaken for our ultimate reality. But Melville, in his opening sentence, spills the beans. He invites us to consciously participate in the artifice of naming — to be in on the joke — and so perhaps start to see through the joke of our own so-called identity.

As the book progresses, this joke plays out as the Ishmael persona's undisguised flimsiness. Normally, a fiction writer strives to make any first-person

---

*   A strong contender for second place is Gabriel García Márquez's *One Hundred Years of Solitude*: "Many years later, as he faced the firing squad, Colonel Aureliano Buendía was to remember that distant afternoon when his father took him to discover ice."

narrator a convincingly solid person, with a realistically limited point of view. Narrators can't see around corners. They're not telepathic. They can't report on conversations they don't hear or actions they don't witness, or on other characters' unspoken thoughts. But Ishmael can. Whenever the pretense of the persona becomes inconvenient, it's just quietly dropped. "Ishmael" melts into a free-floating, omniscient awareness, seeing remote scenes and hearing characters' most intimate ruminations (rendered, just for fun, as Shakespearean soliloquies).

This makes him an Ishmael in the deepest sense — an unmoored wanderer. He spares us the usual recitation of his family history, schooling, marital status, and so on (what Holden Caulfield calls "all that David Copperfield kind of crap"), because it doesn't exist. He has no backstory. The name Ishmael means "God has heard." Melville's Ishmael is not a character with goals to achieve, desires to fulfill. He's a voice to be heard, a playful authorial puppet with only one foot in the story, never more than half-invested in the pretense of personhood. Like Walt Whitman, he is "both in and out of the game and watching and wondering at it." One of this book's great marvels is the sense of happy, weightless freedom that pervades the narrative voice, even in the face of horrors.

Captain Ahab is fully invested in personhood and, it follows, fully immersed in horrors. He also is named for an Old Testament character, a king who encounters the prophet Elijah and scoffs at his prophecy that "the dogs will lick up your blood — yes, *yours*." Kings don't like to be reminded of their mortality. In the Bible, in Shakespeare, in myths and fairy tales, they're usually personifications of the illusory separate self, a.k.a. the ego, especially when they're tyrants like Herod or usurpers like Claudius and Macbeth. Their illegitimate occupation of the throne is the ego's arrogation of the sense of I-am from the boundless, nonpersonal awareness-space. To defend their crown, they'll fight to the death against every perceived threat: Herod orders the Slaughter of the Innocents, Claudius plots the murder of Hamlet, Macbeth dispatches one real or imagined rival after another. And they are ultimately destroyed because frightened, reactive ego turns out to be insubstantial. It's the fever dream from which we finally awake.

That's why, despite his grandiosity, the king always feels wounded and besieged. Our wounded ego's nagging sense of mortality and incompleteness is the goad to find timeless completeness in the only place where it can be found — in the infinite (right here). Ahab's wound, of course, is his missing leg. To restore his completeness, he must hunt down Moby Dick. For all his raging against the White Whale, his obsessed pursuit is the lover's pursuit of the beloved, the devotee's pursuit of the divine. The whiteness of the whale is the whiteness of the one clear light, from which multihued creation emerges and back into which it ultimately merges.

That includes our created personas. Like Ishmael standing watch on the masthead, we all fear this merging with completeness because we sense, correctly, that it will be the death of the separate self we think we are. Yet we pursue it because we sense, also correctly, that only in merging will we at last find fulfillment: 'tis a consummation devoutly to be wished. And like a token of our destiny, our wounded ego already contains the essence of that infinite. Ahab's artificial leg is made of whalebone.

•

Over many decades and in too many countries, we've seen how a wounded, vindictive king will fight for his crown at all costs — determined, if he is to be destroyed, to destroy the kingdom in the process. If the captain must go down, he'll bring the ship down with him.

That's what Ahab does. In the final, furious hunt, Moby Dick wrecks the whaleboats that pursue him, as well as the *Pequod*. From the last sinking boat, Ahab hurls a harpoon, but the line attached to it catches him around the neck and he vanishes into the sea. As the great whale dives, he leaves a whirlpool, into which everything and everyone — almost everyone — is apocalyptically sucked. Ishmael is the sole survivor.

All this has been fated since the scene, ninety-nine chapters earlier, when Ahab summons the crew to the quarterdeck, divulges his crazed mission, and unites them in a frenzy of assent, chanting "Death to Moby Dick!" The scene bears an eerie resemblance to the chants of political vengeance with which our modern mad captains incite their followers. Afterward, Ishmael considers the enigma of Ahab's success.

> How it was that they so aboundingly responded to the old man's ire — by what evil magic their souls were possessed, that at times his hate seemed almost theirs; the White Whale as much their insufferable foe as his; how all this came to be — what the White Whale was to them, or how to their unconscious understandings, also, in some dim, unsuspected way, he might have seemed the gliding great demon of the seas of life, — all this to explain, would be to dive deeper than Ishmael can go.

"Deeper than Ishmael can go." Yeah. The "evil magic" whereby such dangerously damaged leaders can draw such passionate support is a deep mystery.

But consider this:

It's hard work being good boys and girls. It's frustrating to be constrained not only by the laws of the land but by the laws of physics, logic, and math. Gravity, morality, legality — all such a drag. How refreshing then, how exciting, to have an avatar of transgression, someone who offers us the vicarious thrill of breaking every law with the gusto of a pro wrestler breaking a folding chair over the referee's head. As we've seen, people will follow such a leader even when — *especially* when — he leads them to self-destruction. There's no kick to the Kool-Aid unless it's poisoned.

Transgression is just clumsy transcendence. It's the wrong answer to the right question: What shall we boundless souls do about these intolerable boundaries? It's one more way of getting blotto, like bingeing on drugs, drink, doughnuts, or family-wrecking sexual adventures. Those are all headbutting assaults on our perceived prison bars, which yield some temporary numbing but with a lot of collateral damage. The sages' solution is to undream the bars out of their illusory existence — to wake up to the freedom of our unconstrainable beingness, which makes following a few rules of the road no big deal.

In the old days, a few monks could go into the jungles or hills, sit communing with the infinite, and keep the cushions warm for the next generation while the rest of us went stumbling about our business. But now we're too dangerous to keep stumbling. We're all on the *Pequod*, there's an epidemic of destructive transgression, and transcendence may be the only effective medicine.

•

With a nod to the Book of Job, Ishmael says, in this book's epilogue, "And I only am escaped alone to tell thee." From a Dharma perspective, his survival makes sense. He's the weightless narrative voice, the unembodied witnessing awareness. Everything that's constructed — bodies, projects, nations — must eventually deconstruct, as the Buddha said just before his own body finally broke down. So it's good to do the fire drill before the fire. While we still have this precious human nervous system, it's good to practice tuning it to that unconstructed and therefore indestructible silence at our depths. Yes, concludes Ishmael, in this world we're subject to the whirling storms of every kind of calamity:

> But even so, amid the tornadoed Atlantic of my being, do I myself still for ever centrally disport in mute calm; and while ponderous planets of unwaning woe revolve round me, deep down and deep inland there I still bathe me in eternal mildness of joy.

19. I'm Nobody

EMILY DICKINSON

In India, a saint is someone who has woken up. Rather than a martyr or a miracle worker, a saint might be completely ordinary and inconspicuous on the outside, while quietly living a life of enlightenment within. One of my teachers once said that trying to understand a saint by tracing outer events is like trying to know a person by studying their footprints in the sand.

Studying Emily Dickinson's footprints has been a growth industry for over a century and a half, ever since the neighbors in Amherst, Massachusetts, started noticing that she was seen less and less outside her parents' big yellow house, and eventually not at all. As they passed by on Main Street, admiring her expertly cultivated gardens, they might strain to catch a glimpse of her in the white dress that, in her later years, was said to be her only outfit. The neighborhood children got the closest to her, gathering below her second-floor bedroom window, waiting for her to lower a basketful of her excellent baked goods via rope and pulley. In return, they would send up a daisy or a clover. All that time, Dickinson was quietly discovering boundless awareness. "The Brain," she wrote, "is wider than the Sky."

As a schoolgirl she was bright and spirited, and in her one year of college at Mount Holyoke she was outspoken, challenging the pious Christian attitudes the teachers expected. Then things began to change, and for reasons that are murky, she came home and stayed. She never married but lived out her life with her stern father (a lawyer, legislator, and treasurer of Amherst College); her depressed, sickly mother; and Vinnie, an also-unmarried sister.

When not busy in the kitchen or garden, Emily wandered through the fields with her "shaggy ally," a brown Newfoundland named Carlo. She played the piano and sometimes wrote original compositions. Alone in the attic, she read Shakespeare aloud. She had a few hopeless, drawn-out obsessions with older men, some of them married, who lived inconveniently (or perhaps all too conveniently) far away. She wrote them letters.

She also wrote letters, hundreds of them, to Susan Dickinson, the beloved school-days friend who married Emily's brother Austin and lived with him in the house next door. Sue may or may not have been the main object of Emily's romantic passions; theories abound. We know that Emily wrote to her, "I would nestle close to your warm heart. Is there any room there for me? Or shall I wander away all homeless and alone?" We also know that Sue was tormented by Austin's very public, yearslong affair with an attractive neighbor.

Theories also abound as to why Emily's reclusiveness deepened over time: perhaps due to romantic rejection, or the shock of the Civil War, or her mother's growing invalidism, or autism, or even the death of her dog. Eventually, she holed up in her bedroom whenever visitors came to the house. She cracked the door open to hear her father's funeral.

Today, Dickinson would probably be diagnosed with agoraphobia (fear of public or open places), accompanied by panic attacks ("terrors," as she called them in her letters), triggered by the deaths of an astonishing number of people close to her, four of them in her fifteenth year alone. So yes, her solitude was arguably pathological in origin. But that doesn't diminish the awakening or the poetry that grew out of it. If we knew as much about the primal traumas of all the venerated saints and buddhas as we do of hers, we'd probably find that she has plenty of company. People who are doing just peachy in their outer lives are generally less driven to look seriously within.

A *wounded* Deer - leaps highest -
I've heard the Hunter tell -

As with most of us, then, whatever awakening Dickinson experienced seems to have been mixed with the residues of neurosis. The divine light doesn't necessarily wash all those residues away. The sting gradually drains out of them, but quirks remain.

What matters is the poetry that came from that mix. Few of Dickinson's contemporaries got to read it. Letters she sent to friends would often contain a poem or two, but only ten were published during her lifetime, in newspapers — anonymously and in mutilated form, thanks to editors who tried to "fix" them. Her early aspirations to be a published poet were soon discouraged. Until 1886, when she died in the big yellow house at age fifty-five, no one knew she'd been producing and squirreling away a huge trove of poems.

Vinnie, whom Emily had instructed to burn all her papers, went through her bureau drawers and found, along with a lifetime's worth of letters, some forty handmade booklets with about eight hundred poems meticulously copied into them. And there were more poems, hundreds of them, on loose sheets of stationery or on scraps — the inside of a used envelope or the back of a chocolate wrapper. There were nearly eighteen hundred poems in all, none with titles, more than half of them written in a creative rush during the five years of the war. Vinnie burned the letters and kept the poems.

Dickinson's handwriting has been likened to fossilized bird tracks. It's mysteriously peppered with very short horizontal lines, barely more than dots. Sometimes they seem to function as an all-purpose punctuation mark, sometimes they seem like an idiosyncrasy of penmanship that's best ignored. (They're transcribed here as hyphens.) Not expecting publication, and living in her solitary world of field and garden and second-floor bedroom, Dickinson had quietly gone her own way. Both poetically and spiritually, her way was radical.

•

Consider this two-line bombshell from 1860:

> Not "Revelation" - 'tis - that waits,
> But our unfurnished eyes -

Dickinson grew up in an era of intense spiritual ferment, with competing denominations, from Shakers to Mormons, proclaiming belief in their own version of ultimate truth. But in this poem, with the cool confidence of one who doesn't just believe but sees, she dismisses *everyone's* version with a droll pair of quotation marks: "Revelation."

What she sees is precisely what the awakened sages have always seen, that the real ultimate truth is not a revelation. Anything that's revealed has *content*: a message (that is, a thought), or a feeling, or perhaps a sensory experience. Maybe it's sublime, celestial content: a hundred thousand angels singing hosannas as God whispers the Message of All Messages in your ear, or a hundred thousand volts of kundalini energy surging up your spine and lighting up your chakras like a Christmas tree. But that's still content, and therefore it's not It. It's specific, x rather than y, and therefore it's bounded, finite. Our longing is for the infinite.

Dickinson calls It "our unfurnished eyes": not anything we experience with the eyes or other senses, but rather the awareness-space within which all seeing, all experiencing, happens. It's empty, uncluttered by objects, like an unfurnished room. This, of course, is exactly what happens in sitting practice, when awareness — the eye, the I — temporarily disengages from objects and rests in itself. We're like the sun that's been shining on object after object but now simply abides in its own light. We enjoy unfurnished, luminous freedom, and as awakening grows, that enjoyment persists, even when meditation ends and our eyes are once again furnished.

This is a subtle Dharma insight, and for Dickinson it wasn't book-learned. Apparently she was a natural, inclined to spontaneous inward settling during her long stretches of quiet solitude ("Silence," she wrote, "is Infinity") and the time she spent communing with the natural environment.

> A flask of Dew - A Bee or two -
> A Breeze - a caper in the trees -
> And I'm a Rose!

She did know about the Transcendentalists, just seventy-five miles away in Concord. She admired Thoreau's work and treasured a volume of Emerson's poetry. Once, on a visit to Amherst, Emerson himself dined next door at Dickinson's brother's home, and Emily was invited. But she didn't show. Perhaps her neurosis prevented her, or perhaps, having so deeply tasted the transcendental, she just didn't need to bother about the -ism.

Dickinson's highest poems demand the perspective of samadhi to decode them. Otherwise, we're left scratching our heads over, say,

> I taste a liquor never brewed -
> From Tankards scooped in Pearl -

That's a koan. The taste of a liquor never brewed is the same thingless thing as the sound of one hand clapping, or the face you had before your parents were born, or Keats's ditties of no tone. It's the flavor of no flavor, and it gets you higher than high. Beyond all the somethings of the senses and mind, it's sublime no-thing, straight up. The tankard is empty, but like unfurnished empty awareness, it's luminous, pearlescent. By the end of the poem, Emily's sloshed, like a common drunk leaning against a lamppost — only, in her exalted state, she is "Leaning against the - Sun!" Emerson, in his library of imported Eastern scriptures, may have read the Vedic hymns to Soma, the intoxicating beverage of the gods, but Dickinson guzzled the stuff.

•

In Tibetan Buddhism, Dickinson's unfurnished eyes are called "naked awareness." That expression always reminds me of a counterculture slogan from the sixties: "Warning — I Am Naked Under My Clothes." Like our body under its layers of fabric, our awareness remains inherently naked under its layers of thinking, feeling, and that rough weave of habits and tendencies called "personality." Meditation, which is often mistaken for a process of *creating* pure awareness, simply uncovers it.

But *how* do we uncover it? Dickinson knows that too.

> Not knowing when the Dawn will come,
> I open every Door

We can't know when or from what direction the light of samadhi will dawn for us. So we remain omnidirectionally open. That's about as concise a meditation instruction as we could hope for. Elsewhere, she puts it this way:

> I cling to nowhere till I fall -
> The Crash of nothing, yet of all -

Here the operative word is "fall." Any effort to create a nonagitated state of mind is itself a form of agitation, and therefore self-defeating (a crucial point that's missed by many meditators). So don't try to concentrate or dive within. Rather, let yourself *fall* within, as naturally as you fall asleep or fall in love. As with sleep or love, our role is just to get out of the way.

Naturals like Dickinson know this without being told; falling overtakes them irresistibly and unpredictably. In fact, these two lines occur in the middle of a poem that's not about serene contemplation but mourning. Sometimes extreme emotional distress leaves us with no choice but to let go. Then we learn the same lesson as hardworking meditators when, at last, they run out of moves: surrender. Cling to nowhere. Hold to no reference points, no set ideas about what is what, where you're going, or how you'll get there. You're not the driver. Cling to no imaginary steering wheel or map. You are, as Dickinson writes elsewhere:

> Done with the Compass -
> Done with the Chart!

Don't try to chart your course. Just be, and when you find yourself reverting to some effort or plan, simply relax your grip. Don't try to figure it out. Here Dickinson has clearly replicated, within her own experience, Keats's discovery of negative capability. In Japanese Zen it's called *shikantaza*, "just sitting." And unprompted, in its own sweet time, gravity takes over. Falling happens.

What do we fall into? "The Crash of nothing, yet of all." As we fall we implode and our world of experiences implodes with us, all things silently crashing into no-thing. All forms crash into emptiness. Afterward, we return to the world of forms, but gradually we come to see that the forms are still empty, and always were. Then the empty us glides frictionlessly through the empty world…like butter. That's a lot of fun.

This is what religion is supposed to do for us. At its best it does, but the best happens rarely. When Dickinson was fifteen she was caught up, along with many of her friends and relatives, in one of the waves of dramatic Christian conversions that swept through the region. But she was too ruthlessly self-aware for it to last long, realizing that her leap of faith had been artificial — strenuous leaping rather than natural falling. By the time she was twenty-two, she could write:

> Some keep the Sabbath going to Church -
> I keep it, staying at Home -
> With a Bobolink for a Chorister -*
> And an Orchard, for a Dome -
> …
> God preaches, a noted Clergyman -
> And the sermon is never long,
> So instead of getting to Heaven, at last -
> I'm going, all along.

We have to love her audacity, her matter-of-fact heretical testimony that divine communion, which people seek in church, she finds spontaneously in wordless outdoor solitude. We have to love her dry wit as she answers the unspoken objection that true spiritual uplift requires a duly ordained pastor. Her pastor is God, whom she meets wherever she goes and who has, after all, a pretty solid reputation (he's "a noted Clergyman"). Unlike the pastors in town, he gives no long, boring sermons. His truth, empty of content, is conveyed in a moment, each moment, in silence.

Churchgoers believe, or at least hope, they are "getting to Heaven, at last." They endure their tedious services and struggle to live virtuous lives with the goal of "getting" (earning, attaining) some promised next-world blessedness. Emily is not getting but "going," eliminating the middlemen with their wordy revelations and taking the do-it-yourself or, rather, the be-it-yourself approach. It entails no doing, no pursuing blessedness, but instead

---

*   With a songbird for a choirmaster.

THE DICKINSON HOME
ON MAIN STREET, AMHERST

naturally finding it "all along," in every inch of our goings through this world. As the Vietnamese Zen master Thich Nhat Hanh wrote, "Peace is every step." The pious who try to sweat their way to heaven, like meditators who try to sweat their way to peace, miss the goal by pursuing it.

Subtly strengthening Dickinson's sense of spiritual authority here is her favorite rhythmic pattern, called *ballad meter*. It consists of alternating lines of iambic tetrameter (four stresses) and iambic trimeter (three stresses), rhyming on the second and fourth lines.

> A-*one*, a-*two*, a-*three*, a-*four*,
> A-*one*, a-*two*, a-*three*,
> Ba-*dah*, ba-*dah*, ba-*dah*, ba-*dah*,
> Ba-*dah*, ba-*dah*, ba-*dee*.

In New England by Dickinson's time, this had become the standard meter for hymns. So, even as she disses the church, she echoes its sound, borrowing from it a sort of instant Sunday-morning solemnity — you can almost hear the organ music — plus, perhaps, a dash of irony. (A quick way to check whether a poem may be hers is to see if you can sing it to the tune of "Amazing Grace." Or, alas, the *Gilligan's Island* theme.)

Even more central to her style is the deliberate plainness, the precociously modern, unsentimental, "unladylike" toughness of language, seventy years before Hemingway made such a splash with it. We can hear it especially in some of her blunt opening lines, which ambush the reader much as John Donne's do: "Talk not to me of Summer Trees," or, "I had been hungry, all the Years," or, "I send you a decrepit flower." This tough language is not just a pose or style. It buttresses a give-it-to-me-straight psychological toughness, as in this:

I like a look of Agony,
Because I know it's true -

Or this:

A Bird, came down the Walk -
He did not know I saw -
He bit an Angle Worm in halves
And ate the fellow, raw

This was a radical choice in an era when prose and especially poetry were expected to be flowery. American writers were still trying to prove that, here in our frontier outpost, we could sound like sophisticated Europeans, with elaborate, complex sentences and lots of polysyllabic, Latinate words. Why just walk when you can *perambulate*? Why merely lie when you can *dissimulate*? Walt Whitman's *Leaves of Grass*, published in 1855, helped advance a more earthy, honest American voice, but (as we'll see) its erotic content made it *too* earthy for polite society. Dickinson wrote to a friend, "You speak of Mr. Whitman. I never read his book, but was told that it was disgraceful." She had to find her avant-garde style, like her spiritual insight, on her own.

•

The gossip and speculation around Dickinson's private life have spawned books, plays, films, and recently a streaming TV series portraying her as a sexy-strong Girl Power heroine with suspiciously modern dance moves. It's all an attempt to discover who this strange person was, to guess her secret. But she's told us her secret: she wasn't a person at all.

I'm Nobody! Who are you?
Are you - Nobody - too?
Then there's a pair of us!
Dont tell! they'd advertise - you know!

How dreary - to be - Somebody!
How public - like a Frog -
To tell one's name - the livelong June -
To an admiring Bog!

This poetic embrace of nobodyness is often interpreted biographically, as Dickinson's affirmation (or sour-grapes rationalization) of her own anonymous life — a condemnation of fame and, perhaps, a fantasy of romance with a similarly anonymous soul mate, in a hermitage built for two. But I think we can take her at her word. "Nobody" means not an individual: in Buddhist terms, anatta, "not-self." She's disavowing not just ego*tism*, self-importance, but ego, the very notion that we're a self, a separate entity neatly wrapped up in a bag of skin. Any sensible adult will deny being a *special* person. Far more profoundly, she denies being a person.

This, as we've seen, was Shakespeare's secret, that "There was no one in him." It's the secret of all the sages. And as we keep falling into the deliciously empty, open space where we thought our individual self was, it becomes *our* secret. Sooner or later it becomes clear that the alleged somebody-thing was never a thing at all. It's just patterns of activity, a bunch of doing, and behind them is not a doer but limitless being.

That discovery annuls our feelings of deep neediness. Yet it is, shall we say, *chummy* to meet another person who's in on the secret of nonpersonhood. It's like hearing all the others at the slumber party snoring away, thinking we're the only one that's awake, till someone winks at us from across the room. *Well, hi there!* That's what happens in the second and third lines: "Are you - Nobody - too? / Then there's a pair of us!" The childlike, peekaboo-ish tone helps make the point: Being nobody is simple and innocent. It's not weird. It's not, as writers like Beckett imagined, terrifying. It's the way into the kingdom of heaven. It's jolly fun — so much fun that we'd love to share it with other playfriends.

Yet, in the fourth line, we see the problem that can arise if we overshare the secret, one that many a Dharma bum has encountered after trying, in the first flush of excited discovery, to explain the experience to others. "Don't tell! they'd advertise - you know!" In the history of awakening, many comedies and tragedies of errors have come about this way. The most tragic cases wind up with someone being crucified. But just having a more-or-less distorted version of your nobodyness "advertised" — having it made a spectacle, whether you're condemned as a heretic, dismissed as a fool, or exalted as a guru — is a kind of crucifixion. It's a perversion of personless nonstatus into extraordinary status, the agony of becoming a caricature. So keep your head down.

In the second stanza, Dickinson describes the alternative to nobodyness, the business-as-usual of being somebody, and finds just the right word: "dreary." It's such a lot of work, constantly hustling to prop up something that doesn't exist. (We can never stop or we'll melt back into nobodyness, and then we'll die, right?) To maintain our myth of somebodyness, we have to keep reiterating it: send out those press releases, post those Instagrams. Listen to most people talk about politics, art, religion, sports, love, anything, and you'll realize that they're talking about themselves. Whether stated or unstated, it's all "*I* think," "*I* feel," "*I* want," "*I* fear." It is, in fact, as repetitious as the croaking of frogs on a summer night. In the brilliant joke that concludes the poem, what the frogs croak is their own name, and they all have the *same* name: "I. I. I. I."

Yep, you're special. Just like everyone else. And if by chance you succeed in croaking "I" a little louder than the rest, your reward is what's known as fame: the admiration of a bog of frogs. Mazel tov.

•

Not all of Dickinson's poems reach this level of insight and of art. Eighteen hundred poems is a lot, and she doesn't hit it out of the park every time, but neither does Shakespeare — just try reading *The Merry Wives of Windsor*. Not expecting to be published, she left behind a lot of tiresome dear-diary stuff about her romantic martyrdom ("Each Scar I'll keep for Him," and so on), which finally comes to life when it lapses into sexual fantasy ("Wild nights - Wild nights! / Were I with thee"). Some pieces are lightweight quips, made for the amusement of a friend, not for the ages. Some are developmental work, the experimentation that all artists must do in the course of finding their art. But when she hits it, boy, does she hit it.

She wrote, famously and extensively, about death. She saw so much of it that at some point she knew she had to come to grips with it. The first step (for anyone) is to acknowledge its inexorable reality — the fact that death is really, truly coming for everyone you love, and everyone you don't, and you. Logically, of course, we all know that we're not the one lucky exception to the death rule, but psychologically we give a little inner chuckle and decide that *sure* we are. In Tibet in the old days, they cured that chuckle by having each new monk who joined the monastery build his own coffin and sleep in it every night.

In the opening of her best-known poem, Dickinson confronts Death's inexorability, but with a lighter touch than the Tibetans — with a little pun.

Because I could not stop for Death -
He kindly stopped for me -

Don't have time for Death? Too busy being busy with your Very Important Busy-ness? No problem. Wherever you are, like a kindly, courteous carriage driver, Death will make a special stop for you. He may not be on your sched-ule, but you're on his. He leaves no passenger behind.

The other step for Dickinson was to put aside religion's smiley-face bro-mides. (*Don't worry, in heaven you'll be happily reunited with Grandma and Grandpa and your puppy.*) She knew she had to take a more rigorous, empir-ical approach, to get as close as she could to a direct, unflinching experience of what it means to die. She had to meditate on death, gazing at it steadily, without interposing any concepts, till her gaze penetrated its visible surface.

For that, she had to use not the physical eye, but insight, intuition, both of which mean "inner gaze." True, it's easy to mistake our hopeful or fearful fantasies for inner gaze, unless we've been graced with extraordinary clarity and honesty. Dickinson was.

What may be the most powerful of her death meditations was written in 1862. It begins:

> I felt a Funeral, in my Brain,
> And Mourners to and fro
> Kept treading - treading - till it seemed
> That Sense was breaking through -
>
> And when they all were seated,
> A Service, like a Drum -
> Kept beating - beating - till I thought
> My mind was going numb -

The inner gaze here is so strong, it's as if the poet has rediscovered a forgotten scientific instrument, employed by sages thousands of years before the mi-croscope and telescope: the *introscope*, which allows her to look inside and connect with the essential truth of things we think of as outside. She doesn't just see or hear the funeral. She *feels* it — viscerally, palpably — in her mind, or as she writes in the first line, "in my Brain," invoking the physicality of that organ to vouch for the solid reality of her experience.

The endless "treading - treading" of the mourners in the first stanza, and the drumlike "beating - beating" of the funeral service in the second, may feel familiar. They're oppressive, and they go impossibly on and on, as funerals often seem to do. (It's the opposite of time flying when you're having fun.) One result, which may also feel familiar, is that the mind goes numb. We can't think anymore and just glaze over. But where the rest of us check out is where sages and poets check in. For Dickinson, this numbing is like the anesthetic before the operation. It permits her to cut deep. With the mind sidelined from crowding the air with its usual imaginings, now she can expand the reach of the senses to regions that are unimaginable: "Sense was breaking through."

And then I heard them lift a Box
And creak across my Soul
With those same Boots of Lead, again,
Then Space - began to toll

In the third stanza, the service is finished. The poet hears — not sees — the mourners "lift a Box" to carry it out. That's strange. The lifting of the casket is a hushed activity. But now the poet's entire sensory capacity has been squeezed into the auditory sense, which becomes extra-vivid. At the same time, her consciousness ("my Soul") begins to melt out of its old boundaries. As in certain dreams, the point of view is slippery and diffuse. The treading of the mourners resumes (feeling as cold, heavy, and dark as "Boots of Lead"), and the church's floor creaks, but now the melting, oozing Soul seems to be both under the wooden floor and inside the wooden casket as much as it's witnessing from the wooden pew. The numb mind's concepts of "self" and "other" blur and melt, merging the mourner and the mourned.

As all the Heavens were a Bell,
And Being, but an Ear,
And I, and Silence, some strange Race,
Wrecked, solitary, here -

From an objective point of view, the next thing that happens is the tolling of the church bell. But that point of view belongs to the living. As the poem's witnessing consciousness continues to diffuse and expand, its experience is that (at the end of the previous stanza) "Space - began to toll" as if "all the Heavens were a Bell." This is the beginning of the journey through what Tibetans call the *bardo*, the transitional dimension between dying and whatever's next, be it rebirth or nirvana. The body, as it's perceived by others, is dead, but the senses take a little more time to withdraw from this world. As confirmed nowadays by science (and by those who work closely with the dying), the last sense to go is hearing.

So any notion of a bell or any other solid, visible entity is now gone. The world of sight, touch, smell, and taste is gone. What's left is sound: the tolling filling all of space, the Heavens themselves tolling. And the experiencer that experiences the sound has been refined to pure hearing ("And Being, but an Ear").

Then even sound and hearing go. What remains is "I, and Silence, some strange Race, / Wrecked, solitary, here -": some primordial sense of I-aware, consciousness devoid of anything to be conscious of, absolutely solitary, in an absolute vacuum of absolute silence. The word "Wrecked" is a pun that reflects the opposing perspectives of the two worlds we're traveling between. In the world of the living, a box is being carried away, containing the wreckage of a body. They call it "dead," but "dead" is a concept that only the living can entertain. Meanwhile, the person formerly known as living is shipwrecked on an unknown shore, like Robinson Crusoe, the only one of his race, a stranger in a strange, silent, landless land.

That might seem as far as we can go on this journey, but Dickinson has one more stanza's worth of inner sight:

And then a Plank in Reason, broke,
And I dropped down, and down -
And hit a World, at every plunge,
And Finished knowing - then -

Even the far shore of perfect, solitary silence is, in a way, *something*; we can, at least abstractly, conceive of it. So even that conceivability must go ("then a Plank in Reason, broke"), that last little rug must be pulled from under our feet ("And I dropped down, and down"). In the now-distant land of the living, the mourners have moved to the cemetery, where the coffin is lowered into the ground. But we, like Alice falling down the rabbit hole, are plunging down some transdimensional elevator shaft, and every floor that rushes past is a possible world, a universe, a rebirth. Where will we stop? What floor will we get out on?

That we cannot know ("And Finished knowing - then -"). That's the next life. It all depends on what we grasp at as we fall. Or if we're one of the rare souls that has attained enough equanimity to refrain from grasping and just enjoy the freedom of the free fall, we don't get out at any floor. We're done with the cycle of rebirth and redeath. That's final nirvana, and if it sounds like a loss in any way, that's only from the perspective of those who aren't there.

This is pretty much the lay of the land as set forth in the Bardo Thödol, the so-called Tibetan Book of the Dead, used by Vajrayana Buddhists since the eighth century as a manual for navigating their way through the transitional dimension. The Bardo Thödol is much longer and more detailed, with elaborate descriptions of the hallucinatory splendors and terrors that lurk in that elevator shaft, which one should calmly cruise past while following the Clear Light. (Please keep your hands and arms inside the car till the ride has come to a complete stop.) It's striking how one solitary woman in a big house in Amherst, using only her untutored, unguru'd introscopic gaze, managed to see much the same terrain.

•

There's only one authenticated photograph of Emily Dickinson, taken when she was about seventeen, posing beside a table, with a handful of flowers and a book at her elbow. We're tempted to gaze at it, to crank up our own intro-scope and try to penetrate the surface, to deeply know the consciousness that gazes back through those eyes. We know she was an intrepid, lone astronaut of inner space, and not much more.

But there are intriguing glimpses. Dickinson's beloved sister-in-law and next-door neighbor Sue eventually had three children. Emily doted on her nephew and two nieces, and their garden and orchard became a magnet for the local kids. At least for a while, she was joyfully alive in their world, even as she retreated from the world of adults. They called her Miss Emily, and they never forgot the tiny, frosted, heart-shaped cakes and the chocolate caramels she would make and bring or send over, along with a letter or poem for Sue. Half a century later, one of the boys, MacGregor Jenkins, wrote:

> She was not shy with [the children]. She was a splendid comrade and a staunch companion. Her ready smile, her dancing eyes, her quick reply made us all tingle with pleasure when we were near her.... We knew the things she loved best and we sought the early wild flowers, a flaming leaf, a glistening stone, the shining fallen feather of a bird and took them to her, sure of her appreciation of the gift as well as the giving.

In one of Jenkins's recollections in particular, this sweetly domestic Miss Emily and Dickinson the visionary poet seem to converge:

> She had a habit of standing in rapt attention as if she were listening to something very faint and far off. We children often saw her at sunset, standing at the kitchen window, peering through a vista in the trees to the western sky — her proud little head thrown back, her eyes raised and one hand held characteristically before her.

If we really want to know what Emily Dickinson was about, we finally need to forget about her and explore as she explored. We could start just like this: standing in rapt attention, perhaps with one hand held before us, listening to something very faint and far off.

20. I Am Large

WALT WHITMAN

Emily Dickinson and Walt Whitman are the nonidentical twin pillars of American poetry, opposite in almost every way.

She came from prim Puritan stock. He came from free-thinking Quakers. She was the reclusive Myth of Amherst. He haunted the newly bustling streets of mid-nineteenth-century Manhattan, "hurrying with the modern crowd as eager and fickle as any." She was a miniaturist, fashioning hymn-shaped little verses on discarded scraps of paper. He was a maximalist, whose lush lines sprawl, unconstrained by rhyme or meter, filling page after page like a jungle reclaiming helpless cities.

Even physically, she was "small, like the wren." He was big-boned, red-complected, with hair and beard as unruly as his written lines. Unpublished, she accepted anonymity. He self-published and shamelessly self-promoted; the only things he wrote anonymously were hack work to pay the bills and rave reviews of his own poetry. She's our iconic perpetual virgin. He's our iconic, exuberantly erotic gay (or gay-plus) Papa Bear. There's only one photograph of her. There are hundreds of him — he loved the camera and it loved him. She wrote, "I'm Nobody!" He wrote, "I am large, I contain multitudes."

But in their opposite ways they wind up in the same place. With her penetrating inward gaze, she bores deep into a rose or bee or casket till she arrives at the infinite. He expands outward, encompassing peoples and vistas, the grandness of America and of the universe — and arrives at the infinite.

Whitman's sweeping vision couldn't be squeezed into tidy rhyming stanzas. He knew he needed a bigger boat — a bigger poem with a looser, more expansive form. That form didn't exist so he created it, by echoing the rhythms of nature: night and day, birth and death, the whirling planets, his own pulse and breath. Storm cycles don't rhyme, people don't make love in sonnet form (I hope), but it's all powerfully rhythmic and keeps going for as long as its natural energy demands. Half a century later, French poets would "discover" this approach and call it *vers libre*, free verse.*

The supersized, forty-three-page free-verse poem that embodies Whitman's vision — his Declaration of Resplendence — is "Song of Myself." It also required a supersized protagonist, and he found one right at hand.

> Walt Whitman, a kosmos, of Manhattan the son,
> Turbulent, fleshy, sensual, eating, drinking and breeding

But this version of Walt was made, not born. He was born Walter Whitman Jr., of Brooklyn the son, where he lived in his mother's house on Myrtle Avenue and shared a bed with a mentally and physically handicapped brother. Two of his brothers died in mental institutions and a third drank himself to death. A sporadically employed journalist and second-rate fiction writer who dressed like a dandy of the era, this Clark Kent was a mild-mannered reporter who created his own Superman, then set out to become him.

He started ferrying into New York to immerse himself in the spectacle of the first modern city: new high-rise office buildings, ships from all nations crowding the harbor, opera (he was a big fan), huge waves of immigrants, a budding downtown bohemian saloon scene, tenements, prostitutes, warring

---

* Whitman was also influenced by the rhythms of the King James Bible and the fluid lines of operatic arias. His truest precursor, though, was Christopher Smart, who wrote some very strange stuff a century before Whitman. He was in an insane asylum at the time, and his poetry wasn't discovered till 1939. Google "For I will consider my Cat Jeoffry" and take a deep breath.

street gangs like the Bowery Boys and the Dead Rabbits, and corrupt, divisive politics — the mayor was a shady, pro-slavery real estate developer who favored seceding from the Union. It was an urban tapestry of contrasts such as had never before existed. There Whitman worked as a printer's apprentice, teacher, reporter, and editor, but never for long. He had a habit of being fired for chronic laziness; in photos from that time, he looks like he can barely keep his eyes open.

Then he woke up. It happened in his early thirties. One morning, probably in late June of 1853 or 1854, he had a dramatic samadhi experience that found expression in a torrent of words unlike anything he or anyone else had ever written. *Leaves of Grass* consisted of a dozen poems, of which the first and longest is "Song of Myself." The superhero Walt makes his debut in the frontispiece of the first edition, published in 1855. This deliberately provocative engraving epitomizes the new New York and the new Walt. The uncertain dandy has been reborn as a proletarian street guy, a virile American work-

ingman in an open-collared shirt, without jacket or tie, his hat and hips at an insolent angle: "one of the roughs," he calls himself. This was no way for a poet to pose. Even Thoreau wore his Sunday best for the camera.

This Walt embodies defiance — and seduction. One hand in his pocket, one on his hip, he cocks his head and peers at the reader with a look that says, "So…you gonna fight me or fuck me?" Midway through the print run, Whitman stopped the presses and had the engraver enhance the bulge of his crotch. The picture had the desired effect, generating shock, controversy, and — most important — attention.

·

If you picked up *Leaves of Grass* in a bookstore in Whitman's time and read the opening of "Song of Myself," you'd probably guess that the author was the most arrogant jerk ever to set pen to paper.

> I celebrate myself, and sing myself,
> And what I assume you shall assume,
> For every atom belonging to me as good belongs to you.

That first line is a provocation as bold as the frontispiece.* The second line only makes things worse: this guy is determined not only to sing his own praises but to foist upon us his own unsupported assumptions.

But the third line changes everything: "For every atom belonging to me as good belongs to you." Oh. Apparently what's being celebrated here is not the self in the usual sense of a unique, isolated entity with nice, clear boundaries — an individual, an ego. It's fluid, permeable, communal. We're all simmering together in one big Universe Soup, whose morsels are people, planets, animals, trees, all expanding, contracting, mixing, sharing atoms promiscuously.

Now we can see that "assume" means to *take on*, as when we assume a role or responsibility (or mortgage). We take on the atoms that come our way, and in this shape-shifting, borderless existence they all eventually come our way. So when Walt celebrates the self, he's celebrating everyone. I am he as you are he as you are me — Lennon saw that, but only after the acid kicked in. If that's the nature of reality, though, we should be able to see it naturally. But how?

Whitman answers in the next line, with breathtaking simplicity:

> I loafe and invite my soul

Like Dickinson, he gives us a one-sentence meditation manual, but in his own provocative way. Loafing, laziness, is one of the deadly sins. Here it's a boast, part of the celebration of oneself (and of the new Manhattan culture, where "loafers" were badass street idlers). It's also skillful means. After we've tried everything else, lazing turns out to be the most efficient way to invite our soul, our essence. Just leave off doing and marinate in being, which is the soul.

Of course, that soul is always already here. What we're actually inviting is our recognition of it. As part of that process, we might use an object of contemplation, something on which to rest our attention while settling into the silence: a mantra, a koan, an image of our favorite deity. Keats used a bright

---

* Actually, in the first edition, this line reads simply "I celebrate myself." Whitman added "and sing myself" later. Critics still argue about which version is better, much as they argue about the two published versions of the key line in *Where the Wild Things Are*: "Let the wild rumpus begin!" vs. "Let the wild rumpus start!" (Correct answer: "begin.")

star and a Grecian urn. Whitman makes a point of using something we normally overlook and even trample underfoot.

> I lean and loafe at my ease observing a spear of summer grass.

The poem goes on:

> My tongue, every atom of my blood, form'd from this soil, this air,
> Born here of parents born here from parents the same, and their
> parents the same,
> I, now thirty-seven years old in perfect health begin,
> Hoping to cease not till death.

> Creeds and schools in abeyance,
> Retiring back a while sufficed at what they are, but never forgotten

Here the poet declares his mission, to express cosmic reality in its fullness. Can a mortal tongue do that? Yes, because, like everything else, it *is* that reality, one more carrot in the cosmic soup, made of atoms that have been blood, soil, air, and generations of parents, and in time will be more. And yes, because he places "creeds and schools in abeyance." He puts all religion and philosophy on hold and uses his little-child beginner's mind to see afresh. "Don't seek truth," said Seng-ts'an, the Third Zen Patriarch. "Just stop cherishing opinions."

This clean-slate attitude sets the initial conditions for the poet's daunting task:

> I harbor for good or bad, I permit to speak at every hazard,
> Nature without check with original energy.

Whitman proposes to be like a wide, welcoming harbor (like New York Harbor), capacious enough to admit all vessels without judgment. Then Nature herself becomes his muse, speaking through him, opening all the stops, allowing the vital energy of the universe to pour through him and come out in words. That's all.

•

Whitman kept revising and expanding *Leaves of Grass* for the rest of his life. It's only in later editions that he gave the poems titles and divided "Song of

Myself" into fifty-two sections (suggesting a full cycle, like weeks in a year or cards in a deck). In section 5, he describes the awakening that transformed his life and ultimately transformed our literature.

> I mind how once we lay such a transparent summer morning,
> How you settled your head athwart my hips and gently turn'd over
>   upon me

Whoa! Apparently, we're about to witness an act of poetic fellatio. But in the next few lines we realize that the unnamed "you" is not a human lover, or not *only* a human lover, but an angel of the Lord, the peace-conferring Holy Spirit settling upon the poet in the form of a human lover, just as it settled upon Christ "in bodily form like a dove":

> And parted the shirt from my bosom-bone, and plunged your tongue
>   to my bare-stript heart,
> And reach'd till you felt my beard, and reach'd till you held my feet.
> Swiftly arose and spread around me the peace and knowledge that
>   pass all the argument of the earth

OK then, it's not fellatio (or not *only* fellatio). What's being blown is Whitman's mind. There are two strange and beautiful gestures here. In the first, the angel-spirit French-kisses the poet's heart chakra, signaling that, for Whitman, the way of awakening will be love, the opening of the heart. In the second, the angel stretches out its arms to hold Walt's feet and beard. It's at once an act of tender intimacy and a wrestling pin. Walt wrestles with the Lord, but unlike Jacob, he finds his victory in defeat. He gains the spirit's blessing by surrendering. Love, like any meditative activity, works when we give up our struggle. When we finally stop requiring things to be as they "should," we open to their impossible beauty as they are.

With that surrender comes peace, what Saint Paul calls "the peace of God, which passeth all understanding." It dawns for no reason. It's the silence of simple, nonphenomenal being that pervades all the complexity of phenomena, and sometimes we just tumble into it. It "swiftly arose." The image of the spirit-lover lying crosswise to the poet evokes the *fathom*, a nautical unit of six feet of depth, originally measured (as Whitman would have known) by the span of a man's arms. This sublime peace fathoms us. It sounds us from top to toe, plumbs the depths of our inner space, then overflows to the outer space ("and spread around me"), the kingdom of heaven spread upon the earth.

What arises and spreads is not only "peace" but "knowledge," the perfectly empty knowingness that finally and instantaneously lays to rest all our pesky questions. It surpasses "all the argument of the earth." It makes all our jostling thoughts and theories sound like the jabbering of drunken Smurfs. Requiring no data, derived from no book, it's self-evident, "sure as the most certain sure." And it has ramifications that are also self-evident, as underscored in the next several lines by the insistent, rhythmic repetition of "And" and "I know" (not merely think or feel), like a succession of big waves, rolling ashore and washing away all doubt:

> And I know that the hand of God is the promise of my own,
> And I know that the spirit of God is the brother of my own,
> And that all the men ever born are also my brothers, and the women
> my sisters and lovers,
> And that a kelson of the creation is love

The statement that "the hand of God is the promise of my own" recalls Genesis, "So God created man in his own image." That verse has deep mythic power, but it's rather distant and abstract: it describes a long-ago event that happened to "man," not to us personally. Whitman's version, with its present-tense "is," feels intimate and immediate, so fresh that the paint is still wet. Creation is now and ongoing, cosmic creative energy replicating itself forever, God's hand making my hand, my hand making my poem, and on and on and on.

"And I know that the spirit of God is the brother of my own." The spirit, the essence of God, is as closely akin to my essence as brother to brother. Religion makes formless spirit accessible by giving it form: God the King of the Universe, God the Father, God the Mother. Whitman gives us God the Brother, a wonderfully egalitarian relationship. *Bro!* And since we're all that spirit, the same relationship must extend through space and time to "all the men ever born...and the women." You're my sister on my God's side.

"And that a kelson of the creation is love." A kelson, or keelson, is a structural board that runs above or alongside a ship's keel. Love is not merely a passing emotion that arises, when we're lucky, out of fragile human relationships. It's a stout timber, an infrastructural element of the creation itself, the spine of the universe. Saint Paul says God is love. Not lov*ing*, not a big person who feels a lot of that nice emotion. God — that which makes the galaxies, spins them, and *is* them — is nonseparateness, intimacy beyond intimacy, love. No one can persuade you of this, but when you see it, you see it.

After such a declaration of lofty truth, what's left to say? We can't look any higher, so now — as a sort of quiet coda to that grand spiritual climax — Whitman looks down, to the minutiae of the natural world, the humblest things of the ground.

> And limitless are leaves stiff or drooping in the fields,
> And brown ants in the little wells beneath them,
> And mossy scabs of the worm fence, heap'd stones, elder, mullein and
>   poke-weed.

This is the kind of firsthand, extreme close-up discovery that you probably won't find in the Bible, or for that matter, the Vedas, the Quran, or the Buddhist sutras. You *will* find it in Zen writings, and like Whitman, you may have found it in your own adventures in consciousness (possibly as a child on long afternoons, poking aimlessly and timelessly at those ants and stones). Anytime you think you've seen the Great Big Truth, here's how to test it: it must also be visible in all the smallest parts. God is in the details, literally. Look down at the brown ants or the mossy scabs of the worm fence. If your experience is, "Yep, there too," then your truth passes the test. If it's in the drooping brown leaves as well as the stiff, healthy, green ones, and in your own healthy or drooping body, it passes the test.

This kind of awakening has visited many, but Whitman gives us a precise, keen-eyed account. At last the reporter had found the story he was born to report.

•

"I am the poet of the Body and I am the poet of the Soul," Whitman writes. Because everything is the expression of the infinite — of God, of love, of the soul — everything is sacred, including the body, including all its odors and all the parts we hide.

> Welcome is every organ and attribute of me, and of any man hearty
>   and clean,
> Not an inch nor a particle of an inch is vile, and none shall be less
>   familiar than the rest....
> Divine am I inside and out, and I make holy whatever I touch or am
>   touch'd from,
> The scent of these arm-pits aroma finer than prayer,
> This head more than churches, bibles, and all the creeds.

Accordingly, Whitman leads us on a reverential tour of his body parts. It's sometimes amazingly graphic, as it passes from blood to semen to breast to brain to penis and testicles.

> If I worship one thing more than another it shall be the spread of my
> own body, or any part of it …
> You my rich blood! your milky stream pale strippings of my life!
> Breast that presses against other breasts it shall be you!
> My brain it shall be your occult convolutions!
> Root of wash'd sweet-flag! timorous pond-snipe! nest of guarded
> duplicate eggs! it shall be you!

As the tour continues, it becomes impossible to tell whether we're beholding the body of the poet or of the reader ("it shall be you") or of the world. Hay in the field or hair on his head, trickling maple sap or trickling man-sap, brooks and sweat, genitals and wind — it's all a mash-up.

> Mix'd tussled hay of head, beard, brawn, it shall be you!
> Trickling sap of maple, fibre of manly wheat, it shall be you!
> Sun so generous it shall be you!
> Vapors lighting and shading my face it shall be you!
> You sweaty brooks and dews it shall be you!
> Winds whose soft-tickling genitals rub against me it shall be you!…

> I dote on myself, there is that lot of me and all so luscious

If we lose sight of this sense of bodily sacredness, parts of the poem start to border on soft-core porn — particularly section 11, with its vignette of "twenty-eight young men" bathing in a stream, apparently hunky laborers on a break. A rich twenty-eight-year-old spinster, her fine clothes and home in contrast to their naked bodies and bucolic setting, spies on them from her window. The coincidence of the number twenty-eight suggests an invisible connection between her and the men, as well as the four weeks of a woman's menstrual cycle. The primal inner tides that drive us to mate and reproduce surge across the artificial barriers of class and propriety. (This is seventy years before Lady Chatterley went there with the gardener.) When, in her imagination, the spinster breaks free from her inhibitions and joins her fantasy harem, it's with pure joy.

> Dancing and laughing along the beach came the twenty-ninth bather,
> The rest did not see her, but she saw them and loved them.

> The beards of the young men glisten'd with wet, it ran from their long
> hair,
> Little streams pass'd all over their bodies.

An unseen hand also pass'd over their bodies,
It descended tremblingly from their temples and ribs.

Here, with his usual plain language and eye for the right simple details, Whitman makes us see the toned bodies of the men as the rivulets of water, glistening in the sunlight, run between their deeply cut muscles. Our own imagination has joined Whitman's, which has joined the spinster's. We're completely in league with her as, trembling with virginal timidity, she slides her hand down the men's bodies, past their temples and ribs, and keeps heading south. Then at last, as in any juicy bodice-ripper, demure feminine reticence gives way to a frenzy of orgasmic liberation. One advantage of imagination is that you can ravish all your twenty-eight lovers at once.

The young men float on their backs, their white bellies bulge to the
     sun, they do not ask who seizes fast to them,
They do not know who puffs and declines with pendant and bending
     arch,
They do not think whom they souse with spray.

Whitman's own sexuality is a perennial question, shrouded in Victorian evasions. There's some thin evidence of involvement with women, and thick evidence of men, usually unlettered rough-trade types: bus conductors, cab-drivers, longshoremen. The flamboyant Oscar Wilde once visited him from England and said years later, "The kiss of Walt Whitman is still on my lips." Whitman himself was stubbornly unforthcoming. Late in life, when confronted with the plainly homoerotic elements in his work, he denounced the idea as "terrible...damnable...morbid." He also claimed, unconvincingly, to have fathered six illegitimate children.

But that's the Whitman who lived in our world. More important, and far more interesting, is the über-Walt that is the consciousness of the poems: "hankering, gross, mystical, nude." In this matter, as in others, he is bigger than the one who created him. He is *omni*sexual — he wants to merge ecstatically with everyone, everything, the universe, God. Don't you?

•

The sexual frankness of *Leaves of Grass* got it banned in Boston — to the delight of Whitman, who guessed correctly that that would boost sales. Reviewers called it "coarse," "reckless," "lawless," "indecent," "vulgar," "beastly," "degrading," a "gathering of muck," "vilest imaginings," "natural imbecility," "gross obscenity," and "stupid filth." But the book has other themes that, in the mid-nineteenth century, must have been pretty baffling. Nowadays our more expansive perspective, which Whitman helped pioneer, makes it easier to hear them.

Today, for example, the "power of now" has gained enough currency for people to hear —

> There was never any more inception than there is now,
> Nor any more youth or age than there is now,
> And will never be any more perfection than there is now,
> Nor any more heaven or hell than there is now.

Many people today have a sense of the deep rightness of things-as-they-are:

> The moth and the fish-eggs are in their place,
> The bright suns I see and the dark suns I cannot see are in their place,
> The palpable is in its place and the impalpable is in its place.

Many suspect that we're bigger than one little body or one little lifetime:

> All goes onward and outward, nothing collapses,
> And to die is different from what any one supposed, and luckier.

> Has any one supposed it lucky to be born?
> I hasten to inform him or her it is just as lucky to die, and I know it.

> I pass death with the dying and birth with the new-wash'd babe, and
>   am not contain'd between my hat and boots

There are enough people with enough deep meditative experience — who perhaps have struggled to describe it to friends — to appreciate the beauty and subtle precision of this description:

> Apart from the pulling and hauling stands what I am,
> Stands amused, complacent, compassionating, idle, unitary,
> Looks down, is erect, or bends an arm on an impalpable certain rest,
> Looking with side-curved head curious what will come next,
> Both in and out of the game and watching and wondering at it.

There's enough mellow, Zennish relaxation in the air to hear —

> Do I contradict myself?
> Very well then I contradict myself

And there's been enough yearning for crazy anarchic freedom, enough generations of Beats and hippies and yippies and punks, enough rock 'n' roll to hear —

> Unscrew the locks from the doors!
> Unscrew the doors themselves from their jambs!

We also have a yearning for a wider, more inclusive democracy, of which Whitman is the prophet. ("Not till the sun excludes you," he writes in a poem addressed to a prostitute, "do I exclude you.") We see it particularly in section 15 of "Song of Myself," where he leads us on another tour, this time of diverse people in diverse places participating in diverse activities. At a time when Romantic writers were still fetishizing mad geniuses and knights of the Round Table — the cult of the extraordinary — Whitman celebrates the sacred ordinary.

> The duck-shooter walks by silent and cautious stretches,
> The deacons are ordain'd with cross'd hands at the altar,
> …
> The lunatic is carried at last to the asylum a confirm'd case,
> (He will never sleep any more as he did in the cot in his mother's
>   bed-room;)
> …
> The quadroon girl is sold at the auction-stand, the drunkard nods by
>   the bar-room stove, *
> The machinist rolls up his sleeves, the policeman travels his beat, the
>   gate-keeper marks who pass

On it goes, line after line, a panorama of 1850s American society and an astonishingly lucid act of remote seeing: "The squaw," "The connoisseur," "The canal boy," "The bride," "The opium eater."

In a juxtaposition that can't be accidental, "The President" immediately follows, and rhythmically echoes, "The prostitute." Whitman's vision of democracy is both political and sexual, but most of all it's a democracy of spirit, in which all citizens of the universe are equal because they're all the same

---

* Quadroon: one-quarter Black.

essence, "all just as immortal and fathomless as myself." That's implied by the consistent rhythm and the repeated initial "The" that unite this whole section: "The spinning-girl," "The farmer," "The Wolverine." All people in this nation, all beings in this universe, are points on the rim of the mandala of existence. At the hub of the mandala is the self, which we each call "I," and spokes of radiating equivalence connect this I to all other beings.

> And these tend inward to me, and I tend outward to them,
> And such as it is to be of these more or less I am,
> And of these one and all I weave the song of myself.

•

There were people who appreciated *Leaves of Grass* from the beginning. Whitman sent a copy of the first edition to Emerson, who responded with a letter of high praise. Without asking permission, Whitman promptly turned it into a promotional blurb; Emerson was not amused. In 1856, Thoreau spent a month in New Jersey on a surveying job. One day he, along with Bronson Alcott and another friend, ferried over to Brooklyn to visit Whitman, who chatted with them in his untidy, book-strewn bedroom, with drawings of buff Greek gods pasted to the walls, the bed unmade, the chamber pot indiscreetly visible. When Thoreau asked whether Whitman had read the Asian sacred texts, he replied, "No: tell me about them." The meeting was at times awkward, but Whitman gave Thoreau a copy of the new second edition of *Leaves*, which was even spicier than the first. The virginal Thoreau was torn between shock and admiration, but back home in Concord he made a point of carrying the scandalous book around conspicuously, as a flag of defiance.

Whitman spent the Civil War years — his early forties — in Washington, volunteering at the makeshift hospitals set up in government office buildings, overflowing with horrifically maimed and dying soldiers. Amid the piles of amputated limbs and the stench of festering wounds, he comforted the young men, brought them little treats, and helped them write letters to their families and sweethearts. That work aged him rapidly but made him respectable, earning him the moniker "the Good Gray Poet." His poem commemorating Abraham Lincoln's death, "O Captain! My Captain!," showed he was capable of writing perfectly adequate, not particularly interesting rhyming verse. "O Captain!" became his greatest hit; in later life he grew weary of having to trot it out at every public reading.

Whitman suffered a debilitating stroke in 1873 but lived another nineteen years, much of it bedridden in a brother's house in Camden, New Jersey, where he prepared the final edition of *Leaves of Grass*, now grown from the original dozen poems to some four hundred. He received visits from admirers, designed his own mausoleum, and contemplated his leave-taking from the world.

But he had written his most profound leave-taking years before, at the end of "Song of Myself." After that epic celebration of the individual as cosmos, how could he make his exit? It took a messenger from the sky to usher him offstage, to summon him back to the raw, wild churn of existence out of which he, like all of us, had briefly materialized.

> The spotted hawk swoops by and accuses me, he complains of my
> gab and my loitering.
>
> I too am not a bit tamed, I too am untranslatable,
> I sound my barbaric yawp over the roofs of the world.

Then, as the day melts into dusk and the poem melts into silence, the poet himself melts, dissolving into the elements. When someone who loves you dies, if you can get quiet enough and clear enough you may notice that they don't go anywhere. They simply delocalize; they dissolve back to the beingness that they, and we, have been all along. Their essence, now free of the cast-off body and personality, is everywhere. It's up to you to find it. Whitman, the lover of the world, remains ever-findable.

> I depart as air, I shake my white locks at the runaway sun,
> I effuse my flesh in eddies, and drift it in lacy jags.
>
> I bequeath myself to the dirt to grow from the grass I love,
> If you want me again look for me under your boot-soles.
>
> You will hardly know who I am or what I mean,
> But I shall be good health to you nevertheless,
> And filter and fibre your blood.
>
> Failing to fetch me at first keep encouraged,
> Missing me one place search another,
> I stop somewhere waiting for you.

21. Ah, Buddy

J. D. SALINGER

Coffee was unknown in Europe until about the year 1600, when the first beans were imported from North Africa to Venice. Before that, throughout the Middle Ages and into the Renaissance, we can imagine nobles and peasants alike, stumbling about listlessly, peering around corners and behind bushes, muttering, "There must be something else...but I don't know what it is."

That's Holden Caulfield's situation. The anxious, depressed sixteen-year-old narrator-hero of J. D. Salinger's *The Catcher in the Rye* is the embodiment of what my teacher Maharishi used to call "the restlessness of the seeker": the roiling unease of one who finds life profoundly unsatisfactory but doesn't know what's missing. He can only vaguely sense that what's presented as the Good Life, despite its comforts and rewards, is somehow shallow and inauthentic — "phony," to use Holden's word — relative to some as-yet-undefined higher truth, some deeper delight.

This is the life of quiet desperation that Thoreau said the mass of men lead. Usually it's a chronic, low-grade condition that can be conveniently ignored till some crisis, such as a career meltdown or the death of a loved one, renders it acute. But since sensitively tuned adolescents like Holden live in a state of perpetual crisis, their turmoil serves as a nice, dramatic metaphor for our own quieter, less photogenic restlessness. In this sense, *Catcher*, the quintessential novel of adolescent discontent, isn't about adolescence at all.

We see this in the scene at Rockefeller Center, where Holden and the vacuous Sally Hayes, in whom he has a flickering, half-hearted romantic interest, go ice-skating and then sit down for Cokes. Holden imagines out loud going to college and marrying Sally, and the conventional adult existence he'd be stuck in.

> We'd have to go downstairs in elevators with suitcases and stuff. We'd have to phone up everybody and tell 'em good-by and send 'em postcards from hotels and all. And I'd be working in some office, making a lot of dough, and riding to work in cabs and Madison Avenue buses, and reading newspapers, and playing bridge all the time.

Now, none of this, taken item by item, is inherently oppressive. (I've heard bridge is a lot of fun.) But if it's the totality of your life, then yes, all that *stuff* — without the offsetting spacious freedom of boundless Nonstuff — is oppressively claustrophobic.

To the extent that the book *is* about adolescence, its timing was fortunate. It was published in 1951, just as the word *teenager* was coming into wide circulation, and with it the idea that the teen experience is a thing to which attention must be paid. Before that, it was generally considered an awkward transitional passage to be hurried through, head down, as quickly and quietly as possible. Now postwar prosperity was ramping up, suburbs and television were proliferating, and the kids had something good and vapid to rebel against as well as the luxury to rebel against it.

By the time I started teaching English, in the late seventies, *Catcher* was a high school standby. My students were always surprised to learn how old it was. Every generation of teenagers thinks they invented sex, anxiety about sex, fart jokes, swearing, smoking, and cynicism about their lame parents and teachers. From the opening sentence, Holden's narration, with its repetitions and evasions, feels like their inner voice.

> If you really want to hear about it, the first thing you'll probably want to know is where I was born, and what my lousy childhood was like,

and how my parents were occupied and all before they had me, and all that David Copperfield kind of crap, but I don't feel like going into it, if you want to know the truth.

The book's premise is simple. Bright, underachieving Holden flunks out of his Pennsylvania boarding school — not the first school he has flunked out of. He takes the train north to New York and hangs around the city for three days before going home to face his parents. Salinger casts a lonely pall over the journey by having Holden set forth in the dead of a December night.

> When I was all set to go, when I had my bags and all, I stood for a while next to the stairs and took a last look down the goddam corridor. I was sort of crying. I don't know why. I put my red hunting hat on, and turned the peak around to the back, the way I liked it, and then I yelled at the top of my goddam voice, *"Sleep tight, ya morons!"*

In its backhanded way, this gesture makes Holden's mission clear. As Saint Paul writes in Thessalonians, "Let us not be like others, who are asleep, but let us be awake and sober." Holden wouldn't know to put it this way, but he's on the trail of awakening. His hunting hat signifies his commitment to the search, and wearing it backward signifies his willingness to go against the grain, to separate himself from the others, the sleepers.

But when he yells, *"Sleep tight, ya morons!,"* Holden crosses the line between separation and contempt — the kind of wiseass contempt that teenagers are famous for. On the spiritual path, that's a rookie mistake. The stubbornly immature keep doubling down, condemning the stupid world for failing to appreciate their suffering and their genius, for not showering them with attractive girlfriends or boyfriends who find their problems fascinating, for telling them to go clean their room. If they read *The Catcher in the Rye*, they mistake it for an invitation to indulge in Holden's worst tendencies, to persist in their unwinnable war with the world.

·

But Salinger has other plans for his hero. Having set forth from the land of the sleeping, Holden must now cross the no-man's-land of seeking. This is challenging territory, where we've lost the security of our old quasi-blissful ignorance and have not yet reached the real bliss of awakening. (As they say in India, we've left the hut but have not yet reached the palace.) Salinger depicts this psychological landscape as a succession of bleak train stations, seedy hotels, and lounges with bad dance bands. At its lowest depths, it's a landscape of despair.

> It was lousy in the park. It wasn't too cold, but the sun still wasn't out, and there didn't look like there was anything in the park except dog crap and globs of spit and cigar butts from old men, and the benches all looked like they'd be wet if you sat down on them. It made you depressed, and every once in a while, for no reason, you got goose flesh while you walked. It didn't seem at all like Christmas was coming soon. It didn't seem like anything was coming.

As Holden crosses this land, he has lots of random encounters with people — kind and unkind, bright and stupid, helpful and dangerous. Mostly they add to his confusion. Seeking some clarifying wisdom, he calls on a former English teacher, who instead of helping makes a pass at him. Back in the hotel, he makes a date with a low-rent prostitute. In theory, or at least in male fantasy, a prostitute could be a wonderful ministering angel of sexual healing (as in Leonard Cohen's "Sisters of Mercy"), but this one, ironically named Sunny, is so surly and stupid that Holden can't bring himself to connect with her, even physically, and he sinks deeper into depression.

In fact, the only really wise, pure, admirable people in Holden's world are children, specifically his sister Phoebe, who is ten, and his brother Allie, who died at eleven. If taken literally, that's a gloomy prospect for us adults — we're all doomed to corruption. Taken as a metaphor, it points to a way out of the darkness. Jesus says we can enter the kingdom of heaven by being *like* little children. This often happens spontaneously. Perhaps we're making art or playing with our kids, or we're in the woods or in the ocean or in love. One way or another, we relax our grown-up plans and defenses and sophistication, and just be simple. We just be, and we let everything else just be. Then whatever we've been doing takes on the friction-free, lighter-than-air, everything-A-OK quality of transcendence.

Throughout the book, occasional flashes of this transcendence light up the dark. For example, in the depressing Edmont Hotel's depressing Lavender Room, Holden finds himself dancing with a depressingly dopey blonde tourist. But she's a great dancer:

> She was one of the best dancers I ever danced with. I'm not kidding, some of these very stupid girls can really knock you out on the dance floor.

He asks her:

> "You know when a girl's really a terrific dancer?"
>
> "Wudga say?" she said. She wasn't listening to me, even. Her mind was wandering all over the place.
>
> "I said do you know when a girl's really a terrific dancer?"
>
> "Uh-uh."
>
> "Well — where I have my hand on your back. If I think there isn't anything underneath my hand — no can, no legs, no feet, no *any*thing — then the girl's really a terrific dancer."

There it is. Everything becomes like nothing: delicious nothing. In Buddhist terms, form is revealed to be emptiness. Years ago I saw André Watts play some piano concerto with an impossibly wild, high-speed finale. Of course, his technical skills were at the tip-top virtuoso level. But at a certain point there was suddenly nothing there: no skill, no speed (because no time), no piano, no playing, no player, no listener, "no *any*thing," as Holden says — just a sort of weightless *whhhhhhhh*. I've experienced the same thing when face-to-face with awakened sages. Some words were being said, but there was no one saying them, or hearing them. However it happens, it's the same *whhhhhhhh*.

This sublime transcendence can also be found in precisely the kind of ordinary, bourgeois routine that Holden fears: "making a lot of dough, and riding to work in cabs and Madison Avenue buses, and reading newspapers." That's the meaning of the Zen saying, "Before *satori* [realization] we chop wood and carry water. But after satori we chop wood and carry water." If we just add the element of transcendence, we can persist in the most mundane of routines and it no longer closes in on us. It all becomes weightless, spacious, liberative. Like Holden's blonde dance partner, it's OK if it's dopey.

Another aspect of this essential, sanity-saving innocence is conveyed near the end of the book, when Holden sneaks into his family home one night, avoiding his parents. He finds Phoebe "sitting smack in the middle of the bed, outside the covers, with her legs folded like one of those Yogi guys." Clearly, this child is cast as a sage. She has dance music playing softly on the radio and Holden wants her to dance with him, but she insists that he first take off his shoes (as one does before entering a temple or ashram). Her name evokes a sweet little songbird but also Phoebus Apollo, the god of sunlight and of divine, healing truth.

In appropriately childlike terms, Phoebe speaks exactly the truth that

Holden needs to hear. He goes on one of his sad, negative rants — two pages' worth — till she interrupts him to say, "You don't like *any*thing that's happening." That stops him in his tracks. Phoebe has busted him for projecting his own toxic attitude onto the world. She's challenging him to open his eyes and see the world and its people innocently, as they are, in all their unaffected, inescapable goodness and beauty.

Immature seekers operate only on the principle that the kingdom of heaven is inside us, per the Gospel of Luke. In pursuit of inner nirvana, they withdraw from the allegedly crappy outer world, with its cigar butts and globs of spit. But mature seekers know, per the Gospel of Thomas, that the kingdom is both inside us and outside us, that the grace of nirvana embraces everything we thought was the enemy of grace. That's a more advanced vision. It takes longer to see, but it's crucial. Otherwise, start looking for a cave.

Holden receives one more version of this wisdom, and it's the juiciest. Throughout the book, he's been pondering the ducks in Central Park, and what happens to them in winter when their lagoon freezes over.

> I wondered if some guy came in a truck and took them away to a zoo
> or something. Or if they just flew away.

He asks occasional strangers about the fate of the ducks, but none are helpful. The question becomes a kind of koan, a puzzle that Holden must solve to solve the problem of his own life. The question inside the question is, What is a sensitive seeker like Holden to do in a cold, bleak world? Fly away, escape? He does fantasize about hitchhiking out west and working anonymously at some rural gas station, pretending to be "one of those deaf-mutes." He knows that's "crazy," but what's the alternative? Wait to be carted away to some zoo-like institution? In fact, by the story's end, we realize that he's been narrating it from a sanitarium, where he's recovering from the breakdown that the whole book has been building to.

At one point, though, Holden gets into a vomity-smelling cab and asks Horwitz, the hypertensive driver, about the ducks. At first he responds, "How the hell should I know? … How the hell should I know a stupid thing like that?" But then he changes the subject to fish, as if Holden has been asking the wrong question all along.

> The *fish* don't go no place. They stay right where they are, the fish.
> Right in the goddam lake.… They get frozen right in one position
> for the whole winter.… Their bodies take in nutrition and all, right

through the goddam seaweed and crap that's in the ice. They got their *pores* open the whole time. That's their *nature*, for Chrissake. See what I mean?

Holden *doesn't* see what he means, at least not right away. Horwitz means, or rather, Salinger, speaking through Horwitz, means: No, don't try to flee from the world (don't duck out of your problems), and no, don't wait to be rescued. Take the third way, the Dharma way. Stay right where you are.

Horwitz's parable of frozen fish taking in nutrition through their pores may not be scientifically precise — just for starters, I'm pretty sure there's no seaweed in the Central Park lagoon — but it's a highly precise meditation instruction. Don't try to split your experience between "good" (the smell of the wafting incense) and "bad" (the sound of the barking dog). Without judging or filtering, without favoring or resisting, simply rest in the midst of it all. Open your pores to it all. In fact, I've sat with Buddhist lamas who use the phrase "Open all your pores" as part of their guidance. They encourage their students to meditate with eyes wide open, to more rapidly erase the imaginary line between "meditation" and "life," between the kingdom "inside" and the kingdom "outside."

Then whatever shows up to the five senses is fine. Whatever thoughts or feelings show up, fine. By being innocently present to whatever presents itself, you discover that it's all a present, all nutritious and delicious, the kingdom of heaven spread upon the earth. In the Tibetan tradition, this approach is personified by Garuda the Space Eagle, whose name means "devourer." He's always shown triumphantly feasting on venomous snakes — representing the "bad" experiences we usually try to avoid — and metabolizing them into enlightenment. The venom makes his feathers shine.

Does Holden get it? Does he reach the end of the spiritual path by the end of the book? No, but he reaches the end of the beginning. After twenty-five chapters of gloom, there's finally a moment of cathartic ecstasy, while he sits on a bench in Central Park watching Phoebe ride the carousel. It begins to rain.

GARUDA

My hunting hat really gave me quite a lot of protection, in a way, but I got soaked anyway. I didn't care, though. I felt so damn happy all of a sudden, the way old Phoebe kept going around and around. I was damn near bawling, I felt so damn happy, if you want to know the truth.

But the decisive scene is just before this one. Holden has made up his mind to head west, but first he arranges to meet Phoebe outside her school to say goodbye. She appears, "dragging this goddam big suitcase with her" and insists that she's going with him. Moved by her gesture, he at last says, "I'm not going away anywhere. I changed my mind." That's when we know the healing has begun, with the commitment to remain right where one is — like a fish in the ice, like Buddha Gautama beneath the tree — and against all odds, to find the boundless OK-ness of things just as they are.

·

Meeting your favorite writer should probably be disappointing. Writers put the best of themselves into their work, and when it goes really well — when most of their stars are out, as Salinger once put it — something comes through them that is somehow *better* than themselves: wiser, funnier, more life-expanding, more magical. (Reading it later, they say, "Jeez, where'd *that* come from?" Then they wonder if they'll ever be able to do it again.) So if meeting writers is a letdown, it means they've done a good job.

That's what generally happened to the earnest pilgrims who made their way to Cornish, New Hampshire, to stake out Salinger's driveway and pester him about the meaning of life. What they found was a grumpy, half-deaf old man, annoyed at being harassed by people who refused to believe he'd put everything he knew about that subject, and more, into his books.

Salinger just wanted to do his job. When the success of *The Catcher in the Rye* threatened to make him a celebrity, he moved from New York to his Cornish farmhouse so he could write undisturbed, and he lived there till his death in 2010. With rare exceptions, he gave no interviews, but he was neither a hermit-sage nor a wacko recluse. He had friends (well, a few). He had, eventually, three wives and two children. Despite his experiments with alternative diets, he had a weakness for flame-broiled Whoppers. He liked to watch sports, Hitchcock films, the Marx Brothers, and *I Love Lucy*.

He was an NYU dropout from a family of Jewish cheese merchants. He had once courted Eugene O'Neill's debutante daughter Oona. (She was dating Orson Welles at the same time, but dumped them both to marry Charlie

Chaplin.) Salinger was also a World War II veteran who had fought in the D-Day landing and the Battle of the Bulge and had walked into a concentration camp at Dachau just after liberation. He later told his daughter, "You never really get the smell of burning flesh out of your nose entirely, no matter how long you live." He was hospitalized for combat trauma and soon afterward took up Zen practice.

Then, in 1951, the same year that *Catcher* was published, he started studying Vedanta, the pinnacle system of Indian philosophy, with its direct pointing to boundlessness through insight and meditation. His teacher was Swami Nikhilananda, who taught just two blocks from the Park Avenue apartment where Salinger had grown up. The swami also led summer seminars in an idyllic Victorian cottage on an island in the Saint Lawrence River. That seems to be the place where Salinger's spiritual flame was most incandescently lit, and which inspired him to find his own rural refuge in New Hampshire.

Eventually Salinger had other spiritual enthusiasms, but Vedanta was his mainstay. He became good friends with Swami Nikhilananda and wrote him letters over the years, sometimes lamenting his lack of spiritual advancement. But at some point he realized that even if he never became an awakened sage himself, perhaps, if most of his stars were out, he could create one on the page.

Salinger's sage is Seymour Glass, whose name is a pun and a query. What happens when we see more, when our vision penetrates deeper than other people's, as if looking through glass? Can we handle that much vision without shattering like glass? Can we live in a world that wasn't built for buddhas, and can that world live with us? These are the questions that Salinger explores through a series of Glass family short stories and novellas, most of which were published in the *New Yorker* between 1948 and 1965, and later collected in three books.*

Seymour is, like Salinger, a traumatized war veteran, and in his first appearance ("A Perfect Day for Bananafish"), he's trapped in a marriage to a woman who understands neither the darkness he has confronted nor the light it has spurred him to reach. Her name, Muriel, is also a pun. Like a mural, she's prettily painted (her defining activity is doing her nails), but communicating with her is like talking to a wall. Seymour's response ultimately is to blow his brains out.

---

*   They should be read in order: (1) *Nine Stories*, (2) *Franny and Zooey*, and (3) *Raise High the Roofbeam, Carpenters, and Seymour — An Introduction*. Then, if you really want to follow Salinger into deep space, go online and find the June 19, 1965, issue of the *New Yorker*. It contains the uncollected (and, some readers conclude, unhinged) story "Hapworth 16, 1924."

But his end is his beginning. Salinger, for the rest of his writing life, continued to revisit and reevaluate Seymour in absentia, through the legacy and recollections of his singular family. We eventually learn that Seymour was the eldest of seven brilliant children, all of whom were star contestants on the radio quiz show *It's a Wise Child*. He was also the family guru, deeply immersed in the enlightenment texts of East and West, and took it upon himself to spiritually educate his younger siblings.

He had long earlobes like the Buddha's. He failed to show up for his own wedding, not because he was afraid or upset, but because he was too happy. Once he told his brother Buddy, "All we do our whole lives is go from one little piece of Holy Ground to the next." He wrote in his diary, "I'm a kind of paranoiac in reverse. I suspect people of plotting to make me happy." The more fully his portrait as a young buddha is fleshed out, the more imponderable his suicide becomes. But ponder it we must, and his family must. It becomes another koan.

Perhaps the easiest way to explain his suicide, or explain it away, is to attribute it to Salinger's initially sketchy understanding of enlightenment. It's heavily marbled with bad Emersonism, where the sage is, by definition, a brilliant nonconformist in heroic conflict with the mediocrity of society. That reduces enlightenment to an attitude, a slightly more sophisticated version of Holden's *"Sleep tight, ya morons!"* The real thing is deeper than that. It's the silence that we *are*, and which everyone else is. While wannabe buddhas scramble to shore up their fragile edifice of attitude, real buddhas relax in the Great Ease. Through the various Glass family members, Salinger eventually hashes these things out.

Of course, it's easier for us to judge Salinger's understanding now, with sixty-some additional years of awakening practice under our collective belt. That's partly thanks to Salinger himself, who had the chutzpah to inject unapologetic Dharma teachings into elite literary fiction, and from there into a thoroughly unready American society.

In 1953, with Joe McCarthy at the height of his loathsome power and "(How Much Is That) Doggie in the Window?" at the top of the Hit Parade, the *New Yorker* published "Teddy," whose ten-year-old main character spouts straight-up Vedanta philosophy. Teddy is on a trans-Atlantic cruise with his family and is, if anything, a more perfectly realized sage than Seymour. In a modern equivalent of Christ's Sermon on the Mount or the Buddha's Discourse in the Deer Park, Teddy gives a sort of Chat on the Deck Chair, in which he explains to a skeptical but curious adult how our multi-lifetime enlightenment journey works. (In passing, he recalls a previous incarnation as a yogi in India who was lured off his spiritual path by a woman.) Teddy says that no one should be afraid to die, since "Everybody's done it thousands and thousands of times," and by the end of the story he shows that his fearlessness is not just talk.

All this post-*Catcher* work, freed from Holden's carping adolescent voice, is richer, more sophisticated, with convoluted, playfully self-conscious sentences that keep getting longer, loopier, and funnier.

> By the time Seymour was in mid-adolescence — sixteen, seventeen — he not only had learned to control his native vernacular, his many, many less than élite New York speech mannerisms, but had by then already come into his own true, bull's-eye, poet's vocabulary. His non-stop talks, his monologues, his near-harangues then came as close to pleasing from start to finish — for a good many of us, anyway — as, say, the bulk of Beethoven's output after he ceased being encumbered with a sense of hearing, and maybe I'm thinking especially, though it seems a trifle picky, of the B-flat-major and C-sharp-minor quartets.

In one droll gesture, Salinger, speaking through Buddy Glass, the family's resident writer, says, "Please accept from me this unpretentious bouquet of very early-blooming parentheses: (((()))))." That bouquet might well be Salinger's model of the human mind, which his prose aspires to reproduce: thought within thought within thought within thought, at the inmost core of which is perfect, fragrant emptiness. In that same spirit of dizzy, trippy fun, Buddy also reveals that he is the author of *The Catcher in the Rye* and several other works that we had foolishly attributed to Salinger.

Finally, when the Glass geniuses realize how they can stand to live with the rest of us — by holding us in love rather than contempt — the stories become moving. In *Franny and Zooey*, Zooey Glass, Seymour's youngest brother, has to talk his sister Franny down from a life crisis. She's convinced that her chosen profession (acting) is pointless, and that, in this world of shallow people, anything we might do (action) is also pointless.

In answer, Zooey tells her about the time he was about to appear on *It's a Wise Child* and Seymour insisted that he shine his shoes first. When young Zooey objected — no one sees your shoes on the radio — Seymour told him "to shine them for the Fat Lady." He never explained who the Fat Lady was, but Zooey had his own vision of her.

> I had her sitting on this porch all day, swatting flies, with her radio going full-blast from morning till night. I figured the heat was terrible, and she probably had cancer.

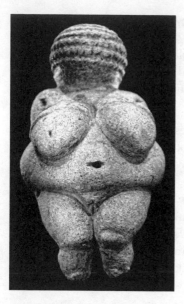

GOD THE MOTHER (VENUS OF
WILLENDORF, PALEOLITHIC
LIMESTONE FIGURINE)

At the same time, considering Seymour's cosmic perspective, it's tempting to connect the Fat Lady with God the Mother, the Infinitely Voluptuous One, who, in the ancient traditions, births us all, feeds us all, *is* us all.

Zooey tells Franny to act for the Fat Lady. Then, talking to himself as much as to her,* he adds something that may be helpful to remember when *we* find our fellow earthlings unbearably vapid and our life on earth weary, stale, flat, and unprofitable.

There isn't anyone *any*where that isn't Seymour's Fat Lady. Don't you know that? Don't you know that goddam secret yet? And don't you know — *listen* to me, now — *don't you know who that Fat Lady really is?*...Ah, buddy. Ah, buddy. It's Christ Himself. Christ Himself, buddy.

The Fat Lady, we could say, is all beings, with all their suffering, which is always as real and important as our own. And all beings, no matter how easy it may seem to dismiss them as too bourgeois or ignorant, too woke or MAGA, too *x* or *y*, are exactly the sacred that we seek. Ah, buddy. Christ Himself, buddy.

So here's the wisdom you might have received if you'd accosted Salinger on his driveway...and if he'd turned up his hearing aid to listen...and if, for once, he didn't mind repeating what he'd already spelled out in his books. Whatever you do, offer it up. Negotiating peace in the Middle East, taking out the garbage — doesn't matter, offer it up, to God or infinity or the universe. Offer it up to the Fat Lady. Then it doesn't matter if what you do is big or small, or if it succeeds or fails. You're doing it not for the result but for the offering. What matters is that you act impeccably. Shine your shoes.

---

* As all spiritual teachers do, by the way.

22. Look Again

KEY, ROGERS & FRANKLIN · THREE ANTHEMS

> "Begin at the beginning," the King said, very gravely,
> "and go on till you come to the end: then stop."
>
> — Lewis Carroll, *Alice's Adventures in Wonderland*

A word before we come to the end…

I hope our little excursion has helped open your eyes a bit wider to the radiance of the infinite, not only everywhere in literature, but everywhere in everything. Perhaps you'll be inspired to find the Dharma of gardening or drumming or software development, or whatever you get up in the morning and do. It's there, guaranteed.

You may also be inspired to continue your Dharma explorations in literature. We've only looked at English-language writers, but there's plenty to find in, say, Sappho, Sophocles, Lady Murasaki, Dante, Cervantes, Sor Juana,

Proust, Rilke, Kafka, Neruda. There are also those who wrote in English but whom I couldn't include without this book running to many more hundreds of pages. Just for starters, juicy prospects include Edith Wharton (*The Age of Innocence*), James Joyce (*Ulysses*, if you have a year to spare, and *Finnegans Wake* if you have several years), and the poetry of Elizabeth Bishop and William Carlos Williams.

One place to go next could be Vladimir Nabokov's *Pale Fire*. The whole story is told as a series of apparently insane footnotes to a 999-line poem, which begins with this stunning image of a bird meeting its death and/or nirvana:

> I was the shadow of the waxwing slain
> By the false azure in the windowpane;
> I was the smudge of ashen fluff — and I
> Lived on, flew on, in the reflected sky.

JACK KEROUAC, CIRCA 1956

I'm also leaving you on your own with Jack Kerouac. Kerouac lived and wrote such a hopped-up mix of revelation and commotion, of luminous joy and baffled joyride, that it's probably best to jump right into *On the Road* or *The Dharma Bums* or *Visions of Gerard* without anyone trying to sort it out for you. Let Jack be Jack. But I've felt his spirit hitchhiking its way through this book. Most of the writers here lived some version of Kerouac's beat-up, beatific adventure, dancing or stumbling their way "to a plank where all the Angels dove off and flew into infinity."

•

We can't conclude our exploration without considering the one literary work that, here in the USA, is experienced the most times by the most people, year after year: our national anthem. It is, we could say, our national mantra, the one sound in which, by tradition, we join our voices and our hearts to collectively vibrate our shared American essence, whatever that might be.

That's the idea, anyway. But "The Star-Spangled Banner" has, understandably, fallen on hard times. Francis Scott Key, the lawyer and presidential advisor who wrote the words after witnessing a battle in the War of 1812, did own half a dozen slaves. True, he freed them all during his lifetime, but he also prosecuted people for possessing abolitionist literature. On the other hand, he represented (pro bono) freedmen and slaves seeking their freedom, and he convinced a newspaper editor that slavery was "radically wrong." Once again, people are complicated.

There's also that notorious bit in the third verse:

No refuge could save the hireling and slave
From the terror of flight, or the gloom of the grave.

This couplet has been widely assumed to celebrate the indiscriminate murder of enslaved people. But that makes no sense: they were, after all, considered valuable property. Rather, it celebrates the killing of enemy soldiers in battle, some of whom were mercenaries ("hirelings") or former slaves. (Black soldiers fought on both sides.) In fact, the word *slave* here may well have nothing to do with involuntary servitude. For centuries, it was an all-purpose insult. Several characters in Shakespeare, none of whom are enslaved, are called "drunken slave," "mindless slave," "devilish slave," "cold-blooded slave," "rascally slave," and so forth. Banquo's last words, addressed to the thug that Macbeth has sent to kill him, are simply "O slave!"

In any case, the second, third, and fourth verses exist on paper, but for at least 150 years they haven't been part of the mantra as Americans sing it. In Isaac Asimov's short story "No Refuge Could Save," an intelligence officer in World War II exposes an overprepared German spy by discovering that he knows all four verses, as no real American would.

The anthem does sound like a triumphant military tune — a confident, assertive march. But on a closer listen, it yields some major surprises. It's actually a waltz, and it asserts nothing. Rather than marching in a straight line toward the next conquest, it sashays and whirls in 3/4 time, in unpredictable directions, and it ends with a question mark. Like a koan, it's a question that's perpetually unanswered: open-ended, ever-unfolding.

It's not GI Joe stuff. This country, in fact, is a woman. The name America — our nation's *bija-mantra*, our seed or essence mantra — is female. The deity form that embodies her is the gigantic Liberty goddess in New York Harbor. Our macho national posturing is like the *travesti* roles of nineteenth-century opera, in which a female character poses as a male to accomplish some daring feat, such as rescuing her husband from prison. In the end she reveals her true nature: the compassionate, nurturing qualities of female wisdom.

America obviously has a lot of macho, warlike history. We've done both necessary things and terrible things. As Senator Cory Booker puts it, "If America hasn't broken your heart, you don't love her enough." But now, for a happy finale (our continued survival, and the world's), it's time to shed this man-drag and revert to essence: to summon our mother wisdom and feed the hungry, care for the earth and water and air, make peace, and perhaps even help lead others to deepest peace. The Statue of Liberty's pose is not static. She's in midstride, going places, leaving broken shackles and chains at her feet. Her full name is *Liberty Enlightening the World*, and rays of light emanate from her head, indicating the wide-open crown chakra of the awakened.

The history behind the anthem is well-known. On September 3, 1814, Key and another American boarded a British ship in Baltimore Harbor to negotiate on behalf of President Madison for the release of some American prisoners. During a polite dinner with the British officers, Key and his companion overheard the plans for the imminent bombardment of Fort McHenry. Now they knew too much and were required to remain onboard till morning. If the Brits took the fort, which guarded the city of Baltimore, they'd have a good chance of retaking their former colony.

Through a long night of heavy rain and constant bombardment, the two Americans waited anxiously for the dawn to reveal that the Stars and Stripes still flew over the fort. That morning, Key wrote the poem "Defence of Fort McHenry," which was soon set to the tune of an old English drinking song, "To Anacreon in Heaven," a melody so popular that it had already been used for more than eighty songs.

BOMBARDMENT OF FORT MCHENRY

But there's a resonance to the anthem that goes deeper than this history. "O say can you see" is the question we've been asking throughout this book, the question repeatedly asked in the Dharma. Do you truly *see*? Do you perceive the ultimate reality of your world and of your own existence? That's been hard during our dark night of ignorance, but now, "by the dawn's early light," with the first glimmers of our awakening, we catch the first thrilling glimpses.

Yet there's some déjà vu to those glimpses. If the darkness were really all-enveloping, we'd never be able to see our way out of it. We wouldn't know what to look for. But because the infinite is our own nature — more truly *us* than our body, thoughts, emotions, or personality — we have a primal memory of it, like the oldest of old friends. We recognize it, re-cognize it. We've seen it before, "at the twilight's last gleaming."

This familiarity is dramatized in a story about Gautama, the Buddha-to-be. After his years of starving and torturing his body in his quest for enlightenment, Gautama suddenly remembered something that happened when he was seven years old. His father and his father's workmen were plowing the fields, and the boy was left sitting in the shade of a rose-apple tree. In that easygoing summer's-day state of mind, left quietly by himself, perhaps lulled by the repetitive motion of the plowmen back and forth across the field, he slipped naturally into samadhi.

This memory showed him that his strained approach to awakening was counterproductive, that the direct path is to let yourself settle naturally. Straining overshoots the mark. With that insight, Gautama accepted the meal offered by the village girl Sujata, then sat down under the fig tree to meditate till he became Buddha, the awakened one.

I've found over the years of teaching meditation that when people have their "first" clear taste of transcendence, they often say something like, "Oh — *that!*" They find themselves recalling an earlier first taste from childhood, when with no training or intention at all — while, say, riding their bike in the morning light or playing alone in the backyard — they settled into their own being, just like young Gautama. It's the most natural thing in the world, and it's the first step into a life of enlightenment.

That life is embodied here by the flag, with its "broad stripes and bright stars." The stripes, fiery red and cool white, suggest the horizontal plane of life, the material world, with all its vying dualities of war and peace, contraction and expansion, assertion and acceptance (as on the hat of Dr. Seuss's cat). The stars, floating in their dark blue field, suggest the vertical plane, the transcendent heavens to which we aspire, the unchanging beingness that is the silent witness of all the turbulent change (like Keats's bright star). Together, the stars and stripes make up the wholeness of life, Krishna's Yogastah kuru karmani.

Firmly established in the boundless sky of universal being, act boldly on your particular battlefield of doing.

Until we're firmly established, that vision keeps getting lost in the darkness and confusion of "the perilous fight." But even then we may get flashes of it. That's portrayed in the poem's most striking image:

> And the rockets' red glare, the bombs bursting in air
> Gave proof through the night that our flag was still there

Throughout the battle, all of Baltimore was under blackout conditions. The bombs and rockets that Key saw intermittently illuminating the flag were, of course, launched by the British as they shelled the fort. Sometimes it's when the fort of our own life is under attack, illuminated by the incendiary energy of the danger itself, that the vision of wholeness is revealed. It's easy to feel complacently enlightened-ish when our health is good, our kids are happy, our country's at peace, and we've got money in the bank. But the real proof of our unshakable nature comes in the dark night, when our life is most shaken.

When you get sick or get fired, when your big project or your cherished relationship hits the rocks, when you're in a foul mood and all the teachings ring hollow, that's the time to ask yourself, to *look* and ask yourself, *Through all these changes, what remains the same? Amid all this loss, what is it I never lose, and* can *never lose?* That's it, that simple, irreducible beingness, that I-awareness that's aware of foul moods and fair moods and remains untouched by both. One of my Dharma teachers used to say, "Everything that *can* be shaken *should* be shaken." Then what remains is the real thing. Rest in that.

The same holds true for society. Many things about America that we used to take for granted have been shaken. You who read these words somewhere in the near or distant future know more than I do about how it all turned out. Meanwhile, I watch the sky for proof through the night.

> O say does that star-spangled banner yet wave
> O'er the land of the free and the home of the brave?

When I was little, if another kid in the schoolyard or on the bus tried to boss you around, your standard reply was, "It's a free country!" Only years later did it occur to me that kids in other countries might not have that expression. Even when America hasn't deserved it, she's somehow continued to stand for a spirit of freedom that has inspired people throughout the world. Will that spirit survive? Does that banner still wave? We'll see where this waltz takes us.

That question reaches its apex of dramatic tension in the last line, with "O'er the land of the free." Of course, "free" is the word that makes "The Star-Spangled Banner" famously hard to sing, an octave and a half above the lowest note. Actually, "red glare" is sung on the same note, but "free" sounds higher because it comes at the song's climactic moment, because *ee* is the brightest, most silvery vowel sound in our language, and because it's held with a long sustain, like some miraculously levitating orb. It *should* be hard to sing. As we approach it we should wonder, Will we make it? Freedom in this world is not preserved casually, and its name should not be pronounced casually. But when someone gets it gloriously right (like Whitney Houston at Super Bowl XXV), it brings us together in a rare, shimmering moment of communal transcendence.

The bright-starry heaven within us has always been the land of the free, even in countries ruled by mad kings. For those of us in the once-and-future sangha, job one has always been finding that sublime inner promised land and helping others find it. Then comes job two — to grow some outer version of that freedom, on earth as it is in heaven. That's the hard part. That's why, if we can manage it, it's called the home of the brave.

•

But OK, maybe, despite its profound beauty, the days of "The Star-Spangled Banner" as a unifying tune are over. People have been proposing alternatives for years, but the main candidates have problems of their own. "This Land Is Your Land" sounds way too much like socialist summer camp to bring the nation together, and "God Bless America" is Irving Berlin at his cornball worst. It's also a reversion to the barbaric idea of God as a big man with miraculous blessing powers that can be turned on and off like a spigot, and which he should shower on America but not necessarily on those other crummy countries.

For Irving Berlin at his brilliant best, we could consider "Blue Skies." (Cue the Willie Nelson recording, please.) The Prajñaparamita Sutra defines enlightenment as "the spontaneous experience of all possible forms as equivalent to open space." (Not just all forms, but all *possible* forms. We don't have to worry about some new boogeyman exception lurking around the next corner.) This song celebrates precisely that experience, where blue skies are all we see and they smile at us: the spaciousness that surrounds and pervades us is the essence of joy. Some intuition of this open space and this joy is the deep root of the can-do optimism that is probably Americans' most distinctive virtue.*

For a reggae spin on the same theme, we could consider "I Can See Clearly Now," which, right from the title, is an explicit declaration of enlightenment, an affirmative answer to Key's question, "O say can you see?" An anthem should at minimum rouse its citizenry out of the blahs, and if you play either the Johnny Nash or the Jimmy Cliff recording and dance along, it's hard to be depressed. I love the idea of whole stadiums full of people doing that.

Or how about doing a full 180, from Key's battle scene to a love song? We've learned that love is not a crazy, obsessive, exclusive emotion but rather our intimate not-two-ness with every human and seashell and thunderclap in the universe. With that in mind, listen to the gorgeous Harold Arlen–Ted Koehler standard "Let's Fall in Love" as sung by Nat King Cole. Cole's serene baritone is the sonic equivalent of that intimacy. It reveals the song as a Dharma hymn, an invitation to sink, settle, surrender, *fall* — out of our illusory separateness and into our shared God-is-love wholeness. Love, the song says, is our essence, what "our hearts are made of." One line even invites us to find paradise by closing our eyes.

Still, it would be lovely to have an anthem that sprang directly from, and is saturated with, the consciousness of a *bodhisattva* — an enlightened one who embodies limitless compassion for all beings. Arguably, we had such a person who wrote such a song.

A bodhisattva who decided to manifest in twentieth-century America, intent on leading as many people as possible from sadness and confusion into light, might well have shown up not in a church or ashram but on television — and on *children's* television, to reach people while they're still neurologically fresh and pliable. Our TV sage could model a relaxed, mindful pace, allowing plenty of silence to breathe around all the action and words, giving patient little commonsense chats, and perhaps singing little songs to dispel the exaggerated fears that can turn sweet children into warped adults.

That's what Fred Rogers did on *Mister Rogers' Neighborhood*, in 895 episodes from 1968 to 2001. In the great work of enlightening the world, he probably accomplished more than many official buddhas and saints. I

---

*   All the music cited in this chapter can be found on YouTube and elsewhere. Irving Berlin wrote over eight hundred songs, including "White Christmas" and "Cheek to Cheek," but this was his favorite. It debuted in a 1926 Broadway show that flopped, but on opening night the audience demanded twenty-four encores of "Blue Skies," till the exhausted singer could no longer remember the words and Berlin belted them out from the first row.

interviewed him once some thirty years ago, and I can testify that he transmitted the same kind of presence as card-carrying gurus and sages I've been face to face with. At some point, he managed to turn the interview around and make it about me, leading me to a recognition of my own inextinguishable inner goodness. By the end of the session I was in tears, good tears.*

Like "The Star-Spangled Banner," his theme song, "Won't You Be My Neighbor?," poses a perpetually unanswered question. But unlike our current anthem, with its setting of nighttime bombardment, this song is daylit and tranquil. It starts by declaring that it's a beautiful day. In Mr. Rogers's world it's *always* a beautiful day, and it has nothing to do with the weather. Life, as seen with clear eyes, is inherently beautiful — nothing but blue skies do we see.

Where is this seeing to take place? "In this neighborhood," *this* one, wherever we are. That's the key idea of all Mr. Rogers's work: the world as neighborhood, as sangha, the beloved community, something that we're all in together, the universal ecosystem in which we're all citizens. Of course that includes himself. Some midcentury children's TV hosts (like the terrifying Chucko the Birthday Clown) came on with a raucous, condescending "Hey, kids!" but Mr. Rogers used a gentle "Hello, neighbor." And although he was clearly the wise adult in the room, the mister, he started each episode by singing

this song while coming through the door and changing from his grownup's sport jacket and leather shoes to kid-friendly sweater and sneakers. (The sweaters were knit by his mom.)

In the second verse, we go from "a beautiful day in this neighborhood" to "a neighborly day in this beauty-wood." Yes, that's some lighthearted nonsense to get everyone relaxed before we take on hard topics like the death of our goldfish. But it also subtly implies our nonseparateness, in which (per Whitman) "every atom belonging to me as good belongs to

---

* No, Fred Rogers wasn't a sniper in the military. Yes, he was an ordained minister, but he never preached religion: his TV work was his ministry. Yes, he became a vegetarian because he didn't want to eat anything that had a mother.

you." The individual (neighbor), the environment (neighborhood, wood), and the sublime ananda that is the nature of both (beauty) all run playfully together into the one organism they've always been. *Thou shalt love thy neighbor as thyself* — not just as *much* as thyself, but *as* thyself. In the closed system of any neighborhood (home, school, world), the truth of our not-two-ness keeps playing out in the way everything we do comes back to us. What we call karma is the discovery that when the right hand slaps the left hand, they both hurt. So don't.

In the song's bridge, the repeated keyword is "always." Mr. Rogers has always, he tells us, wanted a neighbor like us. Again, it's a declaration of primal, preexisting truth. We're wanted (we're loved) even before we show up. That means our lovability doesn't depend on anything outside the simple fact of our being. As Mr. Rogers often reassured us, "You make each day a special day. You know how? By just your being you."

If only we could all meet on this basis — this recognition of our shared intrinsic divinity — we could save the world. The song, in its final lines, seems to recognize the urgency of this mission, entreating us to "make the most of this beautiful day." The intrinsic beauty of existence presents us with a choice. Like Huck Finn, we've got to decide betwixt two things. We can make the most of this opportunity, open ourselves to that beauty, give up to it, live up to it, let it shine through us in the way we see and treat ourselves and others. Or like so many generations before us, we can turn away from the beauty and pull everyone into another cycle of needless misery.

That's urgent. As the song closes, Mr. Rogers repeats the word "please" three times. He *pleads*, "Won't you be my neighbor?" It all could be so easy.

•

People who spotted Fred Rogers in public were known to break into spontaneous, happy choruses of "Won't You Be My Neighbor?," which puts it well on its way to anthemic status. Still, we can be forgiven if we find ourselves wanting something that, well, rocks a bit harder.

One warm Saturday evening I was riding my Vespa down Main Street in Santa Monica. At a red light I pulled up beside a big, blue Cadillac convertible full of ladies ready to party, twenty-somethings in little black dresses, splendidly dolled up. Their sound system was pumped to 11, they were all bopping ecstatically, and just as the light turned green they sang-yelled in unison with Aretha Franklin, "R-E-S-P-E-C-T! Find out what it means to me!" — and tore off into the night.

So...we have one final nominee.

The premise is similar to that of the Mr. Rogers song. To be good neighbors is to respect one another. But Otis Redding's original 1965 version of "Respect," despite its up-tempo setting and funky horn section, is a lament. The crucial, and surprising, lyric is in the second verse. After all those strutting rock and R&B numbers about how I better not catch you fooling around with another man, here Otis tells his woman, "You can do me wrong, honey, if you wanna," as long as she only does it while he's gone and shows a little respect when he comes home. That's humiliating. His pleas for respect sound desperate, hopeless. He's "got to, got to have it," but clearly he won't get it.

Aretha will get it. She and her sisters (backup singers Erma and Carolyn Franklin) tweaked a few words of the lyric, created a killer arrangement, and injected the song with a whole different attitude, remaking it into a sassy declaration of respect as something they insist on, whether we're ready or not. Thanks to them, the song has been an anthem of civil rights and women's rights since 1967, but it can work as an anthem for us all.

Otis's complaint goes beyond the relationship with his woman. It's really a complaint to life, an admission of defeat and utter futility: No matter what I do, I know I'm screwed. All I ask is that life's relentless malevolence not be right in my face, that it screw me behind my back, but I probably won't be spared even that shred of dignity. When Aretha answers his version with hers, she answers not only on behalf of women but on behalf of life. And yes, she's qualified — come on, she's the Queen of Soul, and ultimately she graduated to Goddess, huge and magnificent at the Obama inauguration, crowned with that giant bow that no mere mortal could get away with.

In her reworking of the crucial second verse, Aretha upends Otis's assumption of malevolence. "I ain't gonna do you wrong while you're gone," she sings, not as a grudging concession, but because "I don't wanna." On the human level, this is · enlightened ethics, morality that's as natural as breathing. The thou-shalt-nots of religion exist to regulate our behavior while we still see others as *other*, ripe for exploitation. As we grow to see them as nonseparate from us, and as we grow unshakably happy without exploiting anyone, the rules and

regs become redundant. No killing? No stealing? No adultery? No problem. I don't wanna.

On the cosmic level, "I don't wanna" means our Goddess is a merciful Goddess, offering us the bounty of existence — as Aretha puts it, all her money, as well as her kisses, sweeter than honey. The Hindus call her Lakshmi, among other names, and depict her with a stream of gold coins flowing from her hands. Virginia Woolf, as we've seen, calls her Mrs. Ramsay, with "plenty for everybody." Salinger calls her the Fat Lady. If you're reading these words, against all odds the universe has raised you, grown you, gotten you this far. If you die in the next moment, that's still been a lot of love.

Gratitude, then, is appropriate. Life is good. If it doesn't look good to you, that's understandable too. When you see only the surface of life, the phenomena in space and time, then yep, there's a lot of unredeemed suffering. Then life's a bitch, not a Goddess, and then we die. Seeing the essential goodness of the nonphenomenal being that underlies all phenomena does take some deeper, clearer vision. That's why it's called enlightenment, and that's the Dharma project.

Meanwhile, as we'll see when our vision clears up, we've been cared for all along. Here's the promise, straight from Goddess, or God, or the universe, whatever inadequate expression you prefer:

> I will lead the blind by a road they do not know; by paths they have not known I will guide them. I will turn the darkness before them into light, the rough places into level ground. These are the things I will do, and I will not forsake them.
> — Isaiah 42:16

And all she asks of you is a little respect. Just a little bit.

What, actually, does that mean? *Re-spectate*: re-look, look back, look again. See what you've overlooked. You don't see the path and the light and the level ground that have been prepared for you? Look again. You don't see God smiling at you through the eyes of your child or your dog, your ex or your unfavorite politician? Look again. You don't see boundless invisible love, silently laughing through each moment, even as you frantically try to change the flat tire on your way to the job interview? Look again. You don't see that banner yet waving, or the imagined boundaries of your own consciousness melting? Close your eyes and look again.

What have we done for these twenty-two chapters but take a lot of old books and look again? Now we've come full circle, back to Blake, who advised us to see a world in a grain of sand and heaven in a wildflower. You don't see that yet? Look again and repeat as needed. Don't worry, God will wait for you: she's got all the time in the world. Meanwhile, look again at yourself and your fellow beings, and if you don't yet see us all as the same one pure light, just assume it for now and treat everyone accordingly.

Kerouac said, "All is well, practice kindness, heaven is nigh."

Simple.

OK then. See you around. Thanks for playing.

Acknowledgments

I am deeply grateful to my agent, Lisa Hagan, for believing in my unusual vision from the beginning; to my editor, Jason Gardner, who nurtured my best ideas and saved me from my worst; and to the entire team at New World Library, for taking such extraordinary, loving care in every step of making this book.

Many friends have aided and abetted this project in various ways, including Katherine Bailey, Fu-Ding Cheng, Cynthia Evans, Jess Fallon, Adam Ferrara, Michael Frederick and Brent Ranalli of the Thoreau Society, Daniel Jackson, the late Bob Morrison (happy trails, my friend), Carl Norman, Lauren Rosenberg, Ted Schultz, Keira Schwartz, Sara Sgarlat, Dave Stanton, and in particular my brother scribblers Michael Ames and Phil Goldberg. Rupert Spira provided important early encouragement and remains an exemplar of impeccable, compassionate pointing to nondual reality.

Thank you also to my sangha brothers and sisters, past and present, east and west, live and virtual, and to my students and colleagues at the Pingry School 1977–2010. A special shout-out to Jim Handlin, who somehow knew I could teach before I did, and to the late headmaster H. Westcott Cunningham III (I didn't make that up), who took a chance on turning an imperfectly refurbished hippie loose in the classroom. Big thanks as well to the students and faculty of Maharishi International University 1973–75, and to my fellow pioneering MIU teaching assistants, a.k.a. the Dirty Dozen.

Thank you, thank you to the family I've been unreasonably blessed with, the whole rowdy Lerea-Dach-Sluyter-Peasley-Rosenberg *mishpucha*.

Deepest gratitude to my teachers, as always, and to the brilliant writers whose work it has been my privilege to contemplate.

And to Yaffa... *Whooooooshhh*.

Selected Bibliography

Abbott, Edwin A. *The Annotated Flatland: A Romance of Many Dimensions.* Edited by Ian Stewart. New York: Basic Books, 2008.

Ackroyd, Peter. *Shakespeare: The Biography.* New York: Nan A. Talese, 2005.

Allen, Charles. *The Search for the Buddha: The Men Who Discovered India's Lost Religion.* New York: Carroll & Graf Publishers, 2003.

Bair, Deirdre. *Samuel Beckett: A Biography.* New York: Harcourt, Brace, Jovanovich, 1978.

Borges, Jorge Luis. *A Personal Anthology.* New York: Grove Press, 1968.

Fields, Rick. *How the Swans Came to the Lake: A Narrative History of Buddhism in America.* Boston: Shambhala, 1992.

Genoways, Ted, ed. "Whitman's *Leaves of Grass* at 150." Special issue, *Virginia Quarterly Review* 81, no. 2 (spring 2005).

Goldberg, Philip. *American Veda: From Emerson and the Beatles to Yoga and Meditation — How Indian Spirituality Changed the West.* New York: Harmony Books, 2010.

Harding, Walter. *The Days of Henry Thoreau: A Biography.* New York: Dover Publications, 1982.

Knowlson, James. *Damned to Fame: The Life of Samuel Beckett.* New York: Simon & Schuster, 1996.

McDowell, Marta. *Emily Dickinson's Gardens: A Celebration of a Poet and a Gardener.* New York: McGraw-Hill, 2004.

Morgan, Judith, and Neil Morgan. *Dr. Seuss & Mr. Geisel: A Biography.* New York: Da Capo Press, 1995.

Reynolds, David S., ed. *A Historical Guide to Walt Whitman.* New York: Oxford University Press, 2000.

Richardson, Robert D., Jr. *Emerson: The Mind on Fire.* Berkeley: University of California Press, 1995.

Twain, Mark. *The Annotated Huckleberry Finn.* Edited by Michael Patrick Hearn. New York: W. W. Norton & Company, 2001.

Untermeyer, Louis. *Lives of the Poets: The Story of One Thousand Years of English and American Poetry.* New York: Simon and Schuster, 1959.

Illustration Credits

Page 1: 1950s USA *Mad* magazine cover, Retro AdArchives / Alamy Stock Photo.

Page 7: Self-portrait, William Blake, pencil with black, white, and gray washes, 1802.

Page 10: *Albion Rose*, William Blake, from *A Large Book of Designs*, copy A, 1793–96.

Page 11: *The Lamb*, William Blake, from *Songs of Innocence and of Experience*, copy AA, object 8, 1826, the Fitzwilliam Museum.

Page 14: *The Tyger*, William Blake, from *Songs of Innocence and of Experience*, 1794, the British Museum.

Page 21: F. Scott Fitzgerald, publicity photograph, from *The World's Work* magazine, June 1921.

Page 25: Zelda Sayre Fitzgerald, studio portrait, 1919.

Page 32: Frederick Douglass, daguerreotype by Samuel J. Miller, 1847–52.

Page 35: *The Shooting of Demby*, from *Life and Times of Frederick Douglass*, 1892 edition.

Page 43: *Krishna Defends Arjuna from Arrow of Snake or Sarpmukhastra*, from *Hindi Gita Press Mahabharata*, date unknown.

Page 44: Henry David Thoreau *(left)*, daguerreotype by Benjamin D. Maxham, June 18, 1856; Ralph Waldo Emerson *(right)*, albumen photograph, circa 1859.

Page 50: S. Margaret Fuller, engraving by Frederick T. Stuart after John Plumbe Jr., circa 1870.

Page 50: Jones Very, likely from a frontispiece of an edition of his works in 1839, re-printed 1881.

Page 51: Bronson Alcott, NYPL Digital Gallery, date unknown.

Page 52: Louisa May Alcott, albumen print on card mount, Warren's Portraits, Boston, circa 1870.

Page 55: Thoreau's shack, drawing by Sophia Thoreau, from title page, *Walden*, first edition, Ticknor and Fields, 1854.

Page 57: J. Thoreau & Son pencil, modern reproduction, photograph by the author.

Page 58: Booby, from "Ornithology," *The Old American Comic Almanac for 1839*, S. N. Dickinson, Boston, 1838.

Page 60: Ellen Sewall Osgood, Sewall Family Papers, American Antiquarian Society, date unknown.

Page 64: Ted Geisel (Dr. Seuss), photograph by Al Ravenna, *New York World-Telegram & Sun*, 1957.

Page 70: *The Cat in the Hat*, Barnes & Noble Booksellers book display in the children's section, NYC, USA, photo by Patti McConville / Alamy Stock Photo.

Page 72: First Lady Michelle Obama reads *The Cat in the Hat* to children in Ms. Mattie's class at Prager Child Development Center, March 12, 2009, during her visit to Fort Bragg. PJF Military Collection / Alamy Stock Photo.

Page 73: *The Calling of St. Matthew*, Michelangelo Merisi da Caravaggio, oil on canvas, San Luigi dei Francesi, Rome, 1859–60.

Page 75: Virginia Woolf, photograph by George Charles Beresford, 1902, restored by Adam Cuerden.

Page 76: Godrevy Lighthouse at Gwithian, Cornwall, desaturized image by Darren Shilson, 2016, St. Stephen, United Kingdom.

Page 87: *The Princess Sabra Led to the Dragon*, Edward Burne-Jones, oil painting, 1866, private collection.

Page 88: Ernest Hemingway, passport photograph, 1923, US National Archives.

Page 91: *Still Life with Apples and Pears*, Paul Cézanne, oil on canvas, circa 1891–92, Metropolitan Museum of Art.

Page 96: Samuel Taylor Coleridge, portrait by Peter Vandyke, painting, 1795, National Portrait Gallery, London.

Page 100: Devanagari schwa, maladroit calligraphy by the author.

Page 103: John Donne, portrait by Isaac Oliver, oil on canvas, 1616, late seventeenth-century copy, National Portrait Gallery, London.

Page 109: *Scenographia Systematis Mundani Ptolemaici*, geocentric model chart, English, 1660.

Page 113: Tara, anonymous Tibetan or Nepali sculptor, date unknown, photograph by the author.

Page 114: Mark Twain, studio photograph by A. F. Bradley, 1907.

Page 115: Huck with rabbit and gun, E. W. Kemble, drawing, from *Adventures of Huckleberry Finn*, first edition, 1884.

Page 117: Pap Finn, E. W. Kemble, drawing, from *Adventures of Huckleberry Finn*, first edition, 1884.

Page 118: Huck in the canoe, E. W. Kemble, drawing, from *Adventures of Huckleberry Finn*, first edition, 1884.

Page 122: Huck and Jim on the raft, E. W. Kemble, drawing, from *Adventures of Huckleberry Finn*, first edition, 1884.

Page 130: John Keats, portrait by William Hilton, oil painting, circa 1822, National Portrait Gallery, London.

Page 133: Grecian urn, John Keats, drawing, based on an engraving of the Sosibios Vase, circa 1819.

Page 139: *The Blue Marble*, photograph by Harrison Schmitt or Ron Evans, Apollo 17 crew, NASA, December 7, 1972.

Page 141: Edwin A. Abbott, studio portrait, date unknown.

Page 145: Sphere, Edwin A. Abbott, illustration, from *Flatland: A Romance of Many Dimensions*, Seeley and Co., London, 1884.

Page 152: William Shakespeare, funerary monument, Trinity Church, Stratford-upon-Avon, photograph by Sicinius (https://commons.wikimedia.org/wiki/File:Monument-ht6.jpg), cropped by the author, https://creativecommons.org/licenses/by-sa/4.0/legalcode.

Page 155: Taijitu (yin-yang symbol), from Yin yang.png, converted to SVG file by Gregory Maxwell.

Page 159: Théodore Chassériau, *Macbeth Seeing the Ghost of Banquo*, oil painting, 1854–55, Museum of Fine Arts of Reims, cropped by the author.

Page 167: Samuel Beckett, caricature by Edmund S. Valtman, 1969, Library of Congress Prints and Photographs Division.

Page 171: Plaque on Library Way (E. 41st Street between Fifth and Park Avenues, New York), sculptor Gregg LeFevre, 1998.

Page 176: Stan Laurel and Oliver Hardy, publicity photo, Hal Roach Studios, circa 1930s.

Page 177: Progress chart by the author.

Page 180: Richard Rodgers and Oscar Hammerstein, press photo, 1945.

Page 184: African American sheriff, Pocatello, Idaho, Corbis, 1903, Smithsonian.

Page 189: Gerard Manley Hopkins, photograph, circa 1889.

Page 191: Robert Bridges, photograph, late nineteenth century.

Page 200: Toni Morrison, "A Tribute to Chinua Achebe," Town Hall, New York City, photograph by Angela Radulescu, 2008 (https://commons.wikimedia.org/wiki /File:Toni_Morrison_2008-2.jpg), "Toni Morrison 2008-2," https://creativecommons .org/licenses/by-sa/2.0/legalcode, 2008.

Page 205: Geoffrey Chaucer, nineteenth-century portrait from the Welsh Portrait Collection at the National Library of Wales.

Page 210: Herman Melville, portrait by Joseph Oriel Eaton, oil painting, May 1870, Houghton Library, Harvard University.

Page 212: Bixby Creek, Big Sur, California (location misidentified as "Monterey, United States"), photograph by Ian Schneider, Unsplash, October 28, 2015.

Page 216: *The Arctic Whaleman; or, Winter in the Arctic Ocean: Being a Narrative of the Wreck of the Whale Ship* Citizen, Lewis Holmes, illustration, 1857, Smithsonian Libraries.

Page 222: Emily Dickinson, digitally restored black-and-white daguerreotype, circa early 1847.

Page 225: Manuscript of the poem "'Hope' Is the Thing with Feathers," Emily Dickinson, 1891.

Page 229: Emily Dickinson Museum, Amherst, MA, front, Daderot, April 18, 2008.

Page 237: Walt Whitman, portrait photograph by George Collins, 1887, restored by Adam Cuerden.

Page 239: Walt Whitman, portrait, from the frontispiece of *Leaves of Grass*, steel engraving, 1854, Library of Congress.

Page 251: J. D. Salinger, illustration by Robert Vickrey for cover of *Time* magazine, September 15, 1961, National Portrait Gallery Collection.

Page 257: Garuda, sculpture, in the Simtokha Dzong, Bhutan, Bernard Gagnon, May 20, 2018 (https://commons.wikimedia.org/wiki/File:Simtokha_Dzong_-_Garuda.jpg), cropped by the author, https://creativecommons.org/licenses/by-sa/4.0/legalcode, May 20, 2018.

Page 262: Venus of Willendorf, Naturhistorisches Museum, Vienna, Bjørn Christian Tørrissen, January 13, 2020 (https://commons.wikimedia.org/wiki/File:Venus_of _Willendorf_-_All_sides.jpg), cropped by the author, https://creativecommons.org /licenses/by-sa/4.0/legalcode, January 13, 2020.

Page 263: Francis Scott Key *(left)*, portrait attributed to Joseph Wood, oil on panel, circa 1825; Fred Rogers *(center)*, photograph by Walt Seng, 1988; Aretha Franklin *(right)*, publicity photo, Atlantic Records, first published in *Billboard*, February 17, 1968.

Page 264: Jack Kerouac, portrait photograph by Tom Palumbo, circa 1956 (https://
commons.wikimedia.org/wiki/File:Kerouac_by_Palumbo.jpg), "Kerouac by
Palumbo," https://creativecommons.org/licenses/by-sa/2.0/legalcode.

Page 266: Francis Scott Key witnessing the bombardment of Fort McHenry, painting
by LTJG James Murray, US Navy, NHHC Photo NH 86765-KN.

Page 271: Fred Rogers, "Mister Rogers' Neighborhood" (circa 1979) PBS File Reference #
33650_192THA. All rights reserved. PictureLux / The Hollywood Archive / Alamy
Stock Photo.

Page 273: Aretha Franklin singing "My Country 'Tis of Thee" at the US Capitol during
the fifty-sixth presidential inauguration, Washington, DC, photograph by Cecilio
Ricardo, January 20, 2009, US Air Force, image 090120-F-3961R-860.

Page 274: Lakshmi image, souvenir from Khajuraho bazaar, juggadery, March 18, 2018.
(https://commons.wikimedia.org/wiki/File:Lakshmi_goddess_(40838437452).jpg),
"Lakshmi goddess (40838437452)," straightened by the author.

Index

Page references given in *italics* indicate illustrations or material contained in their captions.

About the Author

Dean Sluyter (pronounced *slighter*) has taught meditation and led work-shops and retreats since 1970, at venues ranging from Ivy League colleges to maximum-security prisons. A grateful student of sages in several traditions, he has completed numerous retreats and pilgrimages in India, Tibet, Nepal, and the West. Dean's previous books include *Natural Meditation*, winner of the 2015 Nautilus Gold Award for best book on body, mind, and spirit prac-tices. His media appearances have included *Coast to Coast AM*, National Pub-lic Radio, the *New York Times*, *O: The Oprah Magazine*, *Tricycle: The Buddhist Review*, and *USA Today*.

From 1977 to 2010, Dean taught English and developed the Literature of Enlightenment program at the Pingry School in New Jersey. He now lives in Santa Monica, where he teaches meditation, sings with the Westside Thresh-old Choir, plays old songs on the ukulele, and happily zips about on his Vespa. He is married to documentary filmmaker Yaffa Lerea.

More information is available at DeanSluyter.com. For talks and guided meditations, search "Dean Sluyter" on YouTube.